With

compliments

of the

publisher

HarperOne
An Imprint of HarperCollins*Publishers*

With
compliments
of the
publisher

HarnetOne

Dear Prudence

Dear Prudence

Liberating Lessons from Slate.com's Beloved Advice Column

Daniel M. Lavery

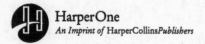

HarperOne
An Imprint of HarperCollinsPublishers

HarperCollins books may be purchased for educational, business, or sales promotional use. For information, please email the Special Markets Department at SPsales@harpercollins.com.

FIRST EDITION

Designed by Leah Carlson-Stanisic

Library of Congress Cataloging-in-Publication Data has been applied for.

ISBN 978-0-06-314036-3

23 24 25 26 27   LSC   10 9 8 7 6 5 4 3 2 1

But all that is morally right rises from some one of four sources: it is concerned either (1) with the full perception and intelligent development of the true; or (2) with the conservation of organized society, with rendering to every man his due, and with the faithful discharge of obligations assumed; or (3) with the greatness and strength of a noble and invincible spirit; or (4) with the orderliness and moderation of everything that is said and done, wherein consist temperance and self-control.

Although these four are connected and interwoven, still it is in each one considered singly that certain definite kinds of moral duties have their origin: in that category, for instance, which was designated first in our division and in which we place **wisdom and prudence**, belong the search after truth and its discovery; and this is the peculiar province of that virtue. For the more clearly anyone observes the most essential truth in any given case and the more quickly and accurately he can see and explain the reasons for it, the more understanding and wise he is generally esteemed, and justly so. So, then, it is truth that is, as it were, the stuff with which this virtue has to deal and on which it employs itself.

—Cicero, *On Obligations*, trans. Walter Miller

I recently got my long-term partner a bidet for his house. I grew up in a country where they are common, and he has always wanted one. He loves it, and often thanks me for buying it. However, he now refuses to buy toilet paper, saying that it's saving him a lot of money. I pointed out to him that I do not want to wash and dry myself with the bidet every single time I use the toilet when I visit him. He offered me a clean, dry shop towel to wipe myself with. What should I do with this—put it on the floor? Hang it up on the rack and hope no one mistakes it for a hand towel? Sneak it into his kitchen and leave it there for him to dry his dishes? I did start bringing over my own toilet paper, but the next time I came over, he had used it all up as Kleenex. So: He refuses to buy toilet paper, has offered me what I consider a gross solution, and will blithely use my supply while I'm gone. I've created a monster. Please help.

—Dear Prudence letter writer, July 2017

Contents

Introduction

What Time's the Next Swan?

I assumed the mantle of Dear Prudence, *Slate*'s resident semi-pseudonymous advice columnist, in November 2015 and relinquished it in May 2021. The first Prudence, Herbert Stein, wrote for a few months in 1997, having previously served as chairman of the Council of Economic Advisers under Richard Nixon. The second Prudence was Margo Howard, a bona fide member of an advice-giving dynasty that included her mother Ann Landers (née Eppie Lederer), her aunt Dear Abby (Abigail Van Buren and sometimes Pauline Phillips), and her cousin Jeanne Phillips, who took over both the Dear Abby *and* Abigail Van Buren bylines in the early 2000s. The third Prudence, Emily Yoffe, ran the column from 2006 until shortly before my arrival in 2015. Editor Jenée Desmond-Harris took over after my departure in 2021. Dear Prudence existed long before my tenure and carries on quite comfortably after me. I have always found a pleasurable sort of reassurance from the inevitable obsolescence of the role, not least because it relieves some of the pressure of trying to offer useful advice to forty strangers a week, fifty-two weeks a year.

The marvelous Walter Slezak (you might remember him as Rock Hudson's wily majordomo in *Come September* or as the villainous Willi in Hitchcock's *Lifeboat*, or then again you might not remember him at all) wrote a charming autobiography in 1962 called *What Time's the Next Swan?* He named the book after a popular story from his father Leo Slezak's turn playing the title role in Wagner's *Lohengrin*:

> It was just before his first entrance. He was ready to step into the boat, which, drawn by a swan, was to take him on-stage. Somehow the stagehand on the other side got his signals mixed, started pulling, and the swan left without Papa. He quietly turned around and said: "What time's the next swan?"

It's the sort of anecdote that appends itself to certain character types once they've reached a ubiquitous level of fame (Groucho Marx, Dorothy Parker, Bob Hope, Oscar Wilde), stories that are better described as plausible than literal. There is always another staging of *Lohengrin* to look forward to next season. There is always another Prudence waiting to take over. If you miss this one, just wait for another swan. You'll be fine.

Advice columnist is not the sort of job one usually trains for, as there are few studios where one can get one's foot in the door by offering miniscule amounts of advice in the mailroom, no Schwab's where agents lunch at the counter and periodically discover savvy newcomers. Landing one of the few nationally syndicated columns is usually a question of luck, proximity, cronyism, and timing, ideally all four. I was no exception; nothing in particular qualified me for the job outside of a general interest in advice-column history dating back to high school, when I'd picked up a secondhand copy of *Since You Ask Me* and taped a rerun of the 1999 made-for-TV movie about Ann and Abby starring Wendie Malick, the Veronica to Christine Baranski's Betty in my psychosexual development.

I was running an unprofitable literary humor website in 2015 when Emily Yoffe left a vacancy in the Prudence chair, and one of the editors at *Slate* happened to like my work and suggested I interview for the job. I did, and I got it. Out of an abundance of caution, I juggled both jobs for a few months until my fingers got sore from all the typing, at which point I quit the unprofitable website, much as a space shuttle sheds its booster rockets upon slipping the surly bonds of Earth before delivering a permanent multipurpose module on the International Space Station. One of the obvious downsides to taking on a job for which one cannot possibly have received any formal training, particularly at the tender age of twenty-nine, is the potential for chaos, so I was particularly grateful to inherit a partially prefabricated persona like Dear Prudence rather than having to come up with a wholly original style from the outset. Whether one comes to Prudence through the Greeks, the Catholic Church, or the Beatles, one has an immediate and instinctive sense of her attributes. Prudence is patient, reserved, discerning, able to judge the right moment to a nicety, endowed with a sense of scale, self-disciplined, forward-thinking, ever on guard against extremes. Philosopher Josef Pieper, one of the twentieth century's clearest students of scholasticism, called prudence the mold and mother of all the other cardinal virtues: "None but the prudent [can] be just, brave, and temperate, and the good is good in so far as [it] is prudent." My own sense of the prudent might differ from the Prudences before and after me (to say nothing of Pieper), but the task, as I saw it, was to incorporate something of my individual values and worldview into the Prudence character, such that the version of myself that offered guidance to strangers every Monday, Tuesday, and Wednesday, with bonus questions available on occasional Fridays, would seek neither to dispense dogmatic and universal codes of conduct nor attempt to remake the audience in my own image. My own faults, as I see them, include a preoccupation with what the neighbors might think, a tendency to filibuster when I feel self-righteous, which is often, too much affection for what I think of as my own cleverness, a desperate and badly disguised desire to please everyone all the time, a tendency to generalize, digging in my heels when I begin to suspect I'm wrong, grudge nursing on a Clara Barton–like scale, carelessness, a tendency to overstate my case and cover up bad motives with sweeter-smelling ones, laziness, and a ruthless impatience with anyone I suspect of shortcomings similar to mine.

Sometimes this made me a very good advice columnist, although one of the more frustrating aspects of advice-column writing is the lack of measurable outcomes. I've never been able to develop a strong sense of what type of person is likeliest to write to an advice columnist, and since so many of the questions I received over the years came through anonymously, I was rarely able to ask for further details, clarifications, or updates if any of them decided to take my advice after all. I decided fairly early on that I would assume good faith on the letter writers' part unless something rang obviously false, although I don't think I had an especially good ear for sounding out that sort of thing, although once someone wrote to me with a question that had been directly lifted from the first half of *Brideshead Revisited*. Luckily for me, I'd read the first half of *Brideshead Revisited*, but I could hardly be expected to go around reading the first half of every book in order to avoid the possibility of being fleeced. Every so often I'd get a letter from someone claiming to have faked a letter I'd answered months or years before, although of course there was no way to verify whether *those* claims might not have themselves been faked. You can see how there might be no end to it if one started worrying about authenticity on that scale. The pleasure of the fake letter, as I see it, is very much like the pleasure of reading an advice column in the first place. The columnist is nobody particularly special except by virtue of their position, possesses no specialized professional or educational training, is not a subject-matter expert, and may hold no personal charm for the individual reader. The columnist is simply *in* the column, standing by and prepared to offer a best guess, with no real lasting authority to worry either letter writer or letter reader.

The letter readers I think I understood a little better, having been one myself for so many years during my commute, slow afternoons in the office, or particularly sleepless nights. It's something akin to the pleasure found in the general genre of "self-help" inasmuch as it offers a project of relentless self-inspection and the hope of endless potential improvement—that is to say, the promise of constant forward momentum at exactly the moment when one feels most confounded or uselessly ruminative—yet without the requisite personal buy-in of a self-help book or seminar or what have you, and in much smaller, more manageable doses. There is also the quiet, private gratification of gawking at someone else's problems without having to commit a vulgarity like eavesdropping or going through their mail. Putting one's oar in is a national pastime, and advice columns provide as healthy an outlet for that shared impulse as any. *At least I'm not the only one with this problem* can feel just as good as *At least I don't have* her *problems*, and the syndicated advice column offers both in spades.

At its best, I think the Dear Prudence column provides readers and writers alike with a dose of what I call "speculative conflict resolution," a chance to walk through the possibility of a variety of life changes, from the minute to the substantial, without necessarily having to commit to any one course of action. The anonymity and distance of the column temporarily remove the stakes from even the thorniest dilemmas. One can imagine oneself taking the advice offered, either in full or in part, and then decide to ignore it entirely, if one likes, or think about trying it in a few months or a few years. From such a perspective, even the "faked" letters, *Brideshead Revisited* included, can be valuable. *What if this really happened? What might I do next?*

So many of the letters I received as Prudence were animated by fear of the seemingly imminent: someone would write in great detail about something they hoped desperately to avoid, but that nonetheless loomed likely, and seek my advice in preventing or forestalling it. Occasionally, I would feel confident in offering a prescription. *Do X and abstain from Y, and Z won't happen. Good luck!* But more often, much more often, I could offer no such guarantee. I suspect most of them already knew that whatever peace and well-being might lie ahead, it could not be won by tightly controlling future outcomes and that, as often as not, the unbearable bolt would have to fall first.

While most of my writing as Prudence necessarily concerned other people's problems, two significant changes in my own personal life found their way into the column: first, I began to transition, and second, I became estranged from my entire family of origin in a highly public fashion that culminated with my father losing his position as the senior pastor of one of California's largest evangelical megachurches. I was hardly alone as a trans advice columnist, of course. Lorelei Erisis has published "Ask a Trans Woman" in *The Rainbow Times* since 2009, and Gianna Eveling Israel's "Dear Gianna" column ran throughout the 1990s and early 2000s in the now-defunct

Transgender Tapestry magazine. But transitioning in the middle of my term as Prudence was, let's say, unusual (none of the other Prudences had done it), and the prospect of changing my byline or hearing my voice change on the weekly show was daunting. With the estrangement I was at least in slightly more crowded company, as the two mother-daughter/sister-niece teams that wrote the Ann Landers and Dear Abby columns have variously fallen out and sometimes back in with one another over the years. Precedence and consensus are both friends to the advice columnist.

As an inevitable result, the kind of advice I gave changed over my five years as Prudence, sometimes dramatically; so too did I begin to attract new kinds of questions, new kinds of advice seekers, and new kinds of free-floating social anxieties.

Like many others of my demographic, I frequently adopt, and just as frequently abandon, relentless programs of self-improvement to signal sociability and reliable middle-classness. I believe I did the right thing in pursuing the estrangement, even as it led to the bewilderingly necessary step of ensuring my father lost his job, but I also think the resultant grief has, on balance, made me a worse person in much of my everyday life. I mean "worse" both in regard to character, as I find myself more frequently irritable, more prone to black-and-white thinking, less patient, less open-minded, more easily startled, and more attached to antisocial and repetitive rituals, and also in terms of efficacy, in the business of personhood—worse at carrying out the basic acts of self-replication, worse at sleeping, worse at waking, worse at participating in the individual elements of a given day. The question of living well, or at least as well as one possibly can after the unbearable bolt has fallen, became one I took very seriously in my advice giving as a result.

Perhaps oddly, this has also produced in me a new kind of cheerful resilience: I believed my life would remain livable only if I could guarantee that the worst thing could not happen. It happened regardless. Endlessly revisiting the psychic wound, the sense that *this can't have truly happened*, makes life impossible, and life must be possible in order to live it. The underside of estrangement, which fell like a bolt over my life, is rumination. My family and I do not speak, and I think about my family all of the time. This is the underside of the rock, where the ants live and move ceaselessly back and forth. There is always something useful to be done after impossibility interrupts one's previously possible life. Being Prudence, judging each moment to a nicety, guarding against extremes, establishing a coherent sense of scale, looking forward, and seeking to be useful to others became a very helpful counterweight indeed. The virtues can hold up a life when beliefs and attitudes falter, when feelings and relationships fall away. And Prudence is the mother and mold of all the other virtues, guiding them each in turn to serve to the best of their abilities. It was a very good job, and I was lucky to have it.

Incidentally, I did get a rare update from the letter writer who'd bought her boyfriend that calamitous bidet, with an even rarer happy ending. She ended up reading both her letter and my answer aloud to him, per my request, and he happily complied by first apologizing and then buying a stock of toilet paper to be made available to any houseguests uninterested in using the bidet. At least, that's what she told me happened. I have no real way of knowing.

Chapter One

Can I Break Up with Him Without Hurting His Feelings?

Letters with an impossible theme: Wanting to end a
relationship without upsetting anyone. The question of
resolving incompatible desires without assigning fault.
The inevitability of occasional hurt feelings. Learning
to live with someone else's disappointment.

Should I break up with my partner?" letters are the advice
columnist's bread and butter, and "How can I break up
with my partner without hurting their feelings, or ideally without letting them know we've broken up at all?" is an especially
popular subtype. It's relatively easy to say "yes" to these letters
as a total stranger with no material investment in these relationships, which might explain this type of letter's perennial

popularity. Often these letter writers are anxious to stress their partner's many excellent qualities (although a sizable minority appear to have no redeeming characteristics whatever), as if in fear that by ending a romantic relationship they will also be delivering a final and permanent verdict on their partner's value as a human being. But "Is this person basically good and deserving of affection, stability, and personal happiness?" is a very separate question from "Do I want to keep dating this person?" Conflating the two does no one any good.

Other familiar subtypes include "Is it rude to stop talking every day to someone who just dumped me? After all, they're being very nice to me" and "Should I tell my spouse that I'm very unhappy about something, even if they might be disappointed?" It can, of course, be deeply painful to contemplate saying something likely to hurt or disappoint someone you care about, particularly if they've been a generally thoughtful and attentive partner. But continued romantic relationships aren't rewards earned by good behavior (though they can certainly be forfeited by bad behavior), and until someone develops a pain-free alternative, the breakup must remain the unfortunately necessary gold standard in the field.

////////////////

Dear Prudence,

My boyfriend of almost two years recently broke up with me, saying he just wasn't ready for a committed relationship. His mom and I still talk all the time, and he's still my best friend, so we text every day. How do I move on? We were at a point where I could envision us building a life together and we talked about it often, except toward the end when he almost stopped talking to me entirely. I'm finding it tough to give up that vision of us I had in my head and embrace our close friendship. How do you think I should handle it?

—Best Ex Forever

///////////

I don't think you two actually do have a close friendship. He dumped you after a period of bewildering radio silence, and he is not doing you any favors by staying in daily contact before giving you a chance to get over the breakup. If you two are ever going to be friends, it's not going to be while you're still picking up the pieces of your shattered romantic dreams.

I think you know what you need to do next, which is why you wrote to me in the first place. You have to stop talking to your ex's mother all the time, and you have to stop texting your ex every day. You'll have to set this boundary yourself, because this relationship you have now is only hurting you, not him. You tell him you're not going to be able to speak for a while—likely a long while—so that you can mourn the end of your relationship and start to figure out a way forward. There's no perfect number to put on this, but I don't think you should envision getting back in touch with him any sooner than a year from now. Any shorter, and you're liable to think, "In another few months, I'll get to be best friends with him again—and maybe he'll be ready for commitment, and see how well I've handled our *breakup, and things will just click, and we'll get back together," which is not at all conducive to the moving-on process. Tell him goodbye, unfollow him on social media, move his number out of your contacts, tell his mom that while you're still extremely fond of her you need some time to yourself, then focus on your other close friends who haven't recently broken your heart.*

///////////

I get variations of this question all the time—so often that I'm prepared to make a general ruling about friendship with exes. Exes can make wonderful friends, and I'm close with some of mine, but I don't know of anyone who's gone from being deeply in love, in full planning-a-life-together mode, to blissfully platonic best friends with no unspoken sense of longing and loss overnight (or even in a few months).

• • •

Sometimes I hear from letter writers who have never been in a romantic relationship but want to be in one very badly indeed. They almost always share their age in the first sentence, and they're almost all convinced that they're alone in having reached that particular milestone without dating at least once. The underlying problem of how to communicate deeply felt personal information without the guarantee of immediate reciprocity becomes more abstract in such cases but remains fundamentally unchanged: *How am I supposed to talk*

about what I want unless I know in advance that someone else
wants the same thing?

////////////

Dear Prudence,

I am a twenty-five-year-old woman, and I have never really had a
romantic relationship. I had a crush in high school that didn't work
out. I went to a college with a significant gender disparity, and
it seemed like all my friends got asked out by the few men who
attended, just not me. I seemed invisible. I ended up dropping out
of that college due to family issues, moved back home for a year,
and worked. My parents had moved away from my hometown at
that point, so there was no one there I could reconnect with. Still, I
managed to make friends. But my romantic life went nowhere. One
guy asked me out, but he was a known creep I had been warned
about. Another guy was younger than me by nearly four years.

Embarrassingly, I've never even been kissed. I feel like
something is wrong with me. I'm still in touch with my friends
from high school and college, so it's not like I can't connect with
people. Yet no guy has ever been interested in me. Is it my looks?
I've been told by a guy friend that I'm a "6.5 out of 10." I've always
been the plain Jane of my friend groups. But I've always made
sure that I have been presentable. Is it my personality? A lot of
my girlfriends say that I am confident and cool to be around,
and they're always in disbelief whenever I mention my lack of
romantic connections. A few of my guy friends have mentioned
that they also think I'm cool, but men have trouble liking me since

all of my friends are "nicer" to be around. According to them, even though I am caring and personable, I'm still too assertive and dominating. One guy even said that I'm too loud and needed to be quieter. At this point, I don't know what to do. I know that there's something wrong with me. There has to be. I have been told over and over that I don't need to be in a relationship until I'm ready, but I have been ready for years now.

I know that the obvious solution is to put myself out there and try dating apps, but I feel like at this point, if no one has ever liked me, then no one ever will. I feel embarrassed by my lack of experience, and with every year, it only gets worse. I feel like I would have to lie to whatever future dates I have about my history just so they don't think I'm pathetic or start looking for flaws that would have repulsed others. Plus, all of my friends in relationships have met their partners organically. I'm jealous that someone could meet them on the street, or in school, or in a club and immediately be interested in them; meanwhile, I'm an acquired taste at best. Any advice would be helpful.

—Never Been Kissed

There's a complicated mix of self-possession and deep despair in your letter. I'd like to start by encouraging you to stop asking your male friends to "rate" you or to offer universal explanations on behalf of all men about why you are or aren't worth dating. They're not capable of offering such explanations, and you're already aware their advice is fairly scattered, sometimes contradictory, and hardly possible to follow even if you wanted to. The fact that they've accepted your premise and are trying to rate you in the first place is a bad sign (as is pointing out how much nicer your other friends are than you, as if you're all in an unending beauty pageant and you've just lost Miss Congeniality again).

I can't help but notice you don't say whether these friends are people you're interested in dating, either. You don't say anything about what men you'd like to date, aside from having had a crush in high school. What do you want out of dating, aside from an outward signal that you are "worth" dating? That's not to say external validation is worthless, or that you must adopt a series of elevated ideals, but it will help to cultivate a sense of what you're looking for beyond a checkmark that announces to the world, "Some man—any man—considers me worth dating." What do you desire in a partner? What interests you, what catches your attention, what do you long for, what do you seek to protect and safeguard and cherish? How do you want to display your interests and affection to others?

You say you feel embarrassed because you believe no man has ever wanted to go out with you, but that's not quite true. I don't say this in the spirit of argument, but I think it speaks to your present state of mind that you seem unable to acknowledge information that doesn't validate your self-deprecation. It's perfectly understandable why you didn't want to go out with the two men who pursued you, but the fact remains that they did express an interest.

You say apps are "the obvious solution" but then dismiss them as somehow insincere or fraudulent in comparison with your friends who met their boyfriends elsewhere. You have assembled a series of elaborate beliefs and touchstones that serve as both self-protection and self-harm. It's the difference between thinking about dating as "I am a pearl of great price, buried in a field, and only someone keen of eye and true of heart will recognize my hidden value and ask me out. If this does not happen, it is because I have no value in the first place" versus "I'd like to date men, which is not a shameful admission of weakness but something true and morally neutral about me."

I fear that asking you to be kinder to yourself will come across as insufficient. But I am certain that mentally beating yourself up and establishing a series of mathematical proofs that demonstrate you're a lost romantic cause will do you no good. You do not have to join any dating apps if the idea causes you too much pain (although I hope you will consider taking a calculated risk on that front), but I wonder if it's the apps themselves or a belief that acknowledging your desires would be an act of public vulnerability so risky as to invite catastrophe. You do not have to pretend to enjoy being single if you would prefer to be in a relationship. But I think it will do you a world of good to stop treating your male friends as romantic authorities when they have merely proven themselves eager to criticize; to handle your self-loathing as a serious mental-health issue that merits careful, attentive, kind treatment; and to consider what kind of life you might like to build for yourself outside of (or, let us say, in addition to) romantic considerations. Good luck.

////////////////

Dear Prudence,
I'm forty-six. I separated from my husband in 2019, and we finalized our divorce during the pandemic. I started dating a hot

thirty-two-year-old and thought it would just be silly and fun.
But we're both deeply in love. I've never had a relationship that
made me feel as completely understood, or had such a strong
physical connection. I can't deny I love him. But we've been
dating for eighteen months, and he's still too embarrassed to
show me his place. I pick him up and bring him home or rent a
room for us. He's unemployed and has no college degree, and
while I think he's a very talented man, his plans for how to get
work are extremely unrealistic. He can't drive and he lives over
an hour away. I've tried to teach him how to drive and he had
panic attacks. I tried to break up with him because I think on
some level, I know I will always have to take care of him. But
he wants to help me, to be involved in my life, to meet my kids
(they did meet once, just not as my "boyfriend," and got along
extremely well). He makes me coffee, encourages me, and wants
to help me around the house; if we gender-swap the situation, is
it not kind of acceptable?

I do worry, though, that I don't respect his goals as realistic.
I've gently nudged him and then thought better and avoided
the subject. What's probably a bigger issue: He's extremely
conservative and I'm extremely liberal, and that has been a huge
source of argument. I think that when it matters, we agree? I also
think there are topics I'll always want to avoid, because knowing
his opinion kind of makes me queasy and I hope he'll change his
mind someday.

What am I doing? I can't stop leaning on him or wanting
him. Everything feels better when we're together. But I have
an awesome career and I'm not unattractive and I know I could

date . . . I just couldn't make myself want to when we broke up. How do I know if it's safe to trust my emotions?

—Love My Coffeemaker

////////////

I'm not quite sure what trusting your emotions looks like in this case, to be honest. It seems like you're using it as a shorthand for continuing to date this guy, which you are of course certainly allowed to do. But you have a number of emotions about him and this relationship, many of them in direct conflict with one another, so I don't think it's possible for you to simply trust your emotions into making a decision.

For whatever it's worth, I don't think it's especially useful to imagine a gender-swapped version of one's present romantic relationship. You don't have a gender-swapped version of your relationship, unless you are both considering transition (as my wife and I did a few years ago, and which I heartily recommend). The question isn't whether any man in your position might be happy dating a woman who doesn't drive or didn't go to college, but whether you're happy with this particular man who won't let you in his house and needs help commuting to your dates. He makes you feel understood and the sex is great, which goes a long way toward explaining why you've been reluctant to end things, but it also sounds like you've been reluctant to seriously integrate him into your life. I wonder if "Is it safe to trust my emotions?" serves as cover here for "I really want to prioritize incredible sex with an attentive partner over values, practicality, and compatibility right now."

Your children liked this guy based on a single meeting as a "friend"; it's unlikely they'll have an identical response once you introduce him as your boyfriend of well over a year. That doesn't mean you can't weather whatever their subsequent reactions might be, just that you should keep in mind that was a one-time, improvised strategy that's unlikely to work again. You think he is unlikely to ever get a job anytime soon and is so resistant to discussion that you've "thought better" of even gentle nudges on the subject. You claim that you two agree "when it matters," but you framed that as a question and without getting into specifics about what actually matters to you. In fact, you say a number of his opinions make you sick to your stomach and that you have to pretend he's going to change his mind someday, despite having received no reason to believe so, just to make your relationship bearable.

I think there's a reason you've needed to keep this relationship in such a protective little bubble—because you know that you won't be able to keep spinning these fantasies of "Maybe it'll all work out because he also makes me coffee" once they crash into reality. This does not mean that you have to break up with him tomorrow. You don't have to break up with anyone you don't want to, even if an advice columnist you've never met thinks you should. But you do have to take everything you know about your boyfriend into honest consideration, even the things you wish weren't true. He is extremely conservative, and he does not seem inclined to become any less conservative after numerous arguments with you. He does not have a job, he does not support himself financially, and he is either unwilling or unable to listen to your suggestions. He does not drive and is presently unable to learn. He does not want you to see his home. You do not want your children to know that you're dating him, and you're worried about the prospect of having to support him if your relationship ever gets more serious. Part of you wants to believe you can overcome these concerns because he encourages you and makes you coffee, and while those are certainly lovely attributes, they're awfully low bars to clear. All of these things are true at the same time. You will have to use your own judgment, your own honest assessment of the situation as it is, not as you wish it could be.

• • •

Some of the easiest questions to address are ones where the answer comes down to "Just tell your partner exactly what you told me."

////////////

Dear Prudence,
What's your advice for when you and your partner were heavily involved in kink when you first got together, but one of you has grown away from it? My partner is an avid role player, but I now find acting out elaborate scenes to be a chore rather than erotic. I feel like I'm letting him down every time I make it clear that kink is something we used to share that I'm no longer interested in. We are polyamorous and we've made the agreement clear that he'll find someone else who's more

interested once more people get vaccinated. Should I just grin
and bear it in the meantime?

—Kink Fatigue

////////////////

*I don't think so! It's one thing to decide you'll occasionally join a
partner in enacting a kink you're not especially into if you've got
the time and the inclination, but yours enjoys heavy involvement
and elaborate scenes, while the most you can muster in response is
the possibility of grinning and bearing it. I think that's an indicator
to put your participation on hold. Your partner may very well be
disappointed that you no longer share this kink, which would be
perfectly understandable, but people's interests sometimes change
over time, and my guess is he'd rather be disappointed while
also knowing what you really want than having you put yourself
through the motions "for his sake." Take a break (indefinitely
or permanently, as you like) from this particular kink, give your
partner the opportunity to talk about his own response, and then
let him figure out how, when, and where to look for other partners
when the opportunity arises.*

////////////////

Dear Prudence,
I've been in a happy marriage for five years. My husband has
always said he wants a football team of kids, but I'm terrified of
pregnancy. I'm not sure what it is exactly. All of it kind of grosses

me out, and I'm having a really hard time trying to get excited about starting a family. He's been ready since the wedding, but I suggested we wait a couple of years (which has turned into five), and now he's starting to suggest we start. How on earth do I get over this pregnancy phobia?

—Terrified of Pregnancy

///////////

Do you want to have children and wish to overcome your fear of pregnancy? Do you want to avoid pregnancy altogether and pursue surrogacy or adoption or fostering? Do you want neither to get pregnant nor to have children? Your aversion to pregnancy is clear in your letter, but I don't know whether you're at all interested in becoming a parent outside of that context. If you want to get over this phobia because you deeply desire to have children, that's one thing, but if you think you need to grit your teeth and get pregnant because it's what your husband wants and you didn't explicitly say "I don't want kids" five years ago, please don't force yourself to go along with something that terrifies and distresses you for someone else's sake, and don't withhold important information he needs to know simply because you're afraid of disappointing him. You're "terrified," you're "grossed out," and you're not excited about starting a family—don't try to downplay your reluctance or make it seem milder than it really is. If your husband is raring to produce a football team's worth of progeny and you're sobbing in the bathroom at the very idea of pregnancy, you two need to figure out if you're compatible in the long term.

////////////

Dear Prudence,

My fiancé and I have been engaged for fifteen months and are planning on getting married this December. I randomly found out from a friend that at one point my fiancé went on a few dates with an ex of mine. Granted, my relationship with this ex was in high school and ended about twelve years ago (and *their* encounter was about nine years ago), but I still can't get over the fact that they were seeing each other. Should I bring it up to my fiancé, who, may I add, is aware of my previous relationship but has not said anything?

—Unexpected Ex Overlap

////////////

Let's look at the alternative to bringing it up: you say nothing; resent your fiancé for never having mentioned going on a handful of dates with one of your exes; and continue to build it up as a betrayal in your mind until your resentment starts to leak out into your relationship in a hundred tiny ways. That is suboptimal, especially since bringing it up is free, legal, and immediately available. So bring it up! You can acknowledge that this all happened a long time ago and didn't involve any wrongdoing, but that you've found yourself dwelling on it and wish that he had said something to you sooner. Saying "I've heard about this, and it bothered me," is not an indelible accusation of wickedness and deceit. Allow your fiancé to hear you out, to offer an apology, to reassure you, to share his own thoughts with you in turn. If you turn it into a forbidden topic, you'll make yourself miserable; if you talk about it, it's likely to return to its rightful size as a distant footnote in your fiancé's history.

• • •

Sometimes, of course, letter writers fear saying something directly to their partners less because they are afraid of hurting their feelings and more out of a sense that the answer is likely to be something between "No" and "Get over it." These people are, I suspect, usually proved right, although in such cases I think it's better to get it over with rather than prolong the suspense. Like Carrie Fisher's Marie in *When Harry Met Sally . . .* , they already know the answer to their predicament; they just want to hear someone else say it. Maybe four or five times. "You're right, you're right—I know you're right."

////////////

Dear Prudence,
My boyfriend of three years doesn't include me in any plans with his close-knit Italian family. In general, I don't expect a lot of contact with them, but I do feel excluded when he doesn't invite me to major family events and holidays. I've told him I'd like to be included. He says he loves me and I'm a priority, but he doesn't want to have to answer difficult questions from his "nosy family members" about our relationship. He also feels my presence would "slow him down" at the events, as he'd have to take time to introduce me, to take care of me, etc. Recently he told me that if

we aren't getting married, I'll never meet his family. I do want to get married, and he knows that. I took that as pretty much the defining writing-on-the-wall moment that this relationship is never going to progress anywhere. He says otherwise and tells me we're meant to be together. His actions and words just don't seem to align. Should I just cut my losses and move on or attempt to talk with him again?

—Time to Cut and Run?

Your boyfriend thinks you would slow him down at . . . family dinners? What could that possibly mean! "Darling, I'd love for you to meet my parents, but I couldn't possibly take the time to introduce you. It would slow me down, and speed is of the essence in these troubled times."

Here is the breakdown, as best as I can tell, of your situation:

1. *You would like to meet his family and also get married.*

2. *He would introduce you to his family if you were getting married, but for aerodynamic and efficiency reasons does not currently have any time to do either of those things.*

It does not bode well, in my professional opinion, but I think it's worth having a final conversation about it. You've been dating for three years; you'd like to marry him someday; and before doing so, you'd like to meet his family. Tell him it's something you take very seriously and are considering ending your relationship over; if he still hems and haws about introducing you to his relatives after that, I think it's a fairly clear sign that he doesn't want the same things that you do.

////////////

Dear Prudence,

I just started dating a guy who is getting divorced. He is smart and funny and considerate and seems to be working hard to deal with his situation well—he simultaneously keeps me informed of milestones (this attorney meeting, that paper filed) yet takes care not to overburden me (sharing sadness/anger with friends and therapist rather than me). He recently went from many-texts-a-day to radio silence for a week. Now we have planned another date and texts and warmth have picked back up. I am inclined to attribute this to the complications of his situation rather than assume he is a hot-and-cold person, which is the type I have come to realize is bad for me. Does that sound likely? I guess I'll know soon either way, right? Just want to avoid heartbreak.

—Hot-and-Cold Running Taps

////////////

This is a question you will have to ask him! I personally could not bear the prospect of total silence for a full week from someone I was dating, no matter how good the reason, but then again, I'm fairly high maintenance. The "complications of his situation" may very well persist for a good long time; getting over a divorce isn't always quick and easy. If weeklong silences are going to be part of

*this relationship, you'll have to decide whether you're interested in,
or capable of, dealing with them.*

////////////

Dear Prudence,

I was secretly in love with a close guy friend of mine for many
years. We're now in our thirties and both married (to other people)
with children. I haven't heard from him in a while, despite reaching
out to him about once a year. I did just receive a response to my
latest message, in which he admitted to pushing me away because
he had been in love with me and it took him a long time to accept
that things were not meant to be! I no longer have feelings for
him and am happily married. I'm just angry with him for only
saying it now. I'm having trouble shaking the feelings of anger and
resentment. I haven't responded yet, and I'm wondering—should
I respond and say, well, I felt that way too? Or just let it go? Even
though I'm angry, I don't know if it is a good idea to basically do
the same thing to him at this point in our lives and make him
reconsider his past actions. But I wonder if being honest will give
us both some closure. Or maybe it would just make me feel better
to tell him the truth, finally. What do you think?

—Tell Him, or Tell Him Off

////////////

*I don't know if closure would be either possible or useful to you
right now. I can understand your anger at his timing, although*

you both sound equally responsible for not disclosing your feelings over lo these many years. What's the good in getting him to reconsider his past actions if you're no longer in love with him? (The answer, I realize, is punishing him for hurting your feelings in the past, which is a perfectly human impulse but not one worth following if you value your peace of mind.) The best possible outcome has already happened. You've both moved on from your never-wholly-avowed feelings for one another; you're happily married with children; and hashing out your potential lost relationship together would only lead to guilt, self-recrimination, and anguish. Better to deal with your anger (and some small satisfaction, surely!) in private, either with a therapist or a closemouthed friend; at most, tell him you wish him the best and hope his family is doing well.

////////////

Dear Prudence,
My boyfriend and I just celebrated our third anniversary. We recently bought a home and want to get married someday. I have one child from a previous relationship, who adores him, and he treats him as his own son. I have been up-front with my boyfriend about things I will not tolerate; dishonesty and cheating are the big deal breakers. My child's father cheated on me, and I left him. Our relationship is strong, and we are happy.

I found out recently that just before our first anniversary, he went to an ex-girlfriend's house after spending some time at a bar that he goes to occasionally. This was before we started living

together, but we were dating exclusively at the time. I assume
he was there either late or spent the night. I don't have details
on that front. I just know that he bought beer and went to her
apartment. I can only assume something happened, especially
since he never mentioned going to a friend's house afterward
(he usually does). I'm crushed. I never knew this before, and had
I known at the time, we would not be where we are today. I am
heartbroken, disappointed, and feel less confident. It wasn't like
we'd only been together for a few weeks—it was almost a year.
I feel he not only hurt me, but by extension, he did a disservice
to my child as well. He is not friends with his ex on social media.
Since two years have passed, should I say anything? Do I keep
this secret to myself? What can I do?

—Unhappily Keeping Mum

//////////////

*If you have the opportunity to trade vagueness for clarity, back
channels for direct conversation, and uncertainty for frank
disclosure, I can't imagine why you wouldn't say something to
your boyfriend. It sounds like you found out this information
from a (possibly misinformed) third party; who better than your
boyfriend to fill in the details of what actually happened? You
trust him, he's given you no cause to doubt his word, and your
relationship is otherwise good, so speak up. Don't lob accusations
or fill in the blanks for yourself, but tell him that you've recently
learned something that makes you uncertain and anxious, and
you'd like him to tell you what happened that night. Then listen*

to whatever he has to say. It may be he admits to something you find unacceptable; it may be that he has a perfectly legitimate explanation; it may be that you two have to fight about this, or break up, or laugh off an unfortunate misunderstanding. But give him the chance to shed light on what is now only a rumor, because I don't think you're going to be able to successfully put this out of your mind on your own.

As an aside: I understand the desire to dwell on feeling hurt in the absence of more information, but whatever happened that night was not a "disservice to your child." This is about you and your boyfriend, and it's unnecessary to insert your son as a proxy into a conversation about your feelings.

• • •

Many of the letters I've received over the years have been variations on "Something about my relationship is bothering me. Should I talk to my partner about it?" Almost always, the answer is yes. But not always.

///////////////

Dear Prudence,

I give a lot of positive feedback and compliments to my family, friends, and my girlfriend. I'm considered a very positive person and was once told by my girlfriend that I was great for her self-esteem. She has struggled with her confidence in the past. Before we became a couple, I constantly complimented her on how beautiful she looked to lift her spirits. The problem is that I am more in love with who she is internally (she is smart, funny, caring, and loving) and not particularly attracted to her externally—but she would never know that, based on my many compliments.

I feel so horrible lying to her about her beauty, but I can't fathom breaking her heart and self-esteem in the process. Please help.

—False Compliments Wearing Thin

//////////////

I am not sure why you got into a relationship with a woman you are not attracted to, but if you're happy with your situation, I'll leave that aside for the moment. Are you telling your girlfriend kind things that you also believe to be true about her appearance, even though they're not backed up by attraction on your part? You can not be attracted to her and still think her new haircut suits her or that she has a lovely smile. Or are you saying things you don't actually believe in order to "boost" her self-esteem? If it's the latter, that sounds awful, and my advice to you is to spend some time in therapy exploring why you've sought out a relationship with a woman whose greatest fear is that she is not attractive despite knowing that you were, in fact, her greatest fear realized. You say you're "considered a very positive person," but there's nothing positive about bombarding someone with insincere praise.

Let me add that I don't think you should share any of what you've shared here with your girlfriend, as it would be unnecessarily cruel. This is something that should be shared in confidence with your therapist. Whether or not you decide to keep dating her, none of what you've told me could ever be helpful to her. It could only hurt.

• • •

While asking your boyfriend's therapist to break up with him for you might not technically be a HIPAA violation, it's unlikely to lead to anything good.

///////////

Dear Prudence,

Over the holidays I got engaged. My boyfriend has clinical depression, and the holidays are rough on him. I was going to break up with him, but I held off, thinking it would be easier after the holidays. Then he surprised me—at his parents' house in front of his whole family—with a ring. I didn't see how to say no without humiliating him in front of his family, so I accepted. I've been trying to break it off ever since, but something always stops me. He had problems at work, and then it was Valentine's Day, and then he had a medical scare. I keep picturing myself marrying him because I don't have the nerve to break up with him. He has a therapist he trusts implicitly. Would it be wrong to ask her to tell him?

—Outsourcing Breakups

///////////

Oh my God, yes, it would be wrong. It would be a violation of roughly every standard of behavior in her profession, and it would be deeply cowardly on your part. You cannot marry someone you do not want to be with just because he has depression and you're afraid of hurting him, but you also can't fob off breakup responsibilities onto someone else just because you don't want to see his reaction. I have sympathy for your plight, I truly do, not least because I think public engagements carry with them an unfair degree of implicit pressure of the kind you experienced in front of your boyfriend's family, and it's clear that you want to be kind. But you absolutely have to break up with your fiancé by yourself. Go see a therapist of your own if you need help mustering up the strength, but don't borrow his to try to get out of this relationship (besides which, I don't believe any halfway decent therapist would ever agree to break up with a client on behalf of that client's partner in the first place). You have to break up with him on your own behalf.

Chapter Two

How Can I Convince Someone They're Hurting My Feelings?

Letters united by the hope that this is all just a big misunderstanding: "I'm sure I just didn't explain how much this hurt me last time." The limited utility of speculating about someone else's intentions. A plea for the end of "love languages." The limits of empathy.

'm not sure how much blame rests with Gary Chapman, the Baptist minister who came up with the "love languages" concept (the idea that there are five primary ways all people express and receive love, including words of affirmation, quality time, giving gifts, acts of service, and physical touch, and that couples ought to analyze their partner's preferred language and use it more often), and how much rests with the subsequent thirty-year game of cultural telephone, but wherever the rot began, it's spread beyond the point of saving. Whenever a letter writer mentions their partner's so-called love languages, it's never in the context of a frank conversation about shared terms and values, but a wholly one-sided exercise in speculation, as in, "I wish my partner would talk to me about his feelings, but I guess there's no point in asking him to, since he fills up the car with gas on the weekends—must be because acts of service is his love language, and asking for words of affirmation would only confuse and disorient him." The five love languages, as they have appeared in the Dear Prudence column, are as follows:

Quality time, as in: "My partner doesn't touch me, or acknowledge my accomplishments or strengths in any way, and he doesn't know much about my friendships or my emotional inner life, and he doesn't anticipate my needs, or do much to thank me when I anticipate his— but he does live in the same house as me, so sometimes he'll be sitting on the couch watching TV or scrolling through his phone while I'm in the room, so I've decided that his love language is quality time, even though he's never said as much. Actually, we've never had a conversation about the love languages; I've just read about them on my own. We haven't had an emotionally complex conversation since before we moved in together, which is why I find myself spending so much of my spare time reading about love languages and relational psychology so I can build up a fort of terminology to reassure myself that he really does love me. Anyhow, he doesn't seem to mind being in the same room as me, which I'm willing to call quality time, because if I don't meet myself in the middle on his behalf I'm afraid he'll never meet me anywhere."

Receiving gifts, as in: "I guess if you think of that quality time we sometimes spend together when we're both in the same room while I'm reading about relationship dynamics as a gift . . ."

Words of affirmation, as in: "Sometimes she says yes when I ask her a question, and there's really not a more affirming word than *yes*, is there?"

Acts of service, as in: "Sometimes he fills up the gas tank when the car needs gas, and I really need to count that as a win."

Physical touch, as in: "The books about gendered communication styles and relational dynamics I read by myself are satisfyingly heavy. If I press one over my breastbone before I fall asleep at night, I can feel a sort of peace-weight slot into my body; not quite restrained, not quite immobilized, not quite held, not quite counterbalanced, but some strange amalgamation of all four. I feel maintained by a steady hand that keeps me

from flying off of the bed and outwards into a thousand
shards. So I think that's probably *my* love language."

• • •

////////////

Dear Prudence,
My boyfriend of a year is hardworking, attractive, family-oriented,
adventurous, and kind, but I feel like our intimacy has been
lacking since the beginning. He is a reserved person, and I believe
his love language is spending time with your significant other,
whereas mine is very much physical and verbal affection. He
does little things like touch my back when he walks past me, put
his arm around me out in public, hug and kiss me goodbye in the
morning, but that's about it. We have sex every couple of weeks
(we spend six nights out of the week together), but we don't
really cuddle. He doesn't really express his feelings toward me
or compliment me besides "I love you." The sad part is, when he
does touch me, I now feel angry and resentful.

After six months together, he said he was sorry we hadn't had
sex in a while and that he wanted to make sure that I didn't feel
he wasn't attracted to me. He is just always tired from going to
work at 4 a.m. When I've talked to friends about this, they think
that I need to make more moves myself, but I feel like the lack
of verbal and physical intimacy has left me feeling too insecure.
To be honest, I feel the most insecure about myself I've ever

been. I don't really like to change in front of him and constantly want to go to the gym. I don't want to tell him he needs to be more intimate with me if he does not want to, because then how natural is that? However, I don't think I can continue a relationship where I feel like I'm not good enough or angry at him when he has no idea. Do you think we could work this out even if we have different love languages?

—Intimacy Issues

////////////

The "love languages" model was created by an evangelical pastor in 1992 to describe broad relational dynamics as he saw them, not a universal empirical observation about human character. So while the idea of love languages can perhaps be useful to some when talking about habits and preferences, it loses all utility when we treat it as some innate, unchangeable aspect of our partner's nature—especially when we make that assumption without ever asking said partner if it's true! Your boyfriend doesn't touch or compliment you as often as you'd like. Having an honest conversation with him about what you want from a relationship is much more productive than assuming "Well, his love language is probably 'being in the same room with me,' which means if I ever asked him to cuddle with me, it would go against his very nature." Everyone is capable of displaying and asking for affection, reassurance, or significant emotional contact. And while different people might have particular preferences, that doesn't mean he's incapable of accommodating yours. I think the real question you need to ask yourself is: "What's *my baseline for considering something important enough to discuss with my partner if I'm angry every time he touches me, feel so self-conscious I don't want to get changed in front of him, and want to send myself to the gym for punishment and discipline, and still think it's not worth bringing up?"*

I understand your fear that if you do bring it up with him, he'll only start touching you to keep you happy, not because his heart is actually in it. But telling him what you want, what you need, what's hurting you, and what's working for you are not demands that he should start going through the motions to meet. It's an opportunity for greater intimacy—even if it leads you to realize you two don't work together long-term. Having a few honest conversations about your disparate expectations and desires for physical touch, possibly even deciding to part ways over a significant incompatibility, is not a bad outcome, and if it makes you feel more confident about stating your needs and desires in a future relationship, so much the better.

/////////////

Dear Prudence,

I love my boyfriend, "Max," but am becoming increasingly worried that we're incompatible. We've been together four years, living together for two. Max struggles to express his emotions and shows his love through acts of service. He cleans our home and cooks most of our meals, and if he knows I'm shopping for a bookshelf, he builds it for me. Caring for me makes him feel good and like he "deserves" me. The trouble is that I sometimes enjoy making my own lunch, I want to contribute to our household, and I sometimes like to buy things with my money. I also want to be told I'm loved, that I'm attractive, that he values me. I feel like a jerk comparing us, because I have a much easier time expressing my emotions, but it frustrates me that even when I prompt him (which I'd be happy doing), Max doesn't really reciprocate compliments.

Like I said: I love Max. The thought of ending our relationship is devastating. But recently a coworker, Jeremy, paid me several compliments over a Zoom call, and I developed a brief but intense crush on him because it felt so good. Max is amazing, but I don't know if we are compatible. I don't know if I'm being selfish or acknowledging that two people can be great but not great for each other. Sometimes I feel hollow and don't think I can live the rest of my life with this ache. Am I being selfish?

—Mum's the Word

////////////

I've reread this letter a few times looking for something "selfish." But here's all I could find: You love your boyfriend, you both look for practical ways to care for each other, you felt good when someone recently paid you a compliment, and you're hurt because the boyfriend you love is sometimes closed off. You haven't described a single selfish act here—just a series of feelings. I've grumbled in the past about the ways the concept of love languages gets in the way of real intimacy by conflating something as serious as "My partner won't tell me he loves me or say he likes my hair once in a while" with "My boyfriend is a bookcase-building robot who is only capable of demonstrating affection through the medium of chores." But love languages aren't some innate quality fixed in our hearts at birth. They're a made-up shorthand for different forms of connection. Max may be a great person, but if you regularly ache and feel hollow because he can't or won't share his feelings with you, all the bookcases and perfectly cooked lunches in the world aren't going to make a difference, and you're not denying some intrinsic part of who he is as a person by saying, "This isn't working for me anymore."

If you don't want to break up with him over this, and he's receptive to the idea of change, you may find couples counseling a useful option as you two reevaluate the basis of your connection and he works to find new ways to open up. But if you tell him that you're starved for emotional intimacy, for hearing "I love you," and for verbal affirmation, and his only response is "Sorry, I can only do acts of service," it's not selfish to say, "I can't live that way."

· · ·

Sometimes the quest to understand a given situation—one's own motivations, one's partner's motivations, one's circumstances and goals and plans—can turn into a useless, compulsive categorization, like a meticulous travelogue where every new day's entry details exactly how lost you are.

//////////////

Dear Prudence,

When I met "Ryan," I knew he had a girlfriend because I met them both at the same time. From the moment I met Ryan, I could tell he was attracted to me, and though I was attracted to him, I put up a lot of barriers to make sure we never got closer than friends. He and I ended up developing a close friendship. We did art together, played music, and talked about just everything under the sun. I always invited his girlfriend to come along, but sometimes it was just the two of us. In an effort to create more barriers, I told Ryan a lot about my past heartbreak over men who were in relationships but actively pursued me without ever leaving their partners, and how I wasn't interested in repeating the same mistakes again.

To make a long story short, after a few months, Ryan ended up telling me he loved me and that he wanted to leave "Ashley." I told him I loved him too but that I wanted a type of love he couldn't give me because he was in a relationship and I wanted to tumble, with no restrictions, madly in love. Ryan said that he wanted the same thing as me and told me that I was the woman he wanted to be with for the rest of his life. I trusted that, considering everything I had told him about my past, he had listened to me when I told him exactly what I wanted.

We started sending love letters to each other. We spent time together reading books out loud and going for aimless walks. We started being physically intimate. Ryan told me he didn't want Ashley to know that he and I were in love because he wanted their breakup to just be about the problems that they had together and not to drag me into it. Ryan then got "confused" about what to do and repeatedly asked me to hold on to what we had, even though he hadn't broken up with Ashley. This went on for six months. He continued to send me love letters. Ryan then decided, to my surprise, to stay with Ashley and cut things off with me. And he hasn't told Ashley about any of this and says he plans to "wait until things get better" between them. I've cut Ryan completely out of my life because he knowingly brought me into a situation I explicitly told him I didn't want. He has lied to me, his girlfriend, and himself.

None of our friends know about what happened, and I feel like Ashley should know so that she's not stuck in a relationship with a man who intentionally lied to her for almost a year (and continues to). Should I tell someone so they can tell her? I know hearing it from me would not be the best idea. I have no intentions of pursuing anything with Ryan in the future, so this is not an attempt to get her to break up with him so I can swoop in. I'm just wondering if this is a situation where I can perhaps share some information so Ashley can make her own decisions about what to do.

—Just Looking Out for Ashley

////////////

I think the best thing you can do, either for yourself or for anyone else, is to stay out of Ryan and Ashley's lives. What you're considering is just another way to continue to tie yourself to their relationship. If there was any part of you that was truly concerned for Ashley's well-being, you would have found your conscience prodding you to tell her sometime in the last year—not just after it became clear Ryan was never going to leave her. It would be better for you to spend this time and energy in therapy trying to figure out what you're getting out of this pointless, painful habit and developing strategies for avoiding similar situations in the future.

• • •

None of this is to say anything against the mere concept of trying to understand one's partner. It's a useful, lovely prospect and ideally part of the pleasure of being in a relationship. The trouble often seems to begin when someone gets mixed up and thinks, "If I can understand why my partner acts this way, and if I feel basically sympathetic about their position, then I can't ask them to change it or consider breaking up with them over it."

////////////

Dear Prudence,
I am a middle-aged male in a relationship with a sweet, kind, successful woman who seems to suffer from a shopping addiction and who can never stop herself from taking home free food. When we first started seeing each other, she wouldn't let me into her home. At first I thought this was because she wanted to make sure we had something real before I met her young daughter (I

have children too), but when I saw her home I realized she had a hoarding problem. At that point I already cared for her very much. I have very serious rescuer tendencies, and I know better than to follow such a path. Now we've been together for almost two years.

Last year, she bought a new home and recruited me to help her move. I pitched in but also gave her space to deal with the masses of shopping bags that had never been unpacked full of duplicate bags of chips and other storage bags, unopened Amazon boxes, stacks of old luggage, etc. I had hoped she would want to pare down on her own, but that didn't happen. She ended up needing a later move-out date and became very distressed as we started moving stale and even decayed food to her building's dumpster. We filled the dumpster and her new detached garage. Evidence of rodent and insect activity was revealed with each peeled layer. Nearly a year after this move, her garage is still stuffed, she hasn't unpacked any of her wardrobe, and new boxes are starting to arrive. I spent a weekend organizing and rearranging her kitchen, but she never committed to the new setup. There's not an inch of open counter space.

I've shared my concerns with her and have been accused of being judgmental and hypercritical. I am terrified that her daughter's nascent compulsivity will blossom into the shame and loneliness her otherwise very sociable mother fosters. After an argument following the exhausting move, she bought self-help books. She seemed committed to cultivating some self-denial strategies. Last week, I visited her place and had my own stress attack when I navigated a cavernous path from her front door to her kitchen. Her attractiveness to me is waning. I love her, want to help her, want to help her child, but I am not a psychotherapist. We recently argued that I'm not moving fast enough, and my question, "Where exactly do I fit in your home?" remains unanswered. Should I stay or should I go? I've been dating on and off for eight years since my divorce, and I'm tired.

—Buried in Boxes

////////////

Let's leave aside the fact that you've grown tired of postdivorce dating, as well as the fact that your girlfriend clearly needs additional help dealing with her hoarding and compulsive shopping, and even your concern that your girlfriend's daughter may adopt some of her more dysfunctional coping strategies. The most important question for you to answer is not "Do I wish I could stop dating and just settle down?" or "Does my girlfriend need help?" but "Am I happy in this relationship, and would I like to stay in it in the future?" Are you getting what you want? You say you don't want to revert to your old rescuer tendencies, which suggests this is a dynamic you've fallen into in the past. Can you see a version of your relationship with this woman where you're not in that exact position? I can't answer that for you, but I can tell you that if she genuinely wants help, there is a great deal of therapeutic, medical, and organizational help available to her. It is simultaneously true that she deserves support and that she

does not need you to be her boyfriend in order to get it. "Where
exactly do I fit in your home?" is a valuable question to ask a
partner, and it's not cruel or insensitive to expect her to give it
some thought. If you decide this relationship isn't working for
you, that isn't a referendum on her worth as a person, nor her
mental health issues.

• • •

There are plenty of cases where empathy and understanding
can become not only counterproductive but even dangerous,
as when it furnishes excuses for bigotry and cruelty. So often homophobia is euphemized as sincere concern or an unfortunate by-product of otherwise-laudable religious piety,
rather than deliberate hostility, and so provides cover for an
astonishing array of violations.

If I could revise anything about my original answer to the
next letter, I'd encourage the letter writer to think carefully
about whether she wants to accept her parents' offer to introduce her girlfriend to her younger brother as her "friend"
rather than advising her to decline it outright. While I still
believe her parents' request was dehumanizing and insulting, deciding to limit contact with one's relatives is an incredibly personal decision, and if the letter writer wanted to
play by her parents' rules at least some of the time in order
to maintain a connection with her brother, especially since
he's still living at home with them, she has every right to do
so. I do, however, always want to emphasize the possibility

of spending the occasional holiday away from one's family of origin when one needs a break—there can be so much pressure about "not ruining" the Christmas holidays, but the holidays come around every year, and we are in no danger of running out of them anytime soon. Besides which, one can no more "ruin" Christmas than one can "ruin" a Thursday.

////////////

Dear Prudence,

I'm twenty-two years old and came out to my parents as a lesbian at fifteen. They are devoutly Catholic and conservative and have struggled deeply with it. For years, they let me know that they prayed every day for God to fix me and forbade me from telling anyone else in the family. Seven years and many fights later, they have definitely progressed. They say they have accepted that this is something that will likely not change and say they are no longer praying to fix it. They have let me tell my relatives and even told some of them on their own. They also ask me questions about my relationships, and my father even had dinner with me and my girlfriend when he visited me at school. They say that just because they believe men and women are fundamentally different and made to complete each other in marriage doesn't mean they are homophobic—they just have religious views about what true marriage is, and I will never have that. We've spent hours going back and forth, and it has all been really painful for me. I also don't know what I can expect from them. It's been so many years and while they have improved, I know I'm not going to fundamentally change their beliefs about my sexuality.

My girlfriend's family is very accepting, and my girlfriend thinks I'm too easy on my parents.

My girlfriend will be in my hometown this Christmas visiting extended family of her own. She's met my eighteen-year-old brother, who loved her. I'd like her to meet my younger brother, who is eleven, but my parents told me they are not okay with him knowing about my sexuality yet and want to tell him on their own terms when he's older. I know he's their child so if they want to teach him that, I guess they have the right. They say they're okay with him meeting Hannah, but only if I introduce her as a friend. He's met my eighteen-year-old brother's girlfriend and was introduced to her as such. Is he at an age where I'm allowed to be mad about this and demand the right to tell him? He's not a baby anymore, and I'm worried that the more years he's indoctrinated into these homophobic beliefs, the less likely it is I'll be able to shake him out of it when he's older.

—Relationship with Homophobic Parents

//////////////

I think it is time, not to be harder on your parents, but to be easier on yourself. For the sake of your own well-being, please stop going back and forth for hours (for years!) with them about whether or not it's a sin that you're in love with your girlfriend, or "merely" extremely sad and a pale imitation of heterosexual love. If your parents are only willing to let your girlfriend meet your little brother

*under the guise of being your "friend," then you should decline
the opportunity. The age of your brother is not the deciding factor
in whether or not you're "allowed" to be angry with your parents.
You are allowed to be angry with your parents right now. You are
allowed to set limits with them. You are allowed to take space and
keep distance between you. You are allowed to say that you're not
going to lie to your little brother about the nature of your sexual
orientation or your relationship with your girlfriend. Your parents
may have the right to teach him whatever they like about sexuality
and religion, but their parental rights do not extend so far that they
can ask you, a grown adult, to lie about your own life to preserve
their homophobic fictions. You should be angry with your parents.
I'm angry with them. Please consider spending Christmas with your
girlfriend's family this year. You don't have to cut your parents out of
your life if that's not what you want, but at the very least know that
you do not have to continue endlessly debating whether or not your
identity is a burden and a tragedy.*

////////////

Dear Prudence,

For more than ten years, I was best friends with an abusive,
controlling man, "Matt." In my early twenties, I moved to a new
city to be closer to him and collaborate together. He put down
my appearance and personality and denigrated any friendship I
had that wasn't with him. He also dealt with extensive, episodic
bouts of depression. About eight years ago, I started gradually
cutting him out of my life, a sort of slow-motion ghosting. Six

years ago, I moved to another city. He sought me out before I left and tried to get me to reminisce, but I said I just didn't feel that close to him anymore. Only after that did I really start to realize how much he'd hurt me.

Two weeks ago he sent me a Facebook message, and I didn't respond. A week later, he sent a long, accusatory message about how I'd wronged him, how I'd deceived him by "giving up on our dream," and how cruel I was for cutting him off, then complained he was going through a breakup and the fallout of a DUI. I told him he needed to seek comfort from someone else and that he had belittled me for years, and then I blocked him. I found out that a few days later he attempted suicide, telling his family that I had told him to "fuck off" when he reached out to me for help. A few people have called and asked for my version, and I've told them. I don't even think his version is that far from the truth. I just don't care. Did I do something unconscionable? Should I have sucked it up and shown more compassion for this person whom, frankly, I have nothing but contempt for?

—Am I Responsible?

////////////

You were extremely compassionate in your response to Matt. The fact that he responded angrily doesn't mean you did something wrong. His cruelty isn't an inevitable result of his depression—it's a choice he makes, and his depression is, while not necessarily irrelevant, not the deciding factor in how either of you behaves, or ought to behave. You encouraged him to seek help and set a reasonable limit. You had no idea he was about to attempt to hurt himself and could not have guessed it. He wants to make you feel personally responsible for his well-being, for his life or death, and if he can't successfully guilt you into doing what he wants, he wants to exert social pressure on you after the fact by blaming you. I'm glad you've been able to clarify things with your mutual friends. My guess is you're not the only one who's seen this particular side of him and that your side of events will carry the day. You did everything right, and you can wish him all the best as he gets support from a great number of people who aren't you.

////////////

Dear Prudence,

When I was a child, I was brutally attacked by a dog. It left permanent scars on my body and on my psyche. I have been in therapy, but that is not a cure-all. I no longer have sobbing fits if I see a dog, but I am still phobic about them. I cross the street if I see one and don't go to people's houses if they have one. I find it easier to lie and say I have allergies because if I tell people the truth, they quiz me or try to prove their dogs are the exception. In college my roommate, knowing my past, dropped a puppy in my lap and I had a panic attack.

I am married to a great man and pregnant with a little boy. He grew up with dogs, and his mother and sister do not accept our refusal to get one despite knowing my past. I have overheard my mother-in-law calling me "vindictive" and "selfish" for denying my husband a dog. My sister-in-law has told me that I need to "process my trauma." I haven't told my husband about these comments yet. I don't know if I should because he will read the riot act to them and refuse to go over for the holidays. He wants to protect me, but I know they will put it on me.

I am stressed at work, stressed over the baby, and sick of this dog issue. How do I handle these people? What can I say to them to get them to understand?

—Not Getting Over It

///////////////

What a monstrous failure to exhibit a scrap of empathy on your in-laws' part! I'm so sorry that you've so often met this response when you've tried to explain that you just can't be around dogs, and that other people have delighted in pushing past your boundaries and making you feel guilty for having residual trauma from a highly significant violent attack in your childhood. The idea that you can simply "process" your trauma away—that it's merely a matter of feeding input into a machine until it's gone—is a ridiculous one, and it suggests that your sister-in-law is willfully misunderstanding what it means to experience trauma. You're able to manage your trauma such that you can live in the world and see dogs from a distance, and that's no small feat. I'm glad to hear that you know your husband will immediately take your side, and while I know you fear being blamed if you tell him, I think it's time. Let him help you draw this boundary and make it clear to his mother and sister that they are not, in fact, "helping" him by trying to make you feel guilty.

Trying to get your in-laws to "understand" shouldn't be your goal, I think, because they already know that you suffered a terrible attack as a child, and their response has been to call you selfish. They understand plenty. They just don't care. The real work should be in communicating your limits to them as a couple—namely, that if they try to revisit the issue again, your conversation with them will be over, and you'll walk away.

//////////////

Dear Prudence,

I'm sort of worried my husband is an asshole. Not to me. To me, he is sweet and thoughtful and very much the wonderful man I married. But, for reasons I can't wrap my head around, he's not like that to strangers. He's polite enough to servers and support staff. But to the bike rider who runs a stop sign? Angry, like the bike rider murdered a puppy. To my mom, who can be a bit tough to handle, he's as patient as can be. To the teenage girl bumping into him because she was staring at her phone walking down the sidewalk? Livid, like she told him she had personally canceled his favorite TV show. Yes, I get it. The world is full of rude people. But my husband takes pleasure in being rude to the people who are rude to him first. I say, ignore it. Focus on the real issues. But he says he's just giving out the same energy he receives. How do I make him stop?

—Always Blowing Up

//////////////

The bad news, I'm afraid, is that you can't make him stop if he doesn't want to, and if he sees his boorish, inappropriately angry responses to everyday inconveniences as justified, then he may not be interested in changing his behavior. But you can at the very least make it clear that you find his anger jarring, inexplicable, and indicative of a deeper problem. I don't know what this conversation will look like going forward. If he's generally polite and not abusing waitstaff or short with your mother, then it may not be the biggest problem in your marriage, but I think you should, if nothing else, pay very close attention to the fact that you're concerned about the way your husband handles his own anger. That's not a small matter or something worth ignoring for the sake of keeping the peace in your relationship.

• • • •

There's also the question of how we want to direct others to understand us, and in what circumstances and to what degree it's even possible to do so. If it were only a matter of providing others with the relevant information and letting nature take its course, that would be one thing (and I'd have answered far fewer letters over the years). But sharing information doesn't always guarantee we'll be interpreted as we might like to be, and information that might be perfectly welcome in one context might be unsuitable or even counterproductive in another. This can be particularly difficult in professional life, where some might want their colleagues to know only the bare minimum necessary to work together, while others might want (or depending on the type of job, even need) to share more; all the more so when someone is just beginning their career and still trying to get a feel for common practices and basic etiquette.

////////////////

Dear Prudence,

I'm currently applying to humanities PhD programs, and several schools ask for a "personal history" statement where I describe how my experiences influenced my decision to get a PhD in my field and how I overcame barriers in my pursuit for higher ed. One of the reasons I'm interested in my field is because I was abused while growing up, physically, emotionally, and sexually, and it relates to my interest in my PhD topic.

I have two worries. One is that sharing my past will be too much information. I read an academic study that said one of the biggest deal breakers in PhD applications is when people "overshare" by talking about experiences being sexually assaulted, etc. My other worry is that I will come off as whiny and performative because in many other ways (financially, socially) I have been very privileged. Many others have had it much worse, and outsiders might never think that I have been abused because I am relatively high-functioning and come from a middle-class family. Should I just skirt the issue, allude to it, or directly come out and say it?

—How Personal Is the Personal Statement?

////////////////

My inclination is that sharing this information in your application is unlikely to help your candidacy and—as you yourself anticipate—may very well backfire.

You're not going into advocacy or social work—a PhD has more to do with research and teaching. Although academic work can certainly be informed by advocacy, it's not the same thing, and I think you should focus on what draws you to that particular type of work. You can express your vested interest in assisting and advocating for survivors of trauma and abuse without going into detail about your personal history in your application. Moreover, you shouldn't feel the need to apologize for the ways in which you haven't suffered or for the ways in which you've been financially privileged as you're presenting yourself as a candidate for doctoral work. Focus instead on what has drawn you to the field and how you think you might be able to contribute meaningfully to it.

• • •

Dear Prudence,

My husband has a coworker he constantly complains about to me. He says that the entire office can't stand her, she's a snitch, etc. However, I just saw messages on his phone with her that are paragraphs long and how he hopes they get to work the same days together. How much should I be worried?

—Husband's Fake Nemesis

I don't want to choose a "concern level" you should set your flag to, but you should certainly talk to your husband about it—starting, of course, with an honest disclosure about just how you came to see those messages on his phone, why you felt compelled to read through them, and whether you two generally have a difficult time trusting each other, and probably an apology, if you two aren't normally in the habit of reading each other's text messages. Then listen to what he has to say, and be honest with yourself about how persuasive you find his explanation. Maybe he has a crush on her or they're having an affair. Maybe he has an unattractive habit of complaining about her to others while flattering her directly in order to stay on her good side. Or maybe both. Whatever the case may be, you can both apologize for having violated his privacy and ask for clarification about a jarring inconsistency.

• • •

In the absence of solid information, it can be incredibly tempting to create a satisfying and cohesive narrative about our partners based on intuition, guesswork, stereotypes, or all of the above. Tempting, but risky.

////////////////

Dear Prudence,
My wife and I have been together for about four years, married for two. We have a good relationship, and I would say are generally a happy couple. Over the last year our physical

relationship has been on the decline. We have talked about it, and she will agree to "make an effort," but that will only last a week before things go back to the way they were. We're both young, but we only have sex about once a month. Even when we do have sex, it feels like she is just not into it. But afterward she denies there's a problem.

I know when she was in college she had a serious relationship with a woman for a year or two. She doesn't talk about it much, just told me that something was "off" and that she wasn't into women. I just can't get it out of my mind that she might be a lesbian. I am having a hard time thinking about how to ask her this, or if I even should. What do you think, and how should I approach this? I have this fear that twenty years down the road she is just going to say, "We need a divorce. I'm a lesbian."

—Afraid She's Gay

I don't think the problem is that your wife is a lesbian, although she might be, I suppose. Anyone might be; we're all subject to Schrödinger's lesbian. She dated a woman once, and things didn't work out between them, in no small part because she realized she didn't want to be with women at all (which is a necessary precondition for lesbianism). I suspect your real fear about the reason behind your dwindling sex life is the possibility that your wife is not attracted to you. If she were a lesbian, you could at least feel it wasn't personal, but you're getting ahead of yourself by imagining she'd only leave you someday to be with women. You and your wife do need to start a conversation together, but I don't think you need to speculate about her sexual orientation in order to get to the heart of your issues.

What you need to talk about is the fact that your sex life has dropped off dramatically, that she hasn't seemed willing to tell you what, if anything, has changed for her, that you haven't made any real progress in rediscovering a physical connection, and that you're feeling insecure, unwanted, and uncertain about her attraction to you. You should also consider proposing to see a counselor together. Maybe your wife has something she's holding back from you. Maybe she's perfectly happy with the state of your sex life, and you'll have to hash out your respective needs and how you can meet one another's. Whatever's going on, you should make it clear when you talk to her that this isn't just a matter of wanting to have more sex: that this has been difficult for you in your marriage. You're afraid that her apparent loss of interest in sex with you means there's something significant she's not revealing. That's the conversation you need to have—not "Are you sure you're not gay?"

Chapter Three

Just One More Thing . . .

Letters with a twist: Withholding the most
important information until the very end.
When your real problem is not the problem
you think you have. Learning to see the
forest for the trees.

Some of my favorite letters involve an unexpected plot twist. Maybe the letter writer is hoping to sneak in something just under the wire. Or they don't yet have a sense of what their problem is, and they're throwing everything at the wall to see what sticks. Or they've got a flair for the dramatic and want to go out with a bang. Sometimes they want to underplay their hand in the hopes that it'll help them get what they want.

////////////

Dear Prudence,

My wife and I have been married many years, with all the ups and downs that long-term married couples are familiar with. She will soon go to a sunny resort with her girlfriends and is looking forward to relaxing and having fun. I would like to suggest to her that if the opportunity arises to have an erotic encounter, she shouldn't feel guilty. At the same time, I don't want her to feel like I am pushing her away or that I expect reciprocation. We still have the hots for each other. Should I even raise the subject, and if so, how [can I] do it tactfully and lovingly?

—If the Opportunity Arises...

////////////

It's fine, if potentially fraught, to raise the possibility of one-off encounters with a long-term partner, but right before your wife boards a plane probably isn't the best time: "Have fun with the girls! If you want to have sex with someone on your trip, I'm okay with an open marriage. Call me when you land." If you want to talk about it, talk about it; don't just tell her what you want without giving her the chance to consider the idea or tell you how she feels about it first. It's also a bit disingenuous to phrase your interest in this as a generous offer:"I could take it or leave it, the idea of you sleeping with someone else. I just thought I'd let you know that it would be fine with me, in case you've secretly been cherishing the thought but felt guilty about it. Because I would hate for you to feel guilty for even a moment. Not that I'm interested in the idea. I am not. This is purely born out of

my deep consideration for your hypothetical feelings." You have to
acknowledge the fact that this interests you; you can't try to mitigate
a possible rejection by pretending you think this is what she wants but
has been feeling too ashamed to bring it up with you.

I'm sure you can find a way to bring this up lovingly, but I'm less
sure about how to make it tactful. This is not a tactful subject! It's a
bold request, and one that she might very well reject. Make it clear
that you're happy with your sex life the way it is (it sounds like you
are), and this is a potential bonus, rather than something you think
you need in order to stay happily married. Tell her that it interests
you, but if it doesn't interest her, you won't push her on it. Then
really don't push her on it.

If you bring it up, you run the risk of her being angry or hurt
at the very idea. If you don't bring it up, you run the risk of never
finding out she's into it too. It's up to you to figure out whether
this is worth the risk. Either way, you're lucky enough to still be
attracted to and in love with someone you've been married to for a
long time. Congratulations!

• • •

It's a little cheap, but the further along I went into my Dear
Prudence career (and my thirties), the more I enjoyed the
increasingly rare opportunities to stress my relative youth,
as when the next letter writer enjoined me to remember
the Chuck Robb congressional scandal before venturing to
advise him. Being only five years old when the story broke
(*story* might be a strong word—a woman named Tai Collins

claimed they'd had an affair, while Robb refused to confess to anything more serious than a hotel-room massage, then carried on being a congressman for another decade), I had neglected to follow Robb's career in any meaningful way, but I dutifully looked it up before deciding it had nothing to do with the question at hand. Chuck Robb is nothing but a red herring, as far as I'm concerned.

////////////

Dear Prudence,
My twenty-six-year-old son is engaged to a twenty-seven-year-old "massage therapist." She goes to clients' homes to provide her services. I am fifty-eight years old, and unless a masseuse is affiliated with an athletic team or training facility, a masseuse is a near-sex worker. Remember Chuck Robb? And a massage parlor in my neighborhood was just shut down for this reason. My son is not concerned about this. I realize they are adults, and having expressed my views, I now need to back off. However, the thought of my future daughter-in-law fondling naked men, or other women, creeps me out.

—Disapproving Dad

////////////

I do not remember Chuck Robb. Masseuses often pay clients in-house visits. You are behaving absurdly. Stop imagining your daughter-in-law fondling naked men, and your troubles will be over.

• • •

I have a soft spot for the unselfconscious fetishist, and as someone who's quit smoking on at least twenty separate occasions, I have a soft spot for the next letter writer, even though I'm not part of his target demographic.

////////////////

Dear Prudence,

Although I myself do not smoke, I have a real fetish for women who smoke. I try to always carry cigarettes with me, just in case someone (preferably an attractive female) is looking for one. Well, this plan worked; a single woman bummed a few cigarettes from me, and now something is developing (maybe just a friendship, but I'm hoping for more). When she realizes that I don't smoke, however, she'll wonder why I keep cigarettes. Would there be any good way to answer this question without scaring her off?

—Smoking Fetish

////////////////

This is oddly charming! It's not a very wholesome habit, obviously, but you don't need me to remind you that smoking isn't healthy. It isn't, at all. Better to quit. Everyone who's still at it, please quit at once.

But in the meanwhile, it doesn't sound as if you leap across the paths of good-looking women to stuff cigarettes in their mouths, which is all to the good. You simply lurk around bar entrances and roped-off smoking sections in the hopes that someone attractive will approach you. (What do you do while you're waiting to be asked for a smoke? Do you pull a cigarette out and pantomime lighting it? Do you pretend to text someone? What are you going to do when everyone is vaping and analog cigarettes are obsolete?)

You have two options, as I see it, both with this particular woman and with other babely furnaces in the future. Well, three: You could quit handing out cigarettes to attractive women, which has to be at the very least expensive, to say nothing of the dangers of constant secondhand smoke. This is, I think, your best choice. But if you insist on doling out cigarettes to the women who catch your eye, we're back to two choices. If she asks you about it (and she may not; perhaps she is very self-absorbed!), you can gently lie and say that you keep an occasional pack on you to be social or that you've just decided to quit. Call it an eccentric, oddly chivalric affectation. She might find that plausible. But she might not.

Or you can say that you find it's a great way to meet the type of woman you're interested in. (I'd save the word fetish for after you've established that she's interested in dating you.) She might find that off-putting! But she might not.

* * *

I have less of a soft spot for meddlers. I can understand the impulse, of course; much like smoking, the world would undoubtedly be a better place if no one gave in to the urge to read someone else's correspondence, but the desire to snoop is fundamentally human. But what great love story, what tale of professional or personal success, ever began with "I was reading someone else's emails at work . . ."?

////////////////////

Dear Prudence,

I work in IT support for a large corporation. Last week I got a call for assistance in fixing an executive's email account. During the course of the incident, I read some of the emails. It turns out that she uses her work email for personal business as much as for work; there was one long conversation with a friend about how she was attracted to a woman working in the mailroom. This caught my eye because the younger woman is my sister. She was unable to get a job for a long time after college, and I got her the job about a year ago. While grateful to have a job, she's understandably frustrated with the menial nature of it. Also, while in her senior year she came out to me and close friends but has never had a girlfriend— something that also depresses her—but she's shy and doesn't know how to go about dating. I want to tell my lovely, talented sister what I know about the executive's interest. I think that it could be helpful for her to know that someone successful is interested in her, and if something came of it, it couldn't hurt her career prospects either. What do you think?

—Maybe Matchmaker

////////////////////

I can think of about forty-seven different ways this could go horribly wrong. Say nothing. What on earth could your sister do with this information? "Hey, I read one of our executive's emails, and she thinks about you, like, all the time. So, the next time you hand her mail to her . . . make a move." Just because this woman wrote to a friend about her workplace crush doesn't necessarily mean she's available or interested in a relationship with your sister. There's also no guarantee that this executive's romantic interest would actually help your sister's career. Nothing good comes of reading other people's emails. Let your sister work on her romantic shyness and career prospects on her own, and try to forget what you read.

• • •

Sometimes the note of surprise comes not at the end but in the very premise, as when two ordinarily good friends find themselves nearly going to war about a hypothetical that endangers their shared reality and sense of mutual goodwill. Luckily this was the last time the question of altruistic kidney donation ever threatened our shared social fabric, as my answer was so thorough and comprehensive that it settled the matter once and for all.

////////////

Dear Prudence,
This is a totally hypothetical question that a friend asked me and which is now leading to a fight. My friend asked me if I would ever

be a living organ donor to a stranger. I said I wouldn't. My friend
then asked if I would donate to somebody I knew slightly, like an
acquaintance or a coworker. Again I said no. My friend then asked if I
would donate to a good friend (we were good friends). I said no. This
is where my friend got mad. My friend is in perfect health and does
not need a kidney or any other organ. My friend asked why I would
be so selfish. I said that, working in the medical field, I know that
there are no guarantees. You can die or have complications from any
kind of surgery, and donating a kidney is major surgery. Plus, I would
be out of work for a while. I have a host of relatives I would want to
be able to donate to if I had to, including my spouse, siblings, nieces,
nephews, cousins, etc. For some bizarre reason, this has caused a
huge rift in what was a good friendship. Do you think it is selfish to
not want to be a living donor to anybody but a relation?

—Don't Want to Donate

/////////////

*No, I do not think it is selfish to think carefully about your own
well-being and priorities when it comes to deciding which of your
organs you might be prepared to donate to someone else.*

*It is, as you say, a deeply personal medical decision, and I have
no idea why your friend is so determined to punish you for failing
to give the right answer to her hypothetical transplant question.
You are not opposed to organ donation, nor are you suggesting
you would never donate an organ under any circumstance. You
have particular conditions for undergoing a difficult and invasive
medical procedure. I don't quite know what she wants you to say to*

her—"I'm sorry I didn't hypothetically give my kidney to someone I used to know from work"? Tell her you care about your friendship, you're sorry to see this come between the two of you, and you'd like to let the subject drop and move on. If she can't drop it, that's a shame for her, and you may have to keep both your kidneys and your friendship to yourself.

• • •

As a general rule, I'm for autonomy when it comes to one's own organs and one's remains. If someone hasn't specifically asked you to dispose of their ashes after their death, it is good manners not to try to steal their ashes, even if you only want to steal some of them.

////////////

Dear Prudence,

My mom's first love died recently. The plan is that he'll be cremated and then his wife will keep his ashes in an urn. My mom wants to take some of his ashes to their "old spot" and scatter them there, assuming she can do so without alerting his family (and thus adding to their pain). She thinks it will help her mourn and that it will not do any harm to him or his family, especially since she will do it only if she can be sure they will not find out. I think it is disrespectful to his remains and that, if he wanted his ashes to be scattered someplace special, he would have talked about it with his wife. Should I stop her? Is this a strange but otherwise okay reaction to the death of someone important to her, or should I encourage her to seek other ways of mourning?

—Cremation Cat Burglar

/////////////

Yes, you should stop your mother from trying to steal her old boyfriend's ashes, even if it's just "some of them." His family will want all of them. I understand that your mother is grieving, but I think this is a wildly irrational response to grief. Of course, wild and irrational plans are a perfectly understandable response to the sudden loss of someone you loved deeply. I don't fault her for having a mad, daring plan for trying to claim a part of the man she felt she lost. But that doesn't mean she should follow through with her plan. I'm not even sure how she could. There is no way your mother could siphon "just a few" of his ashes unnoticed. She would absolutely be found out, and it would be a shock and a scandal and deeply upsetting to her ex's family. It would harm them and humiliate her.

It may be simple grief, or it may be a sign that your mother's mental condition is not what it was, if she thinks she can pull this off. She needs to find a less intrusive way to mourn their connection, and you might need to have a serious conversation with her about boundaries and her state of mind.

• • •

It's not only funerals that bring out some people's worst impulses, of course. Sometimes it's weddings.

////////////

Dear Prudence,

My fiancé is dead set on two women he was formerly in love with attending our wedding—one of whom he confessed he still had feelings for a month before he proposed. He was infatuated with them for a very long time. They both turned him down for long-term relationships, but not before using him to cheat on their significant others. He was in love with them since high school. He is now twenty-eight. He claims that they are really good friends who only want to see him happy, but they never reach out to him to hang out. Our wedding is planned for November in two years, and we got engaged five months ago. I am against these women attending, but should I give in and let them attend my happy day, since it would make him happy?

—Not-So-Welcome Guests

////////////

Lots of people are able to maintain platonic friendships with their exes, and I certainly don't have an ironclad "Don't invite anyone you've ever slept with to your wedding" policy. But this reads like a parody of a bad idea. You and your fiancé got engaged five months ago. Six months ago he was still in love with another woman, had been for over a decade, and had already had an affair with her once. It's unclear to me whether he confessed these feelings to you unprompted or whether he confessed to her first, got turned down, and then confessed/proposed to you afterward.

Either way, I'm glad to hear you won't be getting married for a few years, because that gives you some additional time to spend in couples counseling together first. A few important questions you should explore with your therapist:

1. *Why did I accept a marriage proposal from someone who was in love with an ex a month before?*

2. *What do I believe changed for him during that month?*

3. *What kind of relationship does my fiancé plan on having with these two exes for the rest of his life?*

4. *Does that make me feel supported, valued, and as though I can trust him not to cheat on me?*

Good luck, and please don't put down any venue deposits until after you've had your first few sessions.

• • •

Sometimes when one finds oneself in an all-around unbearable situation, as in the following letter, it can be tempting to fixate on a single problem at the expense of all the others, as if solving that single nagging issue would make everything else work. But it's like trying to declare victory in Operation after a single move. Sure, you've removed the Butterflies in Stomach—but there's still a Charlie Horse, a Wrenched Ankle, Water on the Knee, Brain Freeze, and the Bread Basket to consider.

///////////////

Dear Prudence,

I'm in love with my best friend. He's married. We started a sexual affair last year. (He and his wife seem to have an unofficial or unspoken understanding about extramarital affairs.) I don't think he knows I'm in love with him, and I don't think he's in love with me. I want him to be happy more than anything. I'll put his happiness over mine every time. (I've never felt that so genuinely, even when I was married. It is an awesome feeling.) I think he really loves his wife, and he seems to want to stay married, so that's what I want for him.

But she is not a good wife! She criticizes him in front of his friends in really emasculating ways. She rolls her eyes, uses mean words, and just generally seems to not enjoy his company. I think it's appalling. What do I do? It's so hard to bite my tongue. Maybe that's hard in part because of my feelings, but it's nonetheless hard, and other friends of his feel the same way. When I hang out with just her, I have a good time as long as she isn't talking about him. It's just that I think she's awful to him. If he doesn't mind how she treats him, then I shouldn't mind, right? I mean, it's not my marriage. Or do I tell her to knock it off? Or do I tell him he doesn't deserve that? Or are there other options? I've gone and fallen in love, so I'm not thinking straight.

—Chide the Bride?

///////////////

I'm not so sure that your friend is a terrific husband. You say
that he and his wife "seem to have an unspoken understanding"

*about affairs, which means that they don't have an actual, real,
go-ahead-and-ask-me-about-my-open-marriage understanding.
Which means that he's been cheating on her for at least a year!
And unless you are unbelievably good at hiding the signs of love
(and most people aren't), my guess is that your friend is perfectly
aware that you're pining away for him and is very happy to keep
avoiding any clarifying conversations about the nature of his
relationship with his wife, his plans for the future, and any desires
or expectations that you might have.*

*His wife may be a generally critical and unpleasant person.
Or she may be an otherwise pleasant person who's unnecessarily
unkind to her husband. Or she may be suspicious that he's
cheating on her and acting out. Or she may be relatively well
behaved and you're looking for reasons to make her a bad person
so you don't feel guilty for having "unofficial or unspoken" sex
with her husband. I truly don't know! But I do know that unless
your friend wants to leave his wife, it doesn't really matter how
unworthy you think she is of him.*

*You've clearly been spending a lot of time thinking about what
your friend deserves from his romantic relationships. I think it
would behoove you to think about what you want and expect from
your romantic relationships. It's great that you've already decided
upon a policy of "His Happiness Comes First," but has he ever
actually asked you to fall on a sword for him? Does he appreciate
and appropriately regard your desire to suffer for him? Would
he, in a word, care? What are you getting out of this relationship,
besides good sex and a sense of yourself as a martyr for love?
What would your life look like if you let yourself want more?*

• • •

I received countless letters from people who arrived at an understanding of their own bisexuality only after getting into a serious relationship with a straight partner, and while their particular circumstances varied widely, most of them had to grapple with the question of what this "one more thing" meant for them in the context of a previously monogamous by default and usually still-loving relationship. Some of them wanted to dismiss it as an irrelevance, and others feared that they would *have* to dismiss it in order to respect their spouse. I've never had a single, universally satisfying answer I could offer any of them, but it always struck me as necessary to at least begin by taking their bisexuality seriously and considering all available options from a position of possibility and freedom, regardless of what they might decide to do or share next.

//////////////

Dear Prudence,

I am a bisexual woman who came out about nine months after I started dating my current boyfriend. We've been together for over two years, I love him dearly, and we live very happily together. He is very supportive of my identity but is not interested in any sort of open relationship. An open relationship is not ideal for me either, but since I didn't realize my own bisexuality until after I'd fallen in love with him, I've been thinking about having a sexual experience

with a woman while still staying in my relationship. We talked about
it together about a year ago, but nothing's happened.

At this point in time, I am trying to discover more about my
queer identity. I have made some close bisexual friends who have
welcomed me into the queer women space. They are lovely and
supportive but all single. When I have tried to talk to them about
my dilemma (a loving and healthy relationship that does not allow
me to explore the physical side of my sexual identity), their advice
ranges from vaguely sympathetic to unhelpful. I don't know how
to reconcile this situation. I don't want to give up my amazing
relationship, but I feel weird in queer spaces. I had a crush recently,
and it makes me sad to think I would never have the experience of
romantically loving a woman. What should I do? I don't want to look
back at my life and feel regret, but I also don't want to give up a
loving relationship for something completely unknown.

—Wanting to Experience My Queer Identity

////////////

In terms of finding queer community, I think you'll be best off
looking for support groups, events, and activities that actively
serve bisexual women, particularly bisexual women partnered with
straight men. It also helps to remember that there are many queer
communities, not just one. Many LGBTQ centers have meetings
specifically for women in your position, so see if there are any
local to you. If you're going to a lot of events geared toward single
women looking to date, cruise, or find a girlfriend while what you're
looking for is support for navigating your thus-far-monogamous

relationship with a man, you're not going to be well served. I want you to find a lot of support and encouragement, and I also hope you can accept that sometimes you may feel "weird" in queer spaces, especially at first. That's not necessarily anyone's fault or responsibility to correct. There's a difference between discomfort and alienation, so if people are rude or dismissive toward you because of your relationship, you have my full permission to either ignore them or tell them off. But "feeling weird" is a subjective experience, one that might have any number of possible origins, so I hope you won't take it as an automatic indicator that you're necessarily in the wrong place or talking to the wrong people. Queer communities are simply composed of various queer people, not all of whom are going to thrill and delight you, and finding out what kinds of people you vibe with and what kinds you want to avoid is part of the process of establishing yourself within the community, not a sign you don't belong.

I do not have any advice for you that will guarantee you will not experience regret. All choices involve some sense of loss, even if it's only the loss of potential. I can't promise you that if you break up with your boyfriend to explore your bisexuality that you'll find a woman you love even more than him. I also can't promise you that you won't eventually feel stifled in a monogamous relationship with a straight man. You'll have to be honest with yourself, and with him, and find a balance that works for you. You may decide that as much as you love him, you need to leave this relationship for the unknown. You may find a form of limited openness that works for the two of you in your relationship. You may also find that this openness makes you want more than just occasional one-offs with

women. You might break up for unrelated reasons. You might stay
together until you die. I'm glad that you've developed loving and
supportive friendships with bisexual women, even if their advice
isn't always helpful, and I hope you can continue to prioritize those
friendships while also giving yourself permission to say, "I'm not
looking for advice right now," once in a while.

• • •

Sometimes I am in the fortunate position of being able to comfortably offer a general ruling, as in the next case: It's always okay to lie to your homophobic parents about your love life if you want to.

/////////////

Dear Prudence,

I am a gay man in my late twenties planning to attend an expensive law school in the fall. Fortunately, most of the costs are covered between scholarships and my savings. Additionally, my parents have a significant chunk of money originally intended for my undergraduate education that was never spent because years ago I chose a lower-ranked school at a full scholarship over more expensive options. My parents have generously indicated that these funds are available to me now.

But they are also deeply Catholic. In recent years, the unspoken peace treaty involves me never sharing my romantic life and them sincerely praying for my return to the church.

However, unbeknownst to them, I am considering moving with a boyfriend (of eight months) to be close to my law school in August. It would be my first time living with someone.

I fear discovery of this situation by my family could prompt bitterness as well as the loss of financial support. Optionally, I could try to conceal my relationship and living situation from them long enough to irrevocably secure the assets in question (six months to a year). This could prove difficult; my parents will want to visit. My (saintly) boyfriend says he's up for whatever I decide. Ultimately, I will have to confront my parents on this topic, but I do not know if now is the best time. Should I attempt deception?

—Not a Lawyer Yet

I think the sooner you can get the money from your parents, the better off you'll be and the less time they'll be able to spend holding it over your head trying to control you. If they've offered you the money and you're in your late twenties, I don't see why they need to hold off (unless it's for tax purposes?)—it's not like you're a teenager starting college and don't have any experience handling money or paying your own way.

If you need my permission not to tell your parents that your roommate is your boyfriend, you certainly have it. You don't have to come out (again) on anyone's timetable but yours, and this is money they've earmarked for your education that would do you real, substantial good. I don't believe it would be dishonorable to postpone conversations about your relationships until after you've secured educational funding if you know they'd try to use money against you. I will say this: I don't think what you're contemplating is deceptive. Your parents know that you are gay. They also know that you don't share details about your romantic life with them because they're homophobic. Continuing to not share details with them is not deceptive so much as the order of the day. I do think you should prepare yourself for the worst and assume it's at least possible they may find out and withhold the money. Have an emergency plan in place for that, even if it means postponing your entrance for a year while you try to find the money somewhere else.

• • •

Some problems involve a series of cascading "just one more things," such that the letter writer becomes tempted to ask for a dispensation, as in, "I know ordinarily you wouldn't advise me to tell my sister-in-law that I'm in love with her, but this is a pretty unusual situation, right?" And the following *is* a pretty unusual situation, but my advice remained the same.

////////////

Dear Prudence,
You know how some people are fine, absolutely unobjectionable, but you just don't click with them? You don't dislike them, but you don't much like them either—you just don't think about them much at all. That's how I've always felt about my sister-in-law,

"Janice." She was kind of dull and a bit smug, but my brother loved her. I passed her the gravy at Thanksgiving and was glad I didn't have to spend the rest of the year with her. Well, now I'm in love with her, and while it's not directly connected, her marriage to my brother is in trouble. (For the record, I doubt that Janice is my soul mate. We're badly suited, whereas she and my brother are usually a power team-up. It's just a whole bunch of stuff at once, and then the pandemic, that's heightened everything. But I *feel* like she's my soul mate.)

I had a really bad car accident a few years ago, lost my job, got dumped, and developed a drinking problem. When I hit rock bottom, my family was there for me, but it was Janice who stepped up the most, who let me cry on her shoulder, who drove me to my physio appointments. So now, lonely, desperate for affection, and still all banged up, I am in love. And it looks like my brother and Janice are going through something. There's a terrible part of me, maybe 5 percent, that wants to take advantage of it. But the rest of me wants to be a good friend, a good in-law, and a good brother. I'm not sure how to navigate this without making things weird, damaging my family relationships, or possibly taking advantage of the situation to get what I want. Should I tell Janice how I feel and then distance myself? Distance myself and just look like I'm ungrateful for all her help? Pretend to be disinterested and just play the role of good brother-in-law?

—Opportunity Knocks but Once

The first thing to do is refocus on the support you can draw from sources that aren't your brother's wife, not because you need to start ignoring her as a matter of principle, but because you need more than one person you can rely on for help. That might mean asking others to drive you to your appointments, looking for twelve-step recovery meetings (or non-twelve-step alternatives), crying on a rotating cast of shoulders, and seeking out ways to help others when you can.

It's not my place to tell you whether you are or aren't in love with Janice. Perhaps more importantly, love can sometimes be accompanied by self-interest or neediness or dislike, even contempt. But you seem fairly aware that your newfound love for Janice didn't arise from reevaluating those qualities of hers you dislike or a desire to care for her the way your brother does, so much as an overwhelming sense of gratitude for her care and attention in your moment of crisis. That doesn't make a strong foundation for a committed romantic relationship.

Prioritizing non-Janice emotional outlets will make it easier to find ways to step back from her (possible) marital crisis without suddenly going cold and ignoring all of her calls.

Don't punish her for being kind to you by withdrawing or by burdening her with an unexpected announcement that you're kind of in love with her, even though you still sort of don't like her and don't think you two are suited for each other anyway. (I'm reminded of Mr. Darcy's first ill-fated proposal to Elizabeth Bennet: "'I might as well inquire,' replied she, 'why with so evident a desire of offending and insulting me, you chose to tell me that you liked me against your will, against your reason, and even against your character?'") Trust that she has friends and family of her own she can turn to for advice and counsel who are better suited than her husband's brother to help her with whatever problems she may be facing in her marriage. Ask yourself if part of your desire to stir the pot comes from any resentment toward the rest of your family for not "stepping up" the way Janice did when you hit rock bottom, and find a therapist if you still can't shake that 5 percent of you that wants to see if you can get an affair going.

• • •

Sometimes the problem of "just one more thing" works in reverse, as when a letter writer fears that their particular needs are going to be the straw that breaks someone else's back.

////////////

Dear Prudence,

For about a year since I graduated with my PhD, I've had some trouble finding a job. I've applied to many, but a lot of jobs just won't take a risk hiring a PhD unless a PhD is required. I couldn't even find tutoring jobs. On top of that, I also had health issues, so working full-time was out of the question. I've finally gotten my health under enough control and was even offered a job. The pay, however, is terrible. I'm debating applying for SNAP. When my health problems started, I lost my job and moved in with my mother. She owes me money from several years ago when she divorced my father and he stopped paying some bills that legally became her responsibility. That's no longer a problem, and my mother has recently gotten back on her feet financially. She started paying for my credit card bills when I went through my savings. I now no longer have any credit. It will be about a month before I get paid, and I'm not sure I can make it that long. I could possibly ask my mom to give me money on top of the credit card payments, but after six months she started complaining every so often that she thought I would be moved out and financially solid by then. I have a feeling she will start saying this more often if I ask her for more money, even if it were just for a couple months. I absolutely believe in the importance of SNAP and have no moral qualms about anybody who uses [it], but I really don't want to take resources away from people who have absolutely no other options. Should I suck it up and ask my mom, or just apply for SNAP?

—Food Concerns

////////////////

It's a mistake to think of SNAP as a limited resource in the same way a bushel of apples is a limited resource. It's not something you can "take away" from someone else, as if someone else applying five minutes after you might hear in response: "We'd love to give you a card, but [the letter writer] just took the last one. Better luck next time!" SNAP is a federal entitlement program, which means that as long as you meet the eligibility requirements, you'll get benefits. There's no need to worry about qualms here. Apply for the program and use whatever

you're entitled to. Take care of yourself, and good luck with your
new job!

• • •

And finally, there is the problem of accumulating a series of "just one more things." The next letter writer is so eager to persuade her boyfriend of the objective rightness of her position that she's convinced it's just a question of marshaling sufficient points in her favor before he's bound to want the same thing she does. If only things worked that way!

////////////

Dear Prudence,

I've been in a relationship for about three months. My partner and I knew each other for about six years and were very close before we got together, and for the most part it's genuinely the best relationship I have ever been a part of: he's funny, sweet, ambitious, etc., but also since we've been friends for so long, he's also really amazing with my four-year-old son. I have a habit of "falling fast" and wanted to discuss the possibility of us moving in together when our leases are up next summer. He currently lives an hour away, and it's just nice to think about a future where we don't have to drive so much to get to see each other. Additionally, his current roommates are financially unreliable, causing him to have to work longer weeks just to make sure he will be able to cover whatever they don't pay. I have a good-paying job and could offer better financial security, but he won't hear it. Even though what we have is super solid, and he tells me all the time about how much he loves me and my son, he says a year from now would be too soon to consider living together. I'm trying to make peace with this, but I really don't understand. I really want to respect his boundaries, but I honestly really feel like I would be the overall better roommate option: I'm financially reliable, relatively clean, and my kid is pretty chill most of the time. Is there a way to broach this topic again without coming across as disrespectful?

—Good Girlfriend, Better Roommate

////////////

The good news is that you don't have to understand your boyfriend's position in order to respect it. If it would help to hear someone else summarize it, allow me: Your boyfriend loves you very much, but he's not ready to start talking about moving in together after a mere three months of dating (even though you've known one another six years), and he doesn't think he'll want to move in together anytime in the next nine months, either. That's it. That's the position: He loves you, he loves your kid, and he wants to take his time before moving in with your kid and taking on a much more involved, quasi-parental role. Before you say again how chill your kid is—and I believe he really is delightful!—deciding to move in with a partner with a four-year-old child is a pretty significant step, no matter how relaxed the four-year-old, and it's naive to suggest otherwise.

I'm sure you are a more responsible roommate than the people your boyfriend presently lives with. But so are many other people, and it's disingenuous to present your position as merely logistically superior ("I pay my rent on time, and it would cut down on our commute if we lived together") when in fact it's what you want for the next stage of your relationship. That's fine; you don't have to apologize for falling fast or for wanting to live with him. But you should acknowledge the fact that it is fast, that it's pretty unusual for couples to plan to move in together after just a few months of dating, and that it might in fact be better for your son to move ahead patiently, building up trust and intimacy and routine over time. You can bring this up again with your boyfriend, but I don't think you should say, "Explain this to me again, because I just don't understand—I'm such a great roommate." Say something more like this: "You know me well enough to know I tend to fall fast; I've known you long enough to feel pretty confident about our relationship. I want to live with you. I think it would be a lot of fun, and I think we'd all get along really well; I also understand why you want to wait a year or longer. But I hope we can talk about the possibility of living closer to one another (without living in the same house) if you decide you want new roommates once your lease is up, and I hope you'll let me know when you do feel ready to move in together."

Chapter Four

In the Family Key

We've got it all: mom problems, sibling problems, in-law problems, kid problems, nephews and nieces who want to borrow money, parents who took out credit cards in your name without telling you, sisters who insist on using you as a surrogate, brothers who wreck your car, contested inheritances, secret half-siblings, demanding stepparents, unpleasant group vacations—you name it.

P artly due to proximity, partly to history, and partly because they're likely to already know your Social Security number, relatives are often at the root of the thorniest problems. They know how to push the most exasperating of buttons. Letter writers often rely on them (or vice versa) for childcare, employment in the family business, or rides to work, and unlike a bad boyfriend or girlfriend, they can rarely be sent packing on the strength of a single breakup conversation. Beyond that, of course, there's an intricate and delicate web of dependence, care, continuity, and shared relationships that tie us to one another that's not so easily cut. Whenever possible, and excepting explicit cases of abuse or endangerment that necessitate emergency action, I've tried to bear in mind each letter writer's particular goals and values when it comes to navigating family conflict, rather than simply counseling estrangement at the first sign of contention.

After all, there's something presumptuous about suggesting to someone that they stop talking to their own mother, even if that someone has particularly sought out my opinion on the subject, so I'm reluctant to recommend it too quickly or too often. Yet this reluctance has been repeatedly tempted in the face of an astonishingly vibrant array of bad mothers over the years. The column has seen countless lousy uncles, terrible grandmothers, insensitive brothers, and troublesome cousins, but some of the most memorable, the real standouts, have been mothers like this one.

///////////////

Dear Prudence,

My twenty-seven-year-old daughter and her best friend, Katie, have been best friends since they were four. Katie practically grew up in our house and is like a daughter to me. My daughter recently got engaged to her fiancé and announced that Katie would be the maid of honor (Katie's boyfriend is also a good friend of my future son-in-law). The problem is that Katie walks with a pretty severe limp due to a birth defect (not an underlying medical issue). She has no problem wearing high heels and has

already been fitted for the dress, but I still think it will look
unsightly if she's in the wedding procession limping ahead of
my daughter. I mentioned this to my daughter and suggested
that maybe Katie could take video or hand out programs (while
sitting) so she doesn't ruin the aesthetic aspect of the wedding.
My daughter is no longer speaking to me (we were never that
close), but this is her big wedding and I want it to be perfect. All
of the other bridesmaids will look gorgeous walking down the
aisle with my daughter. Is it wrong to have her friend sit out?

—Picture-Perfect Only, Please

*I am having a hard time wrapping my mind around this letter. I
encourage you to reread it and to ask yourself that time-honored
question, "Do I sound like a villain in a Reese Witherspoon movie?"
You are, presumably, sympathetic to your own situation and are
invested in making sure that you come across as a relatively
reasonable person, and yet you have written a letter indicting
yourself at every turn. This girl is "like a daughter" to you, and yet
you want to shove her to the side of a family wedding just because
she walks with a limp. Your daughter's wedding will be perfect
with Katie as a full and honored member of the bridal party. Her
limp is not going to "ruin the aesthetic aspect" of the wedding;
it's merely a part of Katie's life. It is not only wrong to have asked
your daughter to consider excluding her best friend over this—it is
ableist and cruel, and it speaks to a massive failure of empathy,
compassion, and grace on your part. You must and should*

apologize to your daughter immediately, and I encourage you to
profoundly reconsider the orientation of your heart.

• • •

The question of keeping someone else's secrets for them is another recurring family theme. Children often ask one parent to keep a secret from another, parents ask their children, siblings each other, and so on; there's a difficult balance to be struck between honoring someone else's wishes wherever possible, acknowledging one's own limits (people rarely go from being indifferent secret keepers to robustly sealed vaults overnight, especially in a pressurized situation like an upcoming wedding or funeral), and weighing the broader needs and expectations the family as a group might share against an individual's.

////////////

Dear Prudence,

My parents are divorced and aren't on speaking terms. My dad has asked my brothers and me to keep his cancer a secret from my mom. We haven't told her, but it's been hard not being able to go to her for support. In a few weeks, they will both be at a big event, and I think my mom will find out about the cancer when she sees him. I don't want her to be taken by surprise, but I don't want to betray my dad's trust. What should I do?

—Big C, Big Secret

////////////

Talk to your father. Tell him you believe your mother is going to put two and two together the next time she sees him, and it will be better for her to be prepared in private than for her to come to a sudden realization in public. If he's still insistent, I think you should respect his wishes, but hopefully you can stress that this conversation may become unavoidable relatively soon and that getting it out of the way now may protect him from a potentially painful public scene.

• • •

Dear Prudence,

My sister and stepsister have always quarreled over every issue you can think of. My sister is a professional photographer and records almost every family function in spectacular style. My stepsister got married recently and decided to skip paying a photographer since my sister "always carries her camera." You guessed it: The photographs came out horribly—red eyes, blurry, and fuzzy. My stepsister had a fit and screamed at my sister. My sister said she had accidentally brought some bad lenses but since no one officially asked her to be the wedding photographer, she hadn't had time to prepare. And it is true—no one asked my sister to be the wedding photographer or offered to pay her. However, my sister has since confessed to me over a bottle of wine that she deliberately chose a bad camera because my stepsister was a "cheap, selfish witch."

I am not sure what to do here. The entire fallout has
most of my relatives talking about what a "bridezilla" my
stepsister was. Even my stepmom apologized to my sister for
her daughter's behavior. Was my sister right? Should I say
anything?

—Not Picture-Perfect

///////////

*I shouldn't laugh. I won't laugh. I'm not laughing now. Nothing
about this situation is funny, and I'm going to take it very seriously.
Here is my official ruling: say nothing. There is nothing to be gained
by telling your stepsister the truth, as you'll only extend their
ceaseless quarrel. What your sister did was passive-aggressive
and slightly mean-spirited, but your stepsister has also learned an
important lesson: if you want professional wedding photos, hire a
professional photographer, and pay them for their work. Don't ask
someone you have a habit of fighting with over everything to do it
for free at the last minute.*

• • •

Sometimes on revisiting an older answer I detect myself taking on an "advice-columny" persona that rings a little false
in hindsight. I still believe it's perfectly reasonable for the following letter writer to stop giving her sister money, and that
her initial plan of extracting a written "promise" from her
pledging to stop asking was misguided, in part because such

a promise is not legally binding and in part because both parties seemed aware the letter writer wasn't really prepared to back it up by saying no again in the future. But *misguided* strikes me as the better descriptive term than "ridiculous or sad," and I missed an opportunity to explore the sisters' underlying fears, anxieties, and needs with compassion rather than sarcasm. That the letter writer's sister is "not good" with money may be perfectly true—it may even be true that she doesn't really like to work (who does!)—but it's not exactly easy to ask for more hours in retail, where many companies go out of their way not to schedule employees full-time in order to avoid paying benefits. And while her sister's habit of borrowing money might be frustrating for the letter writer, and I continue to sympathize with her desire to change it, I don't necessarily think it's a "ploy" to say, "I need $400 for my electric bill," when she really does need $400 for their electric bill.

///////////

Dear Prudence,

I have a sister who has borrowed approximately $25,000 from me. She is recently divorced and does not really like to work. She receives a modest alimony payment and works approximately twenty-five hours a week in retail. My sister and her ex-husband have never been smart with money. They went through bankruptcy in the past couple years. We both received approximately $120,000 in an inheritance when my mother passed away in 2010. My sister has spent all this money. I have spent some of mine on home repairs. In the past six months, I made my sister sign a statement saying she would not ask for any more money. It didn't seem to help. Her ploy now is: "I need $400 for my electric bill" or "I need $600 to fix my car." My ultimate nightmare is that someday she will knock on my door saying she has nowhere to live. I am the sibling who is more like her Depression-era parents. I pay all my bills on time and in full. I also work full-time at a very decent-paying job that is stressful and approximately one hour from my home. I think I have a personality trait where I am "the caretaker."

How can I get my sister to stop being a mooch? Or get myself to say no to every request for money?

—Mooching Sister

///////////////

I read this letter expecting to have to answer the question "How do I get my $25,000 back?" but you seem to have already resigned yourself to your loss and are merely asking for help in not giving your sister an additional $25,000. You must know on some level that your sister's problem is not merely due to lack of funds—there is, I suspect, no amount of money you could give her that would ever end her habit of asking for more. She will find a way to run through every loan, windfall, or second chance that comes her way until she is willing and able to make different choices. Every time you give her money, you're helping her put

*that day a little further off—which is to say, you're not helping her
at all.*

*Asking her to sign a piece of paper promising not to ask for
money again is ridiculous and sad, because you both know that
when she asks you for money, it works. It's worked to the tune of
$25,000, and it will continue to work until you are able to say,
and mean, no without explanation, without apology, without
justifications, without argument. Just no. It may be worth spending
a little bit of money with a therapist in order to figure out why it's so
difficult for you to stop bailing your sister out of her financial black
hole and to devise strategies for sticking to your guns in the future.*

• • •

I could have dedicated an entire chapter to letters from writers who suspect (or sometimes discover outright) that one
of their relatives is attempting to poison them or a pet or a
child or a partner, either by sneaking known allergens into a
group meal or through the addition of laxatives and household cleaners. I'm far from certain in the following case—but
I do wonder.

////////////

Dear Prudence,
My fiancé and I are going to his sister's for Thanksgiving. I share
three cats and a dog with my mom. Without fail, one of them will

get sick just before I travel. Last Thanksgiving my mom had to put down our cat while I was away. She was not happy with me, and I felt really bad. Now it's three days to departure, and the dog is barfing, and the cat is sneezing.... I can feel the guilt already, and my mom is already starting to look at me sidelong. I don't blame her for being resentful at being the de facto pet babysitter, but this is like a macabre joke: I swear, every time I'm gone, something happens with the animals! Any advice?

—Pets in Peril?

////////////

I want to give your mother the benefit of the doubt: surely she is not intentionally hurting any of your animals, and your pets' suspiciously timed illnesses are only a series of improbable coincidences. Find a sitter when you travel, or board your animals at a kennel. Boarding expenses are almost certainly cheaper than veterinary bills. I don't know if you live with your mother or just share animal custody, but consider taking the pets with you full-time when you and your fiancé get a place together.

Would it be possible for you and your fiancé to invite your mother along (with his sister's permission, of course), or at least make separate plans to celebrate with her? It's possible part of the reason she's unhappy is that she has been invited to babysit four animals by herself for the holiday.

• • •

////////////////

Dear Prudence,

My in-laws are unbelievably superstitious. My mother-in-law believes she's psychic, my father-in-law believes her, and my husband—otherwise rational—thinks we can't know for sure and turns remarkably credulous around her. I find the stream of "insights" and ghost sightings grating, but they can believe what they want—until it reaches the end of my nose.

My husband and I are looking to buy a house, and his mother is constantly bothering me with her visions of "dark auras" and "bad vibes" about the houses. She's not even with us. Apparently she can tell a duplex has more ghosts than Disney's Haunted House from two states away.

I'd just tune her out, but my husband says we should listen to keep the peace. Apparently she won't ever visit if the house is "haunted." My husband caving to her is the worst part of it. Is this going to be how it is going forward? It's a house! A mortgage! The only thing to tie us together more would be a child. So I'm wondering if maybe we need to rethink more than just the "haunted house." Or am I being unreasonable?

—Family of Ghost Hunters

////////////////

I agree that if your husband's response to this has been, "Sorry, we're going to have to pass on this affordable duplex until my mom is convinced it's not chockablock with ghosts," then that's a bad strategy. His idea of "keeping the peace" is financially and relationally unreasonable, and you should make it clear to him that while you won't go out of your way to antagonize her or make fun of her conviction that she is some sort of real estate medium, you're also not going to entertain endless requests to put off buying a home until she can sweep it for signs of the paranormal.

You ask if this is how it's going to be going forward. Obviously I myself am not a psychic, but my guess is that if your husband is willing to indulge some pretty intrusive behavior from her about home-buying, then this pattern will probably crop up again, so it's good to address it now. You and your husband don't have to agree on everything, but you do have to deal with your in-laws as a team and back one another up. It's one thing to say, "We can't know for sure" about the existence of ghosts; it's quite another to say, "Because we can't know for sure if ghosts exist, we should pass on every house my mother believes to be haunted." One is a general, open-ended statement about the nature of possibility; the other is granting his mother total purchasing power in your marriage.

• • • •

One of the rubrics I have found helpful in trying to establish whether a relationship is worth preserving (or even possible to preserve!) is to consider whether one would tolerate such a pattern of behavior from anyone besides a relative. That's not the only possible rubric, of course, but if one would never stand for a double-barrel of cruelty and demands for money from a friend, a lover, or a colleague, it can be useful to maintain a similar expectation from one's relatives.

/////////////////

Dear Prudence,

I'm a trans woman. My mom freaked out when I tried to express
how I felt as a kid and always forced me to wear typical boys'
clothes and play with appropriately masculine toys. My Aunt
Diane (her sister) was the complete opposite. Growing up, I spent
at least one weekend a month at her house while Mom partied.
She let me wear dresses and play with dolls and makeup. I had my
own closet and toy box at her house filled with my real clothes
and toys—things that would have been thrown away if they
appeared at my mom's house. She was incredibly supportive and,
truthfully, was more of a mother to me than my actual mother.

Sadly, Aunt Diane passed away a few months ago after a
brutal, but thankfully brief, battle with cancer. I was and still am
heartbroken. Thankfully I have a loving partner and wonderful
friends to help me through the grief. My family has been less
supportive. Except for a few thousand dollars put into a trust for
my half-sister, Aunt Diane left everything to me. She was a very
hard worker and good with money, though I was still shocked by
the amount. My mother and sister were livid when they found
out, feeling that Aunt Diane should have provided more for my
sister, and are now demanding that I split my inheritance with her.
The thing is, my aunt tried very hard to develop a close loving
relationship with my sister as she did with me, but my sister just
didn't care. She's a lot like my mother—very narcissistic and only
interested in people who can do things for her. She once claimed
that spending too much time with Aunt Diane would turn her into a
"freak like me." I'm tired of being hounded by her and my mother,

but I also feel like she shouldn't profit from my aunt's death when she was so dismissive of her while she was alive. What should I do?

—Hounded by Blessings

I think you should stop taking their calls and emails and texts. If all your mother and sister have ever done for you is mock your identity and demand money from you, you should feel free to ignore their future requests with a clear conscience. If they're not able to take no for an answer, then you should feel free to ignore them entirely.

• • •

Every once in a while, I'd hear from a reader who recognized a recently published letter from another advice column or from one of the popular crowdsourced advice subforums on Reddit, and it was always fun to try to puzzle through whether it might have been the same person trying their luck in multiple outlets, or whether two unlucky women caught their fiancé cheating on them with his sister in the same month. One rather hopes for the former in that case, of course, but there's no way to know.

Dear Prudence,
I recently caught my fiancé and his sister together and broke up with him. I'd always gotten a strange feeling about their

closeness, but I didn't believe it until I saw with my own eyes. To my family and friends, it seems like I woke up one morning and decided not to get married. Everyone is pushing me to work things out with my fiancé. Initially, I wanted to keep what I saw between them and me. If I tell people they have an incestuous relationship, it would probably destroy their lives. I know they're barely functioning and terrified I will tell people about them. I'm worried I will seem spiteful if I tell even a few trusted loved ones the real reason I called off the wedding. At the same time, I'm heartbroken too and don't know how much longer I can handle lectures about "letting a good man get away." Should I stay quiet or speak up?

—Too Close for Comfort

///////////

If you are the Reddit user who posted the same problem two months ago, then first: congratulations on getting out of this relationship before your wedding, though I'm sorry you had to find out that way. (If you are not the same person, then I'll take this as a reminder that anything that has happened to someone can and will also happen to someone else.) I can't imagine how crushed and bewildered you must feel right now, and I hope very much you're able to see a counselor about the emotional trauma you've experienced. I understand your reluctance to bring your fiancé's relationship with his sister to light, if nothing else because it would be exhausting and overwhelming for you to deal with the subsequent aftermath and embarrassing questions. I'm also

*sorry so many of your friends would lecture you about letting
a good man "get away" just because you decided not to get
married. If pressed, I think you should tell people that your fiancé
was unfaithful and you couldn't go ahead with the wedding; this
contains enough of the truth that people will understand and won't
press for further explanation but spares you all from the fallout
that would result from dropping the bomb you hold in your hands.*

• • • •

//////////

Dear Prudence,

My sister has six children, ranging from six months to twelve
years old. For many years, my sister and her husband established
our parents as their children's guardians if anything should
happen to them, but this past year my parents' health has
declined rapidly. They're doing okay but need daily assistance
and won't be able to take care of kids. My sister and her husband
have both been in serious accidents themselves.

My husband and I have one fifteen-year-old, good careers,
and busy lives. Our brothers are both bachelors. My sister has
been pressing me to agree to be her children's guardians in the
event of their death. She has several suitable in-laws but doesn't
like them. My husband and I gave it a lot of thought and agreed
that there would be no way we could take on all six. We could
take the two oldest, but my sister got furious at the suggestion.

She accused me of hating her children, wanting to break up her family, and being a "complete failure" of a human being. I told her to calm down, that nothing had happened and likely never would. She said she would take in my child "in a heartbeat," and I said one child wasn't six. Now she's giving me the silent treatment. I don't know what to do, and I'm worried about how this might affect my nieces and nephews. My husband says we can just placate her and say we changed our minds. I don't want to lie.

—Chancy Custodians

///////////////

The major flaw in your husband's plan—aside from the likelihood that already it's too late to placate your sister by saying, "Okay, we changed our minds"—is that in the unlikely, but not impossible, event that something does happen to your sister and her husband, you'll either have to go through with it or tell your entire family that you didn't really mean it. It's not just that the lie would be uncomfortable to live with, although I'm sure it would. It is also probably not going to get you what you want in the short term and could potentially lead to much bigger problems in the future. What you said to your sister was loving, realistic, and helpful, even though it must have been difficult for her to hear. It might have been better to wait for your sister's initial reaction before offering to take the two oldest (and I can very much understand why that would not have struck her as a viable compromise), but your overall position is still consistent with being a loving aunt and sister.

But you're not in a position to argue about niceties with your sister at the moment. Give her a little longer to cool down, as it's clear her emotions are running high and she's not able to discuss exigencies without picturing worst-case scenarios and worst-possible motives. In a few weeks, let her know you're available to talk if she feels ready: "We don't have to talk about guardianship again if it's too upsetting, but I miss you and the kids, and I'd really like to see you again sometime. I know it's painful to contemplate possible tragedies, and I don't take what would happen to the kids if you two died lightly. I'm sorry I hurt you, and I'm here to listen if you want to talk. I can't give you a different answer, because no matter how much I might wish otherwise, we simply can't raise seven kids, but I want to help in whatever ways you'll let me as you try to figure out your plan."

If her response to that is still "You're a failure who's breaking up my family" or "I'd take in your kid if you died," then all you can do is graciously back off and hope she eventually recovers her sense of proportion. It's painful, and I'm sorry you're going through it, but lying to try to fast-forward to the end of this fight won't work.

• • •

///////////

Dear Prudence,
My older sister and I live several states apart. She has made friends with a divorced man around her age from her church. She has had a crush on him for quite a while, though she has never dated and has not even mentioned having a crush on anyone

since a painful rejection in high school. Even though he does not reciprocate, she continues to try to impress him. After fifteen years of having dyed-black hair, my sister asked my mom to bleach it blond based on his suggestion. Apparently she'd had an intense argument with this man when she was about to touch up her roots! My sister fights rudely with anyone who gives her even a little advice, even her loved ones. Now, she's willing to make choices based on what this man says. My cousins, my brother, and I are all worried, but what can we do without driving her defenses up and pushing her away from us and toward him?

—Blood Is Thicker Than Dye

/////////////

Have you tried not giving your sister advice? What about generally respecting the distance she sets, and developing a mutually independent relationship based on reciprocal noninterference? What exactly are you worried about, and what do you hope to gain out of this situation with your sister? Be specific, as it will help you determine what, if anything, you want to do next.

I can understand your concern for your sister's feelings, especially if you're worried she's going to get hurt. But how could you protect her from that possibility? All crushes carry with them some element of emotional risk, but all she's doing right now is occasionally squabbling with this guy and deciding to do something different with her hair. That's fine! She has every right to decide to change her hair color because of a crush even if she declines to change her hair color when her siblings and cousins say, "You'd really make a better brunette." That's not an indication that the sky is falling, or that she doesn't care about all of you. Remember that scene from Father of the Bride, where Steve Martin suggests his newly engaged daughter put on a coat? "Oh, Dad, it's okay, I'm kind of warm," she says dismissively, at which point her fiancé says, "Annie, it is kind of cold out." She responds, "It is?" as if she's hearing the news for the first time, then immediately puts on a sweater while Steve Martin mugs in exasperation for the camera. This is an incredibly common dynamic! It might be annoying, but it's hardly a sign that your sister is losing her sense of self.

You might think your sister is foolish to try to maintain a friendship with this man. But it's her friendship to maintain, it's her romantic risk to run, and there are no indicators that he's a threat to her safety, so you should let her make her own choices as she sees fit. If it frustrates you to see your sister occasionally accept input from her friends that she doesn't welcome from her family, I'd encourage you to reflect on whether you ever do the same thing in your own life. Try to extend that same freedom to your sister, even if part of you wishes you could protect her from all possible pain.

• • •

Sometimes it can be tremendously freeing to let go of the idea that a historically fraught and contentious parent-child relationship is going to suddenly become an emotionally safe and deeply intimate one. "My parents can't handle too much information about my personal life without flying off the handle, so I'm going to keep things relatively light and detach when they're spoiling for a fight" is often a much more readily achievable goal than "This is finally going to be the year where I convince my parents to respect my decisions."

////////////////

Dear Prudence,

After several years of consideration and a year of study with my rabbi, I've set a date for my conversion to Judaism. I am incredibly happy and excited for this next chapter of my life. The only thing that is weighing on me is whether to tell my parents. I grew up in a very strict household where "Children should be seen and not heard" was the rule. As an adult, I've kept most of my life quite private from my relatives, and my weekly phone calls with my parents never stray beyond the weather, work, and what we've been cooking lately. My mother is a devout Christian, and religion has been a source of tension between us in the past. The last time I expressed doubts about Christianity I was a teenager, and I got slapped, then told not to question my parents again. I've mentioned attending a synagogue in passing a few times, and my parents responded with silence or a hasty change of subject.

Is there any value in telling them about my conversion? It feels strange to omit something that is so important to my day-to-day life, but so does the thought of having to explain or justify a deeply personal decision.

—Secret Conversion

////////////////

You have a mostly sustainable arrangement with your parents where you stay in regular contact but rarely share details with them about your innermost thoughts, feelings, hopes, fears, values, or relationships. Deciding not to discuss your conversion with them sounds consistent with the type of relationship you've had for years. That doesn't mean you have to lie about it or worry that they have the same power to control you as an adult as they did when you were a teenager. But it does mean your primary emotional obligation here should be to yourself, and you should only decide to inform them if you think it would be meaningful for you to address it.

The fact that they've largely ignored your experiences with Judaism in the past might actually end up working in your favor if your goal is simply to provide them with a bullet-points update. You can say something like, "Last month I finalized my conversion to Judaism, by the way, which was lovely. I'm thinking of making panzanella tonight, since it's still too hot out to turn the oven on." Your parents can freeze awkwardly and then respond with, "Mmm. That reminds me, I've got to figure out a use for all the summer squash before it goes bad." If they do react badly and try to criticize your conversion or insist you justify your decision, you don't have to give in to their demands—you can hang up the phone. Again, the choice is really yours here. It's simply a question of which type of strained strangeness you'd prefer with your parents. One silver lining is that you have relatively little to lose.

• • •

I never knew, until I took on the Dear Prudence job, just how many families seem to struggle with the question of priceless jeweled heirlooms! I thought it was only the sort of thing that happened in Guy de Maupassant stories but was delighted to be proved wrong.

////////////

Dear Prudence,
My grandmother once had a diamond necklace that was a family heirloom. My grandfather, who didn't know how to keep things in his pants, ended up giving it to one of his mistresses. My grandmother mourned the loss of the necklace until the day she died. Recently, I happened to stumble across the necklace, or what I think is the necklace, on eBay. I questioned my grandfather and contacted the seller, and both parties think it's possible this necklace belonged to my grandmother. I wanted it back, but when I tried to discuss it with the seller, she said she was selling it for a reason and that, if I really wanted it back, I would pay her either the asking price or more. I am not sure what to do next. She has thankfully taken it down, but I feel like I am being blackmailed. Any thoughts?

—Affair of the Necklace

////////////

Let's start with the good news: You're not being blackmailed. A stranger is selling her necklace, which both she and your grandfather believe is "possibly" a gift he once gave his mistress.

The necklace has presumably been in her possession for a fairly long time, and there are a number of reasons this stranger might not want to ask her relative, who may no longer be living, "Hey, did you get this necklace from a man who was cheating on his wife with you?"

If you can afford to buy the necklace, and you'd like to, you can get back in touch and make an offer. But just because you saw something that looks a lot like the necklace your grandfather gave away doesn't mean the stranger selling it should hand it over on demand. If you're still feeling unsettled, I think a more productive use of your time would be to speak with your grandfather about how his cheating and secret gift giving hurt and confused your grandmother, and how that in turn has affected you. But don't try to work through your family's dirty laundry at this stranger's expense.

Chapter Five

The Care and Maintenance of Your Estrangement

On unraveling the ties that bind. Searching for justification in the hopes that someone else might take over the responsibility of kicking off an estrangement. Wells that don't draw water, and finding alternate sources of refreshment. Drawing the line at toenail clippings.

Some domestic problems are easier to address in a few paragraphs than others; *I've been sexting with my wife's aunt for a year. Am I cheating?* has a fairly straightforward yes-or-no answer. Others can feel like trying to uproot a full-grown oak tree by tugging on a single leaf: *Everyone else in my family acts like everything is normal, but I haven't been able to shake this nagging feeling that something's wrong.* If the family has depended for years on a shared "consensus" denial of reality, speaking up can feel like trying to wake a sleepwalker or issuing an invitation to a pile-on. There's the question of shared allegiances in marriage: *Are my partner and I really a team? Or when push comes to shove, am I going to learn that their primary commitment is to their family of origin and that my options are either to join their team or get pushed aside?* There's also the question of whether "preserving the peace" is a worthwhile, pragmatic goal or a short-term survival technique that offers increasingly diminishing returns, especially if that "peace" is dependent on keeping quiet.

It's not always big-ticket, high-profile problems that lead to division, either. Sometimes a disagreement about when and where to clip your nails can lead a letter writer to contemplate divorce from an otherwise perfectly charming husband. And sometimes relatives can wound deeply and instantly in places where friends, colleagues, or lovers might only score glancing blows. When to negotiate, when to revise expectations, when to prioritize self-protection, and when to pursue conflict are often context-dependent decisions that mostly rely on the letter writer's particular and unique goals, whether that's to field intrusive questions less often, buy some time, find people outside the family to talk to, or finally get something off their chest, come what may.

If a letter writer is already contemplating estrangement or is willing to entertain the possibility, I try to stress two things: that one need not commit to estrangement as a lifelong policy if it seems too daunting, and that estrangement (like breakups!) need not serve as a permanent moral referendum on someone else's character. That's not to say one should approach a potential estrangement with the same casual attitude one might take toward a sweater ("I'll keep the tags on, and if I don't like it, I'll just return it Thursday"), but it can make a very daunting prospect seem more manageable if one keeps in mind that estrangement is a malleable and subjective project, not a binding legal commitment, an option rather than an obligation. If the relationship is already unsalvageable, estrangement does not create the rift; rather it provides necessary space and distance from an already painful reality.

/////////////

Dear Prudence,

I'm a married man, and I have been sexting with my wife's aunt for about a year now. We have never sent pictures or done any type of video chat—it's all been hot and heavy texts. She wants to start video chatting, but I am totally against it. I feel like texting is not cheating because it's just text and not sex. But as soon as pictures and videos and live sessions start, then I am cheating on my wife.

My question for you is, am I already cheating just by texting? I'm sure my wife would think so, but in my heart of hearts I disagree, yet I do think videos and live sessions would be crossing the line. Have I crossed that line already? Should I just do it?

—It's Just Text

/////////////

*You are very much cheating on your wife. With her aunt. And there
are reams of written evidence to that effect. You have definitely
crossed that line, and you've crossed it in a monumentally unwise
fashion. I'm not sure what good you think it will do to disagree
in your "heart of hearts" when—not if—your wife finds out. But
I don't say that in order to bolster your desire for an excuse to
find an "Oh, fuck it" moment and just go for it. Your response to
"Yes, you've been betraying your wife in a deeply intimate and
brutal fashion that will absolutely break her heart" should not be
"Oh well, in for a penny, in for a pound, might as well see if I can
get some nudes out of it," but instead, "How can I rearrange my
ethical commitments and stop cheating on my wife with one of her
relatives?"*

● ● ●

Somewhere between "What do I want from my mother?" (often: affection, attention, support, composure, advocacy, reassurance, a "special relationship" somewhat along the lines of the US and the UK during and after the Second World War, whereby uniquely collaborative goals, values, and operations are regularly reaffirmed in both public conventions and private correspondence, in short, a series of very tall orders indeed) and "What is my mother prepared, willing, and able to offer me, given what I know of her history, her character, and her current inclinations?" there is a field of opportunity, if one can make it through the thousand toils, snares, and thickets barring the way.

///////////////

Dear Prudence,

A few weeks ago, I won an award for my volunteer work. I was excited about it, and like an idiot I invited my mother to attend the ceremony. She ruined the evening for me. She was unpleasant to my friends, refused to smile for the local newspaper photo, and was rude to my state senator. On Friday, the local paper ran an article about me and everything I do in the community. Now she is angry at me for bringing attention to the family.

Somehow I thought getting an award for doing good deeds was something to be proud of. Should I tell her that her attitude has ruined my feelings about volunteering in the community? Or just swallow it like I have done so many times in the past? My entire family acts like I am a bad person for wanting notice for my accomplishments. It's not my fault they have accomplished nothing of note.

—Never Good Enough

///////////////

Both of the options you've proposed here—swallowing all of your anger like you've done so many times before or telling your mother that she's ruined the very concept of volunteering—are bad ones and unlikely to result in increased personal satisfaction. The temptation to underreact and pretend nothing happened may be strong, but it's only ever made you feel resentful, slighted, irritable, and ready to explode. The countervailing temptation to blow up now and tell her she's destroyed your interest in ever helping another person again may feel equally strong, if only so you can feel like you've balanced things out, but I think you should try to pursue a more moderate path.

Wait until you've cooled down a little. Talk to some trusted friends first, or write down some of your more intense feelings in a journal— anything that enables you to collect your unfiltered thoughts while you prepare for a real conversation. You can tell your mother that her rudeness at the ceremony hurt your feelings, that you don't feel guilty about "bringing attention to the family" on the strength of your community involvement, and that if she can't get excited about your achievements, then you hope she can at least strive for peaceful neutrality. In the long run, you may want to stop soliciting your family's approval for your accomplishments, given how much consistent pleasure they seem to have derived from withholding it over the years. That well isn't drawing water.

• • •

Well, some things are just unreasonable.

///////////////

Dear Prudence,
My husband has an extremely obnoxious habit that I have spoken to him about several times over the past five years. He will pick at his toenails while watching TV and then leave the remnants on the couch where he's been sitting. I will periodically find large chunks of toenail clippings randomly on our couch, coffee

table, and floor. It's not often, but every few months I will find these lovely gifts. I have explained to him that it is disturbing and gross (and embarrassing if someone were to come over). I have politely requested that he do this in the bathroom. My requests have gone unnoticed and been ignored. I feel disrespected and grossed out. I have begun to passive-aggressively handle this by picking up the clippings whenever I find them and putting them in his coffee cup in the mornings. I know this is wrong, but I find some relief in making him discover his own toenail clippings in his coffee. What else can I do? How can I help him understand that this is neither acceptable nor fair to me?

—End of My Rope

////////////

This question showed up in my in-box well over a month ago, and I just haven't been able to answer it. I can't stop thinking about it, either. The fact that the odds are now fairly good that you two are quarantined or sheltering in place together—well, let's just say that you, dear letter writer, have been on my mind a lot. There's part of me that thinks, "Look, almost every human being has at least one private habit that's sort of disgusting and sort of comforting all in one, and shame isn't a very useful tactic when it comes to changing behavior." And then there's part of me that thinks, "My God, how hard is it to clip your toenails over a trash can, after being reminded every couple of months for the past five years? How careless can one person be?"

The basic tools of the advice columnist are usually some

combination of time, distance, and perspective. But I don't have any surefire techniques for getting someone to pay attention after you've tried reminding them, explaining your feelings, reasoning with them, and pleading with them for half a decade. In your position, I might very well find myself tempted to do the same thing to him and feel simultaneously defeated and a certain thrill of vindictive pleasure. Is your husband an ordinarily reasonable, well-meaning person? If so, I'd try to see if I could use this escalation as an attempt to snatch up some sort of victory: "I need to admit defeat here. This has been so frustrating, and so unmanageable, that I've found myself putting your old toenail clippings in your coffee cup in an attempt to get your attention, because everything else I've done to that effect has failed miserably for the past five years. You know that it grosses me out; you know that I end up cleaning up after you, which I resent; and you know enough not to do it at work or in public—only in places where I'll take care of it for you. I don't feel proud or happy about my actions, but I don't have any better ideas, so I'm asking for your help. I'm clearly missing something. What are you getting out of this? What's going on inside of your head when you pull off your toenails and leave them on the table? Do you find yourself spacing out and forgetting what you're doing? What do you think would be necessary to get this to change? I'm absolutely out of ideas. What do you suggest?"

That's not to say he's likely to immediately chirp: "I never thought of it like that. What a great idea! If I start doing [thing], I know this will never happen again." Expect a few uncomfortable silences and some initial defensiveness, but hold out until he's willing to offer up a solution or two of his own. You've done the

*heavy lifting for the past five years. I think it's fair to ask him to
take the lead now. Good luck. I'm rooting for you.*

• • •

For perhaps obvious demographic reasons, I heard from a great
many more children resentful of their parents and older relatives than vice versa; I treasured hearing from the occasional
resentful grandmother as a rare, unlooked-for gem. Moreover,
I so often found myself advising letter writers to take a stron-
ger tack against their relatives, to draw a firmer boundary, that
it was delightful to be able to counsel de-escalation.

//////////////

Dear Prudence,

My granddaughter "Riley" is getting married late next year. She's
currently putting together her guest list (I heard this through the
grapevine) and is not planning on inviting my childhood best friend,
"Greta." Greta has been overwhelmingly kind to Riley for over thirty
years. She sends Riley checks for every birthday, takes Riley to
dinner whenever she's in town, and generally plays a grandmotherly
role in Riley's life. I hadn't heard of any conflict between the two of
them. But it appears that Riley has forgotten all of this as she builds
the guest list. She and her fiancé are getting financial assistance from
my son for the wedding. It seems cruel to not include Greta when
it's not even Riley's own money! I'm thinking of putting my foot down
and saying I won't attend if Greta doesn't attend either. Greta's been

mercifully quiet about this, but I can tell she's heartbroken. I would be too. What's a grandmother to do?

—Penny-Pinching Granddaughter

/////////////

Threatening not to attend your granddaughter's wedding on the strength of something you heard through the grapevine without having a single conversation with her is likely going to backfire. I understand that you love Greta and that she's been a member of the family for decades, but you don't know that Riley has definitely kept Greta off the guest list or whether she just forgot your friend. You don't know how much financial assistance your son is putting in, what Riley's total budget is, or if the couple merely wants to keep the guest list small. You also don't know how many other people are making guest-list requests, and your granddaughter has not only her own relatives and friends to consider, but her partner's.

Rather than approaching Riley with a demand or an ultimatum, you should frame it instead as a request: "I don't know what your budget or guest limit looks like, and I don't want to impose, but if you're able to make room for Greta, it would mean a lot to us both if you'd invite her." I hope you can try to look at this not as an act of spiteful exclusion. It would be great if Riley could invite her grandmother's best friend to her wedding, but it may not be possible. And if she can't, it's not an irrevocable slap in the face. Riley and Greta can still go out to dinner, catch up on the phone, and stay in each other's lives.

• • •

////////////

Dear Prudence,

My brother died in infancy; the rest of us are all girls. My husband
and I discovered we were having twin boys and announced the
pregnancy and the names as a Christmas present to my father.
Baby One has my last name plus my father-in-law's first. Baby Two
has my dead brother's full name. My father and mother both cried
at the news. My husband and I were so proud—until my sisters got
involved. Both are married without kids, but my oldest wrote me
an email telling me I "hijacked Christmas" and she was "saving the
names for her children." She is thirty-seven and has been married
ten years. My second-oldest sister scolded me for not including the
"family" in the naming tradition. I feel so insulted, but I don't know
what to do. There are no grandchildren on my side of the family,
while my husband had two different "Katies" born the same year.
I think both of my sisters are behaving badly, but I don't want to
push them out of the family lines. What should we do?

—Baby Problems

////////////

Even if your sister were 107 and had been married for 300 years,
"saving baby names" isn't a thing, and she doesn't have a right to
tell other people what to name their kids just because she thinks she

has seniority. I can appreciate that you are hoping to de-escalate the situation, but this isn't something you need to apologize for, and I hope you're able to resist pressure to do so in order to keep the peace. You did a lovely thing that honors your brother and father, and there's absolutely nothing keeping your sisters from incorporating either or both of those names with any future children they may have. They have not been injured or insulted. Nothing has been taken from them, nothing has been ruined or tarnished, and Christmas remains on the date it always was. You can tell them both that you care about their feelings, that you did not name your twins in order to hurt or exclude them, and that you hope they can come to feel, with you and your husband and your parents, excitement and joy about the upcoming additions to your family.

• • •

Dear Prudence,

I am fifty-three. My boyfriend is forty. We have been dating for eighteen months, I spend most nights at his place, and we function well as a couple—with one exception. I've been a complete secret from his mother. For reasons he refused to share, he would not tell his mother I existed. I refused to move in with him because of this. I met his father and cooked dinner for the both of them at my house. I met his friends and went out frequently with them. But when his mother visited, I had to make sure all of my things were out of his place so that she didn't suspect he was in a relationship.

Initially, he said that I should just trust him. And I did not begrudge him the occasional day with his mom. But I finally got tired of being excluded from his birthday, New Year's Eve, and other special events. I told him that he either had to tell her, or I wouldn't keep seeing him, and that I was starting to wonder if there were other secrets he was trying to keep from me. To make a long story short, he took me seriously and told his mom. And her reaction was positive. But as is usually the case with ultimatums, I now feel like a bad person for forcing his hand, and I still feel hesitant to move in together. Is it ever appropriate to give such ultimatums?

—Mother's Secret

///////////////

I think the situation you were in called for an ultimatum, and I'm glad you gave your boyfriend one. Ultimatums aren't always unreasonable. Sometimes they're the quickest, easiest way to figure out whether you're wasting your time. You made it clear that, after a year and a half together, you weren't interested in continuing the relationship if he continued to treat you like a dirty little secret. That was the right thing to do, and you should be proud of yourself for insisting on being treated like a partner instead of a shameful habit.

The reason you still feel hesitant to move in together isn't because you were wrong to set a clear limit. I think it's because you're letting yourself really experience the full weight of your frustration now that you've realized your partner's insistence that all this sneaking around was necessary was total nonsense. He claimed his mother would freak out if she knew, when in fact she seems fine with it. That means he was clearing out your stuff and hustling you out the door every time she visited because he wanted to. What's worse, he's never been willing or able to tell you why he did it. And now he wants you to move in with him without ever discussing that year-and-a-half-long routine—just be grateful that his mother thinks you're acceptable dating material, keep your mouth shut, and move on. The problem wasn't that you offered him an ultimatum. The problem is that he wants you to move in with him without ever talking honestly about why he kept you on the sidelines for so long.

• • •

It's bleakly common, this family practice of forced silence about violent homophobia. People describe it by saying, "Well, they've come a long way" or "This has been hard for her, but she's really trying" or "Things are a lot better than they used to be." It's often paired with dreadful little parlor games like "She can come with you for Christmas, but only if you tell everyone she's your roommate," and the prizes are never any good.

//////////////

Dear Prudence,
I'm a woman marrying another woman this summer. My family knows nothing about it—my mom was very violent and threw me out when I came out at fifteen, and though I was allowed

back into the house after a few days staying at a friend's, it was on the understanding that we'd all pretend I was straight and nothing had happened. I have had extremely limited contact with my mom since leaving at eighteen, and we never talk about my personal life, just things like how relatives are doing and what job I'm at. My dad was always more supportive, though he did not come after me when my mom threw me out and went along with the policy of silence afterward to "keep the peace." He's met my fiancée a handful of times and is very supportive of LGBT rights in private with me and with his friends—just not with my mom, who acts like she doesn't even know I've had a girlfriend for six years. I never told my dad when we got engaged because I feared he'd tell my mom—he has broken my confidence before—and that she would then find a way to threaten or harm me on the wedding day.

I was planning on simply letting my dad know I got married after the event and letting the chips fall where they may. But I am starting to feel very guilty about this, and like I am unfairly cutting my dad out because of his wife's behavior. He always tells me how much he loves and supports me, and I know it will hurt him terribly to not be invited to his only child's wedding. Should I give him a chance and invite him for the sake of preserving what relationship we have? This could ruin things between us. My partner says she'll support whatever decision I make, but I know she thinks he shouldn't come. What should I do?

—Dad at the Wedding

I know you feel guilty at the prospect of telling your dad you've gotten married only after the fact, but let's look first at what you've overlooked from his corner over the years: He watched your mom get violent with you and did nothing. He saw her throw you out of the house at fifteen years old and did nothing. He keeps his support of your sexuality quiet and countenances homophobia around homophobic people like your mother. You believe that he would give your mother information she would use to threaten or hurt you, even if you asked him not to do so. You're not "unfairly" cutting your father out because of his wife's behavior—you're acting reasonably and sanely based on his past behavior.

That doesn't mean I think you should stop loving him or cut him out of your life; you have every right to accept your father's limitations and maintain contact that feels meaningful, safe, and sustainable to you, even while declining to share information with him that you know he can't handle because he'd share it with a woman who wants to hurt you. I believe that he loves you, but I do not believe he is capable of giving you meaningful support as long as he prioritizes his wife's homophobia over your safety. Tell him about the wedding after the ceremony. If that's what ruins things between you, not the fact that he failed to protect you when you were being hurt and neglected as a teenager, then I think that's your father's choice to hurt you, not the inevitable result of leaving him off the guest list.

• • •

////////////////

Dear Prudence,

My brother is a child molester who targets prepubescent girls.
He doesn't deny the things that he's done, but he insists that
he's all better now and no longer has those urges, and besides,
his victims—including one of our nieces—were at least partly to
blame because they were "flirtatious." He's never suffered any
legal consequences for his actions, although he was banned
from a summer camp at which he was a counselor for having an
"inappropriate relationship" with a camper.

A while back, I saw on his Facebook page that he was posting
a lot of selfies with the four-year-old daughter of some friends
that he often babysat for—actually, the term he used was *borrow*.
I immediately messaged the parents and told them that while I
loved my brother, I had to let them know that their daughter was
not safe with him. I stuck to the facts and told them that if they
wanted to tell my brother where the information came from, that
was okay with me. My brother was very angry with me, to put it
mildly. I had already made it clear to him that he wasn't allowed in
my house because I wanted it to be a safe space for our niece. I
now don't want any contact with him.

My problem is his two sons, who are now adults. I am close
with one of them in particular. We FaceTime occasionally, do
things like live-text baseball games, and he goes out of his
way to visit me, independent of any other family functions. To
all appearances, he and his father have a normal father-son
relationship, and I have no idea whether my nephews know that
their dad's a pedophile. Prudie, I feel like an ugly day of reckoning

is inevitable. It will break my heart if I lose my relationship with my nephew because he is persuaded to believe terrible things about me or because he is forced into a position of having to choose between me and his father. I know it's coming, and I don't know what to say or do when it does.

—Ready to Speak Up

////////////

I'm so glad you told that little girl's parents. If your brother has never suffered any legal consequences (it sounds as though he's suffered very few consequences of any kind, aside from being banned from a single summer camp), blames the children he's molested for being "flirtatious," and still tries to find ways to be alone with kids, then he is an active, present danger to every child in his life. You have both the right and sufficient reason to talk to your nephews about their father, especially since he has a history of using friends and family members as cover to gain access to their children.

Tell them both—not just the son you're already close with—the same things you told the parents of that four-year-old girl. He's already confessed to targeting children, and you can stick to the facts. Tell them it's an issue of public safety that they don't enable their father or facilitate his attempts to prey on children. It's deeply concerning that your brother has already molested your niece but it's still a secret from at least part of the family. Everyone who is keeping secrets on your brother's behalf is making it easier for him to hurt children, and that needs to stop. Don't wait for your

*nephews to "maybe" find out some version of events from their
father or some other third party—talk to them today. Get in touch
with a lawyer and a therapist and consider whether you need to
start filing reports. Your brother cannot be trusted to hold himself
to account, and there are more urgent matters at stake than
maintaining interfamily relationships.*

///////////////

Dear Prudence,
I've been low-contact with my abusive dad for several years
now, and my mental health has drastically improved as a result.
I'm a queer trans person (they/them) and would be happiest
never speaking to him again. I am in contact with my mother,
who occasionally gives me updates on his life. I know my mother
was victimized by him in her own right, but she also enabled
and justified his abuse of me and my siblings. Now my mother
is currently dying of a chronic illness, and her prognosis is only
another year or two. I live across the country, although I plan to
move to be closer to her this fall. But I'm already thinking about
her funeral: I don't want to go when it finally happens.

Growing up, I was mercilessly mocked for being too "sensitive"
by my relatives. The environment was incredibly homophobic
and transphobic. I don't like showing emotion in front of them.
I haven't seen any members of my extended family in years and
don't want to. I have one sibling I sometimes commiserate with
about how messed up our childhood was, but we're not otherwise

close. I realize not attending would likely destroy my relationship with my remaining relatives, but I don't want to maintain that relationship anyways. I do feel guilty about not wanting to stay close sometimes, but I'd rather grieve with my partner and my friends, who accept me and love me for who I am. Based on previous interactions, I worry that attending might trigger a mental health crisis. But I also know these people think I'm overdramatic, selfish, and attention seeking. The last time I tried to bring up my panic attacks to my mom, she told me to "just close my eyes if I get scared," so I dropped the subject. What are my obligations here? How do I take care of myself when skipping your mother's funeral is pretty universally seen as an awful thing to do?

—Can't Grieve Together

I sometimes refer to the "gift of clarity" as one of the rare upsides that comes from realizing a relationship has been damaged beyond repair. Your relatives believe you are overly dramatic, selfish, and attention seeking and have mocked you for your suffering in the face of their homophobia and transphobia. I don't think there's anything you can do to change their opinion of you, not even if you were to attend her funeral and behave according to their exact specifications. Given that it is not possible to please them, you have total freedom to disregard their opinions. That doesn't mean you'll be able to immediately free yourself of residual family pressure or misplaced guilt (although you can process those feelings with a therapist, your partner, a journal, and your friends

*at your own pace), but it does mean you're free to make your own
decisions without taking your relatives' feelings into account.*

*You don't have to disclose this plan to your mother if you think
it would hurt her. Right now she's alive, and you're prepared to offer
her support and comfort, so focus on the task at hand. But she
won't be at her funeral, and deciding to keep yourself safe from
the relatives who abused you and enabled your father's abuse
does not harm your mother, nor does it diminish the complicated
but real love you feel for her. You also don't have to tell people
about whether you've attended your mother's funeral, if you think
they'd try to question your decision. This guilt does not come from
some wrongdoing you need to make amends for but is part of the
abusive structure you've worked so hard to get distance from.*

· · ·

One of the clunkier aspects of my own estrangement has
been settling on language that can accurately describe what
my relationship with my relatives has historically been like
and what it is like now. Calling them my "biological family"
seems to imply an ongoing distance, which isn't accurate, as
most of us had been very close indeed. "Family of origin" is
more accurate, but it strikes me as clinical, as if describing a
population study. I could simply use their names, but there's
something about trying to eliminate the language of relationships entirely that seems like wishful thinking, at least for me:
*Look at how much I don't care. Our only connections are haphaz-
ard and arbitrary, sheer accidents of genetics.*

I was a middle child; I had an older sister and a younger brother; I had two parents, both evangelical Christian church leaders and still married. My father was the senior pastor at Menlo Church in Northern California and is the bestselling author of numerous inspirational Christian books. My parents and I were close. My sister and I were close. My brother and I had not been close for some time, partly due to his disgust and discomfort with my transition, and partly for reasons that remained obscure to me. In November 2018, my then twenty-nine-year-old brother offered me a surprising disclosure: that for as long as he could remember, he had been profoundly attracted to young boys; that he had never sought professional help for this compulsion and instead believed that his ongoing work with children as a coach, tutor, and youth group leader was an effective form of ersatz treatment; that this work often involved travel where he spent the night alone with said children, although he also found it difficult to restrain himself from telling those children how he truly felt about them; and that he found the act of mentorship sexually arousing. Perhaps most surprising was his admission that he had told the rest of our immediate family over a year earlier and that they had unanimously supported his decisions, which I confirmed that same day during two separate phone calls with my sister and my father.

In that same month, my wife and I reported to the Elders of Menlo Church that their senior pastor—my father, John Ortberg Jr.—had conspired in secret to provide a person experiencing compulsive sexual attraction toward children with unsupervised access to young people through youth groups. We also reported to relevant local schools, who in turn contacted the police. At the time, we hoped the Menlo Elders would conduct a thorough investigation of the report and make such arrangements as were necessary to protect the community. My father was then placed on administrative leave; in January 2019, Menlo Church published the broad outlines of their investigation.

In our opinion, it was not a thorough one. The investigator did not interview a number of key witnesses, did not disclose the particular nature of the relationship between the then-unnamed volunteer and his father, the senior pastor, and failed to investigate any of the church-related work my brother had performed on international trips with the children's ministry. My father then returned to the pulpit, acknowledging vague regret, but neither he nor the church ever made clear what, exactly, they thought he had done wrong, neither did parishioners learn the full story of his relationship to the volunteer, nor his interest in keeping their strategy a secret.

I published a statement expressing dismay at Menlo's institutional failures. Shortly thereafter, the church held a town hall meeting, where one of my father's employees responded to my comments by claiming that I was "lashing out" at my family and insinuating I was mentally unstable because I had transitioned.

In the absence of institutional accountability, and in the interests of securing an independent, transparent, third-party investigation of my brother's history of unsupervised work with children, I published the following statement:

When we last spoke, [my brother] John Ortberg III admitted to seeking out unsupervised contact with children (including overnight travel) for well over a decade. I believe his unique relationship to my father, John Ortberg Jr., is the sole reason why John Jr. went out of his way to protect his secret and facilitate his continued contact with children. During the conversation where he admitted his sexual obsession toward children, John III repeatedly described his work with children as the most important thing in his life, and described his feelings for the children in his care over the years in deeply romantic terms. He acknowledged difficulty "letting them go" from his care, and said he struggled to avoid telling them "how [he] really felt."

He claimed to avoid working with the group for which he felt the strongest fixation, which is pre-pubescent boys. I know that he has not avoided them. As an adult, he has habitually sought out contact with young boys, both professionally in his past work as a tutor, as a music teacher, and youth group volunteer. My brother only resigned from his positions working with children in November when I said I was going to do it for him. I believe that if I had not threatened to do so, he would never have stopped. I do not know whether he has ever harmed a child, as he claimed.

I do not wish to punish John Ortberg III for a condition he cannot control. However, he can control whether he spends time alone with children he desires sexually. He colluded in a desperately unsafe conspiracy on the grounds of a discredited belief—seemingly derived from the "Virtuous Pedophile" movement, whose values both he and my father defended to me—that close, unmonitored contact with children is therapeutic for pedophiles.

When my parents learned I intended to inform the church staff in November, they sent my wife a message through a third party that my brother was suicidal at the thought of being unable to volunteer with children. Rather than seeking medical attention for him, they wanted me to promise not to say anything, and to imply that I would be responsible for his suicide in the event that I reported. I did not then, and I will not now, accept that responsibility. I hope that my brother is safe, healthy, in treatment, and never alone with another child. I hope that his previous work with children, at Menlo Church and everywhere else he pursued such work, is thoroughly scrutinized.

On July 29, 2020, Menlo Church announced they had accepted my father's resignation, citing "poor judgment." They also hired a third-party organization, the Zero Abuse Project, to conduct a second, publicly available investigation and offer recommendations for future policy changes.

My own estrangement was not an act of personal punishment or an expression of anger I could either decide to take or not, but an indirect result of insisting on external investigation, external accountability, and external consequences. I would not, *could* not, simply take my brother and the rest of our family at their word that their secret strategy was safe or sane and that only people with the last name of Ortberg were entitled to know about it. The estrangement was a moral, an emotional, and a practical reality that I could choose to either acknowledge or deny, but the estrangement began that first day they agreed to keep the secret to themselves.

I heard from many letter writers over the years in ghastly, similar situations, many of them much worse than my own. "Keep the secret and we will love you," the promise goes, "but step outside the family circle and there's no telling what might happen to you." For my part, in my own limited and imperfect capacity as an advice giver, I cannot promise much—I can promise that estrangement is *possible*, that it is survivable, and that other forms of relation and kinship and reciprocity exist on the other side. Beyond that, I cannot say for certain; I cannot guess what gains might come to balance the losses for any given person, if leaving will come to feel like a relief or a suppurating wound or something else entirely, if they will suffer financial or legal or personal consequences beyond their ability to bear, if they will be harassed, manipulated, cajoled, sweetened, or ostracized.

While I cannot predict what estrangement might look like for someone else on the strength of a single letter, as there are at least as many types of estrangement as there are families, I can offer a reassurance that is neither cheaply earned nor lightly given: it can be done, and it can even be good. Not *always* good, nor *thoroughly* good, but one can find real and surprising sources of goodness in it. The condition of estrangement is often very different indeed from the condition of *contemplating* estrangement, an exhausting state that combines the worst of both worlds, all of the guilt and anxiety with none of the peace and freedom. Because the mental work of contemplating estrangement is often so exhaustive and repetitive, it can be easy to assume this is what estrangement will be like too.

For my own part, estrangement has not brought perfect peace or restorative forgetfulness. I do not speak to my relatives, and they do not speak to me; but I cannot forget the things we have said to one another, cannot retroactively sever the relationships we once had. When I am tempted to grow maudlin or resentful, which is often, I redirect my focus from my own feelings (changeable, repetitive, highly dependent on mood and circumstance, disposed toward self-pity) to the facts of the case: my father and brother are no longer in a position to abuse their authority over children, and their entire community now knows the critical information they once kept to themselves. This is a good enough outcome. I carry only the burdens I am responsible for, no one else's. This is a good enough outcome too, good enough at least to close a chapter.

Chapter Six

Wait—Am I in the Wrong Here?

> Letters with an unspoken revelation: the problem may not be what (or who!) you think it is. Learning to reevaluate feelings of certainty. Letting go of the need to win at all costs. Taking stock, abandoning self-justification, learning to eat crow, trying to do the next right thing instead of being right.

I dislike realizing I'm wrong, and I dislike *admitting* I'm wrong even more, but I've come to appreciate the upsides that come with such an admission, because it usually means I get to exit a painful situation more quickly and with more remaining dignity than if I stayed put and tried to fight my way out.

In the spirit of this chapter, I'll begin with an admission of my own: I should not have advised the first letter writer to say in their apology that they'd never again touch the disabled person or her chair without her express permission.

Given their only passing acquaintance prior to the encounter, and given how very badly the encounter went when the letter writer foisted their unnecessary assistance on her, I don't think there's any reason to suggest that in the future this woman might call upon them for help. Nor should I have lightly encouraged the letter writer to look for future opportunities to ask others if they need assistance; I think I deferred too much to the letter writer's desire to be conspicuously helpful when I should have advised them to reflect critically on whether they had ever overstepped similar boundaries with others in the past.

///////////////

Dear Prudence,

I recently tried to assist a disabled person getting out of an SUV onto a wheelchair. At the time, it seemed like she had trouble controlling the chair, and I rushed to help. She was brought to tears as she tried to get me to move away. But then she seemed like she was about to fall again while trying to sit in the chair. In retrospect, I think I might have overreacted. But, again, she insisted that I did not help her. I see that person more or less every day, and I am uncomfortable about the right thing. I don't know if apologizing will make things worse. Is there anything to do to make this right or less awkward?

—Unwelcome Samaritan

///////////////

You say this woman seemed "about to fall again" but not that she ever fell—a detail I believe you would have included had it actually happened. Ask yourself why you did not back off the first time this woman asked you to leave her alone. Did you assume that, because she's in a wheelchair, she doesn't know when she does or doesn't need assistance? There's nothing wrong with wanting to help someone, but there is something wrong with repeatedly ignoring someone saying "No, please stop" until you've pushed them to the point of tears. What you did was neither helpful nor kind, regardless of your intentions, and you do owe her an apology. Apologize for ignoring her when she said she could get out of her own car without assistance, for continuing to foist yourself on her after repeated requests to stop, and for making her cry. Make it clear that you'll never touch her or her chair without her express permission again and that you're making a concerted effort to change your behavior in the future.

In the future, if you see someone who may possibly need help with something, you don't have to squash the impulse entirely; just ask, "Can I help you?" and let yourself be guided by their answer. If someone says, "No, thanks. I've got it," take them at their word and back off.

• • •

There's something O. Henry-ish about realizing you and your friend have both been spying on one another, especially if you want to object to your friend's surveillance but can't do so without revealing your own.

////////////

Dear Prudence,

Recent storms rendered a friend's house unlivable, so we offered her our spare bedroom while her roof was being repaired. She's good company, a polite houseguest, and after feeling so isolated during lockdown, it was nice to have another face around for a few days. We live in an old, multilevel house. It has skeleton keyholes on most of the doors, which give a fairly decent view into the rooms behind them, but only if you kneel down and peer through them. The master bedroom is on the top floor. The guest room, guest bathroom, and linen closet are all in the basement, as is the laundry room. There's a second floor for the kitchen, family room, and dining room. On the last day of our guest's visit, my boyfriend woke me up in the mood for morning sex, after which we went back to sleep. We're not terribly noisy, but I also know from experience that sound doesn't really travel between the different stories, so I wasn't worried about waking our guest. Today I checked my cat's "collar camera." He's an indoor/outdoor cat, so I have the collar camera to track him and anything he runs into outdoors. Early in the morning of our friend's last night in the house, the cat-cam footage showed her kneeling in front of our bedroom door with her face pressed against the keyhole for about twenty minutes. At that point, the cat wandered off and curled up in another room.

I feel really violated, and I'm not sure how to proceed. My boyfriend found it weird and gross but thinks the best solution is just not to invite her over for any more overnight visits. I feel disrespected and grossed out and don't want her in my life anymore. I'd rather present a united front, but I won't force my boyfriend to adopt my position. I definitely can't just pretend this never happened. Any advice about how to start this conversation would be much appreciated.

—Visiting Voyeur

"There's no great way to say this, so here goes: we keep a camera on the cat's collar to keep an eye on him when he goes outdoors, and since he was inside the other night, I know that you looked through the keyhole to the bedroom for about twenty minutes. It made me feel uncomfortable and like you'd violated some pretty basic principles about respect and privacy."

At that point, your friend may have her own response about learning that you were (at least incidentally) filming her during her stay; this doesn't diminish the fact that she was wrong to peer through your keyhole either while you were having sex or sound asleep, but it might raise worthwhile questions that both you and your boyfriend should consider before inviting other guests over. Do people who visit your home know that your cat has a camera on his collar? If not, why not? Do you normally give your guests the opportunity to decide whether they're comfortable spending time in your house with a roaming surveillance system, even if the purpose of that surveillance system is supposedly to monitor problems out-of-doors? Have you ever watched footage of your other guests before when your cat unwittingly filmed them, and if so, did you tell them about it? If not, why not? Do you think they

would regard the review of such footage as a violation of their
own privacy? Would you, if you were in their position?

I don't ask these questions as a "gotcha." None of this
undermines your right to object to what your friend did. This
isn't a zero-sum game where you're only either sinned-against or
sinning. But it might also serve as an opportunity to ask yourself
whether you're overlooking your guests' reasonable right to
privacy when they visit your home, if you're not informing them
that they're being recorded whenever your cat is in the room and
that this footage is being stored and reviewed.

• • •

One of the default positions the column eventually led me to
is the virtue of looking for opportunities not to have a problem
wherever one can find them. That's not necessarily the same
thing as abandoning all critical judgment or avoiding conflict,
but life has a tendency to bring so many unavoidable problems our way that it can really be a gift to say to oneself, "I
simply don't know how this situation is going to end up for my
roommate, and I don't have to solve it for her," thus freeing
up valuable time and energy to spend on whatever one likes.

////////////

Dear Prudence,
My roommate is a beautiful soul. Her wardrobe, not so much.
She wears cheap, often tacky dresses (most of them with a

"geeky" theme like *Star Wars*, *Dr. Who*, etc.) all the time. Many of them are full-length ball gowns with petticoats underneath. Her employers appreciate her hard work and dedication, but I've noticed they never take her very seriously and she's never been put in charge of the department she was trained to take over. I adore her geekiness and think style is personal and subjective, but I know not everyone else sees it that way. Her last boyfriend ended things after she wore an R2-D2 gown to his sister's black-tie wedding, even after he begged to buy her a new dress. She rarely gets a second date. I have tried getting her to try on other clothes, but she seems uninterested. I think it's entirely possible the outfits are a shield for her insecurity. I believe there is someone out there who will love her the way she is, but part of me wonders whether it's time to sit her down and be honest because it's holding her back professionally and romantically, and she doesn't seem to understand why. I'm worried I'll lose my friend. Should I butt out or speak up?

—Say No to the Dresses

I know my answer should be something about how your roommate has the right to be her geekiest and most authentic self at all times, but I agree that floor-length Dr. Who–themed gowns are not always the appropriate choice for weddings or the workplace (depending on the workplace). That said, I'm not sure you're best situated to talk to her about her fashion sense. You say her last boyfriend ended things because of what she wore to a wedding, so presumably she's aware that her sartorial choices are off-putting to some—I don't know what you could say to her that's more effective than "I'm breaking up with you because you wore an R2-D2-themed dress to my sister's wedding." When it comes to work, your theory that her clothes are keeping her from being named director of her department is just that: a theory. You've already tried encouraging her to try other outfits, and she's refused to take the bait. It's up to her employers to say something if they want her to dress differently at work, and it's up to your roommate to find romantic partners who like her style. Despite your claim to love her sci-fi bent, I suspect you don't like (and are perhaps embarrassed by) your roommate's clothes and are looking for a justifiable excuse to call an intervention. You don't have one.

• • • •

It's not "heartless" to enjoy a three-day weekend, especially with the sorry state of workplace protections in this country. I'm certain many an affair has been jump-started by a conspicuous display of unsolicited empathy, such as the next letter writer proposes, so part of me begrudgingly admires the tactic, although as affair-generating tactics go, if the empathetic display *doesn't* work, it tends to leave one looking awfully foolish.

Regardless of its efficacy, however, I still think that it's a bad idea and that this letter writer is sufficiently alienated from her own motivations as to be emotionally dangerous. If you realize you're attracted to an acquaintance, believe both of your marriages to be unhappy, and truly don't want to start an affair, then you won't go looking for flimsy excuses to get closer (and boy, "I never really realized how much Memorial Day means to me—do you need someone to hold your hand at your friends' gravesides?" is as flimsy as it gets). Which leads me to believe that part of the work that the claim "I never would take action" is doing here is providing a noble point of identification, cover, and plausible deniability should the opportunity to "discuss it openly" ever arise on the drive to the graveyard: "You'd never cheat on your spouse who makes you miserable? *I'd* never cheat on *my* spouse who makes me miserable. We have so much in common!"

Feeling excited about a new crush is an entirely human and understandable impulse, but I hope the letter writer took that energy in a more constructive direction.

////////////

Dear Prudence,
My son has recently become friends with a boy whose father is a veteran (two tours in Afghanistan). My son's birthday happens to be on Memorial Day weekend, and when I mentioned a birthday party, the dad said his only plans that weekend were visiting graves of some of his friends, so they would be available. I immediately felt guilty for not thinking of that—like so many Americans, Memorial Day for me is a three-day weekend, and I feel heartless for not thinking of its actual meaning. Is there some way to recognize him for what he's sacrificed and what he must

be going through on that day? I should also mention that we are both (unhappily) married, and we seem to be slightly mutually attracted to each other (we haven't ever discussed it openly, and I don't plan to and never would take action). So, while I'd like to recognize him, I don't want to do it in a way that makes either of our spouses think something is going on. My husband does know that I would divorce him if I could afford to and am only staying to give my stepdaughter a communal home until she graduates high school next year. He also tends to be paranoid that I'm interested in every guy that I talk to, so I don't want to give him any more reasons to be angry and feel justified in his disrespect toward me.

—Just Let Me Respect You

/////////////

Your question is, fundamentally, "Can I use the fact that the man I'm interested in is a veteran as an inside track to a closer relationship?" My answer is, I'm afraid, no. I'm sorry you're stuck in a loveless marriage for another year, and I don't want to belittle the loneliness you must feel, but please don't use that as an excuse to try to start an affair. You don't know the state of his marriage. You can only know yours. There are plenty of ways to acknowledge someone's military service if you want to that aren't based on "Can we have a long, intense discussion of what you must be going through," which is clearly an invitation to increased emotional intimacy. You don't feel guilty about insufficiently honoring veterans; you're romantically interested in your married neighbor and want to know if you can use an

over-the-top dose of empathy to see if he's interested in you too.
I think that's unwise. Focus on preparing yourself financially and
emotionally for the end of your own marriage, and don't borrow
trouble in the meanwhile.

• • •

There are few tastes quite so bitter as a gift soured, especially
when you began with the best of intentions. But the next letter writer missed more than one opportunity to set aside her
annoyance and get what she needed to complete a full family
portrait, and what was once intended as a thoughtful gesture
ended up as an apple of discord.

For my own part, I can't stand by my "I don't doubt that
your friend's stepdaughter is difficult" opener, given how un-
reasonably the letter writer presents herself. It's 2021! It's
not hard to get a family photo to work with.

////////////////

Dear Prudence,
For a friend's birthday, I decided to paint a portrait of her with
her late mother and her adult children (two girls of her own and
a stepdaughter). I contacted all three children back in January to
please send me a picture so I could paint them. I contacted the
stepdaughter (she lives out of state) several times. I even sent
her a letter with a paid-for return envelope for the picture. She
told me she would get around to it but never did.

I finally gave up and did the portrait without her. I know that my friend had a difficult relationship with her stepdaughter growing up. I presented the painting to my friend at her birthday party. She loved it so much that she cried. Later, her husband approached me. His daughter came down to visit, saw the portrait, and threw a fit. She screamed at her parents about how she obviously was not loved or wanted in the family. He wanted me to "fix" the portrait now to include this girl. I haven't brought this up with my friend, but frankly I am insulted, and I think a good slap across the face might work wonders for this brat rather than indulging in this emotional manipulation. She did not want to be in the painting; she has no grounds to be upset now. It would require me to start over from scratch. How do I respond properly here?

—Picture's Not Perfect

///////////////

I don't doubt that your friend's stepdaughter is difficult, and I agree that she was the main architect of her own misfortune by ignoring the deadline and the prestamped envelope you sent her. But I do think that choosing not to find a workaround (say, by asking one of the girl's siblings to supply you with a photo of her, or working off an image from social media) and instead presenting your friend with a picture of all her children except the one she's had the hardest time connecting with put her in a slightly tricky position. I don't say that to discount the hard work you put into this or the generosity of the project as a whole. I just hope it helps you contextualize the girl's response and to soothe that itchy slapping hand of yours. (Slaps very rarely work wonders. Usually they just hurt.)

Given that this girl isn't part of your family, and you did work hard to include her in the first place, all you have to say to your friend's husband is this: "I'm really sorry you've been having a tough time with [stepdaughter] over this. I contacted her a few times about participating and didn't hear back from her. I'm afraid I don't have the time to start over such a big project, but I understand if you decide not to display the portrait in order to smooth things over. I hope you three are able to find a good way to talk this through."

• • •

Another mea culpa! How could I have missed it? "He just annoys me. I don't want people to think it's because of his nontraditional lifestyle." The employee who does a great job 95 percent of the time and has a few careless habits like everyone else but mysteriously infuriates his boss and has—ahem!—a nontraditional lifestyle? If you've found the source of the mystery, circle gets the square.

//////////////

Dear Prudence,
I'm the executive director of a tiny nonprofit and have an employee I dislike. The problem is that everyone else thinks this person is great and can't see his faults. He does about 95 percent

of his job very well and often goes beyond the call of duty. He's excellent with clients and coworkers but makes careless mistakes. Several times he's circled the wrong number in a document or left extra spacing between letters. It's in his job description to lock a closet, but he's forgotten many times. Each time, I call him at home and wait until he comes back to do it, but he just won't learn! Mostly, though, he just annoys me. I don't want people to think it's because of his nontraditional lifestyle, so I just bite my tongue. Others find him innovative and creative, but I just want him to buckle down, pay attention to details, leave me alone, and not make errors. I can't fire him justifiably, but I can't work with him either. We are too small to move him, so what do I do?

—Closet Conundrum

///////////

I'm afraid the problem lies very much with you in this instance. Anyone who does 95 percent of their job "very well" ought to be cut a little slack when it comes to spacing and number-circling. It seems like on some level you are aware that your fixation on his occasional, minor errors is irrational and prevents you from doing your job well—I hope this answer can bring you into full awareness of just how inappropriately you are behaving. If an otherwise excellent employee forgets to lock a closet now and again, it is a wholly unjustified use of your time and resources to call him at his home and make him come back to the office in order to lock it. Either have a copy of the key made or lock it yourself. I have locked many doors in my day. It generally takes about half a second.

*What's more worrisome to me is that you want your employee
to "leave you alone," even though you've never described any
behavior that would fall under the category of "not leaving you
alone." Your desire for him to "not make errors" is, you must realize,
impossible and absurd, and you must take responsibility for your
irrational dislike. The problem is you. You are not biting your
tongue as well as you think you are, and I can only imagine how
difficult you must make life for this employee. You absolutely can
work with him, and if you deserve the position you currently hold,
you will find a way to deal with your bizarre dislike of him on your
own time and create, at the bare minimum, a safe and respectful
environment for him to work in.*

• • •

There are practical reasons to admit you're wrong, principles
aside. If you're desperate for your kids to let you spend time
with your grandchild, but your constant demands to be in the
room during labor are pushing them away, ending your constant demands and backing off is the most straightforward
way to ensure you actually get to see said grandchild.

////////////

Dear Prudence,
My son, Steven, and daughter-in-law, Julia, are expecting their
first child and our first grandchild next month. I had what I
thought was a good relationship with Julia, but I find myself

devastated. Julia has decided only Steven and her mother will be allowed in the delivery room when she gives birth. I was stunned and hurt by the unfairness of the decision and tried to plead with her and my son, but Julia says she "wouldn't feel comfortable" with me there. I reminded her that I was a nurse for forty years, so there is nothing I haven't seen. I've tried to reason with Steven, but he seems to be afraid of angering Julia and will not help. I called Julia's parents and asked them to please reason with their daughter, but they brusquely and rather rudely got off the phone. I've felt nothing but heartache since learning I would be banned from the delivery room. Steven told me I could wait outside, and I would be let in after Julia and the baby are cleaned up and "presentable." Meanwhile, Julia's mother will be able to witness our grandchild coming into the world. It is so unfair.

I've always been close to my son, but I no longer feel valued. I cannot bring myself to speak to Julia. I'm being treated like a second-class grandmother even though I've never been anything but supportive and helpful. How can I get them to see how unfair and cruel their decision is?

—Let Me In

////////////

You can't! You shouldn't! You are entirely in the wrong! I say this in the hopes that, after the initial flush of indignation fades, you will be braced and supported by the realization that you have been acting badly and that you need to change. It's difficult to admit when one's been wrong, but there's nothing quite so clarifying as figuring out how to do better.

Your daughter-in-law is giving birth, which is a pretty difficult, painful, and intimate process. She has every right to plan ahead for just how many people she wants to be in the room for that.

This is not about you. You are going to get to see your grandchild the day they are born. You will get to be in your grandchild's life for as long as you live. Nothing is being taken from you. You are not being snubbed. Your daughter-in-law and your son are drawing a totally appropriate boundary, and you need to stop trying to argue with them about it. Frankly, I can see why they don't want you in the room, if "But I was a nurse!" and "I'm a second-class grandmother" is your response to "Please hang out and read a book in the hallway while the baby is crowning."

Let this go. Do not rob this moment of its joy by keeping score and demanding more.

• • •

It may or may not be true that every family has "a difficult member," but what seems to produce the greatest difficulty is the concerted effort the family puts en masse into downplaying or excusing something like trying to set a relative's dress on fire or having a tantrum over being forbidden to drive drunk simply because it happens at a family event.

////////////

Dear Prudence,

My brother "John" married "Kim" last year. She is a perfectly nice woman, but we don't have much in common and aren't close. At the wedding, her mother got catastrophically drunk, sexually harassed the best man, and then got into a fight with the best man's wife (a bridesmaid). The next morning, when the best man quietly moved tables so he wouldn't have to sit with her, she screamed at him for "shaming" her and tried to stab him with a fork. No one on the bride's side blinked an eye. The rest of us assumed they were just trying to salvage the rest of the day by keeping the peace, but when my brother asked Kim about it later, she said the best man shouldn't have "flirted" with her mom and then "acted coy" afterward just because his wife found out. That's not what happened. We all saw her mother get out of control in front of everyone.

John said to let it go because weddings can get emotional. But then the same thing sort of happened at Christmas when Kim invited us all to their house for a party. This time, her mother tried to set fire to my mother's dress, supposedly for flirting with her boyfriend. Kim said that it was my mother's fault for being too friendly and that her mother had been cheated on a lot. John said that Kim knew her mother was in the wrong but was just really defensive of her.

Now Kim has invited everyone to a birthday barbecue for my brother next month. We don't want to go, but we also don't want to skip my brother's party. Every family has a difficult member (we have an uncle who gets drunk and angry if you won't let him drive), but Kim's mother actually tries to hurt people, both drunk and sober. How can we handle this? Not go? Go and do something if Kim's mother gets upset again? (I wanted to call the police at Christmas, but Mom is worried that will alienate Kim and John. His best friend, the best man at the wedding, has already stopped talking to him because of the wedding day incident, which actually probably could have qualified as sexual assault if he'd wanted to push it, never mind his wife's black eye.)

—Family Freak-Out

///////////

You are, as a family, significantly underreacting to Kim's mom and the people who enable her. (You may also be underreacting to this uncle who gets belligerent when his relatives prevent him from drinking and driving, but we'll focus on Kim's mom for now.) This woman tried to set your mother on fire for talking to a man. She sexually assaulted a man she barely knew while he was serving as the groom's best man at her daughter's wedding. Say the following sentence out loud to yourself: "I'm thinking about going to a barbecue with a woman who tried to set my mother on fire for talking to a man." Does that sound like a reasonable sentence? Would you feel comfortable saying it in front of other people who aren't already weirdly bound up with this woman's bizarre, violent antics? I'm having visions of Kim's mom trying to throw one of your relatives on the barbecue over some perceived slight while Kim and John try to stop everyone from calling an ambulance: "Look, I know things got a little out of hand today, but you have to admit that my mother had a right to the last corn muffin." She's not a little bit rude or a touch difficult. She is dangerous and surrounded by people who treat her acts of wild, unpredictable violence as interesting acts of whimsy.

Do not go to this barbecue. If your brother asks why, tell him that you are not willing to put yourself in the same room as a woman who has a history of assaulting your family members and that it is unreasonable for him to expect you to. If he tries to make you feel like you're the unreasonable one, then let him continue living on whatever fantasy island he's currently marooned on. But don't go join him there. If he wants to meet you for dinner in a restaurant without his mother-in-law, great. If he wants to come by your place sometime for a drink after work, fantastic. But spending time with Kim's mom is a nonstarter.

• • •

Dear Prudence,
I take a couple of trips a year with friends or for work in which there are ample opportunities to cheat. In the past I have taken advantage of this, and so have many of my closest friends, both female and male. When I am home, I am as dedicated a partner and parent as anyone else I know. I do at least 50 percent of the housework and childcare. The same can largely be said for my friends, who also don't seem to have a moral problem with straying from their otherwise monogamous partnerships on rare occasions.

I am happily married and very satisfied with my partner emotionally, intellectually, and sexually. But I can't pretend that makes the thrill of the new irrelevant. I am fairly confident that many, if not all, of us are hardwired for this. But obviously this seems to run against the grain in our society, at least on the surface. I wonder if we are living in a very Victorian-esque time in which these basic and not intrinsically unhealthy desires are shunned because of past principle, or if I, and a large percentage of those I know, should be classified as sociopaths.

The easy answer here is that the only thing I'm doing wrong is being dishonest with my partner. But why hurt someone with this truth if it makes no difference to anyone as long as I'm careful to keep it concealed? If I found out that my partner had been doing the same thing, I would not be angry or hurt, but I know that she does not feel the same. Is something wrong with me/us?

—Don't Feel Bad

///////////

No, I totally get it. Human beings are evolutionarily hardwired to furtively cheat on their partners three to four times a year on business trips. It's part of our brain chemistry. You happen to have evolved a little further than most of us onto a super-enlightened plane where you get to make decisions for your partner without her input or consent, and you're just, like, protecting her from something that would hurt her if she knew, which is pretty brave, if you think about it. You're basically her hero, shielding her from things that would only hurt her because she doesn't "get it" yet. Also, when you're not on business trips, you don't cheat on her. The majority of the time, you're not cheating at all! Plus you do laundry. If that doesn't earn you something on the side, I don't know what does.

I'm not going to "classify" you as a sociopath. You seem to want me to either absolve you entirely or call you a bad person, and I have no interest in doing either. But you know as well as I do that you're making selfish, gutless, easy choices. You have no interest in monogamy, and that's absolutely fine. Just don't pretend you've ascended to a higher plane of existence because of it. You've decided that since you're able to "see through" the fiction of exclusivity, you can act without taking your partner's feelings and desires into account. If you truly believed in the superiority of an open relationship, you'd talk to her about it. You wouldn't treat her like a child who hasn't earned the right to be initiated into your secret knowledge because she's too conventional to get it. It doesn't matter if you wouldn't mind if it turned out she had cheated on you; you admit that you know it would cause her pain if she found out. She deserves not to be lied to. Whether you choose polyamory or an open marriage or flexible monogamy isn't the point—whatever you decide, you have to come by it honestly.

• • •

The inside of our own problem can feel like such a vast and complicated place that it can be tempting to assume that nobody else experiences such a dizzying array of weights and counterweights, regrets and bitter-shot pleasure, abeyances and complications; that everyone else gets what they want in

a straightforward, immediate way as soon as they realize they
want it; that we alone are conducting a tortured symphony of
sentiment with a thousand different musicians while everyone
else is playing "If You're Happy and You Know It" on a child's
xylophone. I do it all the time. I'm never right, but I still do it
all the time.

////////////

Dear Prudence,
Last year, after trying on our own for a year, my husband and I
underwent an in vitro fertilization cycle, despite being told that
our chances were very, very slim. I went in for weekly and then
biweekly transvaginal sonograms, changed my diet, went to
therapy to deal with stress, and administered several shots each
day. And it was worth it: against all odds, we now have the most
gorgeous baby.

Physically, the pregnancy was mostly uneventful, but after
struggling to get pregnant in the first place, every day was scary,
and I frequently had thoughts of something terrible happening.
One would think that all the angst, depression, and anxiety of
fertility struggles would evaporate with a successful pregnancy.
But for me, they haven't.

I still struggle with the unfairness that we had to go through
so much to have a child when others have one or many so easily.
When I see parents in the park ignoring or being snippy with their
kids, I feel rage; it seems they don't know how lucky they are.
I struggle, despite being pro-choice, to be supportive of those

terminating a pregnancy for nonmedical reasons. It feels almost like PTSD, and I don't know how to get past it, especially as we are now, once again, hoping for another miracle. What can I do to move forward?

—Picture-Perfect Parents

////////////////

When you find yourself assuming people you don't know had easy roads to parenthood and take their own children for granted, meet that fantasy with the following response: "I don't know this person. I don't know what her life is like or anything about her relationship to her children outside of this five-minute window today. This person cannot help me with my own feelings of anxiety and fear."

I understand your reflexive instinct to turn your pain inside out and use it to scrutinize other people's actions—it's an instinctive response I often share!—but it's not going to get you anywhere. Whether someone else has an abortion has nothing to do with whether you yourself have a child. You know that on some level, but grief and anxiety have a tendency to cause magical thinking— the idea that an action wholly unrelated to a particular course of events can somehow influence its outcome—as well as the belief that everyone else should act as we do. The thought goes: "If I have struggled to have a child and it's caused me pain, then having a child must be equally important for other people to do, and no one should delay or decide against doing so."

I hope this doesn't sound harsh. I don't think any of us are responsible for the irrational thoughts we catch ourselves thinking when we're in pain, and you seem very aware that this is not a helpful, generous, rational approach to dealing with others. It makes sense that this pain has lingered, that it did not magically evaporate when you finally had a child—pain and anxiety almost never dissipate entirely when the hoped-for outcome finally arrives; they just find a way to suck the joy out of that too. You cannot push these feelings away or will them out of existence with positive thinking.

If the feelings come up, acknowledge them as neutrally as possible: "Right now, I'm afraid I'll never have a second child. I'm remembering how scary it was to try to have the first. I feel alone, as if the world is full of happy-but-careless parents, and no one else shares, understands, or cares about my pain. I'm scared of how badly I want a second child because that does not guarantee I will get what I want. I don't know how to experience joy for other people right now, because I'm so stuck here."

I recommend therapy, certainly, but any time you can take to set aside each day to acknowledge your feelings and not try to fight your way past them, whether that be in a journal, in private meditation, or in conversation with someone you trust, may prove helpful.

• • •

Here it is again—another beautiful opportunity not to have a problem.

/////////////

Dear Prudence,

My daughter-in-law enjoys knitting and crocheting. For her birthday, my husband and I gave her a generous gift card to a local yarn store, for which she thanked us and seemed very pleased. Imagine my dismay, however, when six months later for our anniversary she gifted us with a lovely bedspread, which she told me she made with yarn purchased from the gift card! I told my son that we'd in effect paid for our own present and that he needs to communicate to his wife how improper and stingy this move was. He refuses, saying that her labor and time were also part of the gift. We haven't spoken much since except to discuss our grandchildren, and our DIL has been outright cold. I'm considering writing her a letter directly explaining why this was an improper gift and expressing my sadness that her own parents didn't teach her gift etiquette. My husband wants me to drop the whole thing and pretend like it never happened. Prudie, I don't like the idea of moving on as if nothing happened.

—The Gift We Gave Ourselves

/////////////

But nothing did happen. You received a thoughtful gift that cost more time than money. That's it! If someone gives you a present you don't like, you smile and say, "Thanks, how thoughtful," and then stash it in the back of your closet. You don't ask your kid to complain to the gift giver via a back channel. It's fine if you like to give expensive presents—and can afford to do so—but that's not the only way to show someone that you care. Even if you don't like knitwear, your daughter-in-law spent countless hours over the course of a half year working on something very detailed for you, and you yourself say it was a lovely bedspread. Whether she got the yarn with the gift card you gave her or spent her own money is beside the point; you're acting as if she regifted something when that clearly wasn't the case. Your daughter-in-law's gift was thoughtful and intricate; yours was financially generous and relatively generic. There would be no reason to compare the two if you hadn't insisted on doing so in the first place.

You are grown adults with plenty of money; if there's something you want for yourself, go ahead and buy it—this kind of petty scorekeeping around gift giving is barely excusable when little children do it. Writing her a letter to express "sadness" that her own parents didn't teach her proper etiquette would be wildly inappropriate, out of line, and an unnecessary nuclear option. And it's a guaranteed ticket to make sure you see and hear about your grandchildren way less than you do now. You still have time to salvage this relationship—don't die on this hill. Let it go, apologize for your churlishness, and take yourself shopping if you want a pricey gift this year.

Chapter Seven

Going from All the Way Right to Only Half Right

Letters with an unpleasant theme: Realizing you might have to apologize to someone who still hasn't apologized for hurting you yet. Taking the ball and running too far with it. Acknowledging that even though you were justified at first, you may still have taken things too far and need to walk something back.

I want to be right all of the time; in my natural condition and given the option, I would choose the warm satisfaction of self-righteousness over happiness ninety-nine times out of a hundred. I recognize this impulse is at best maladaptive and have the necessary system of pulleys and emotional riggings in place to counter it, but I feel a keen sense of loss whenever I come across a letter where someone has blundered their way from being entirely, unequivocally right to merely half right or, worse, in a position where they have to apologize to someone they dislike. It is my hope that I can help as many people as possible avoid such a situation; for the rest, I advise facing it squarely and getting it over with.

///////////

Dear Prudence,

I'm a freshman in college, and I have a close friend who is very religious. (I am not.) We talk about boys and such, and she has made several references to what is unambiguously vaginal sex (which she's had with one person). Apart from that, she's given head to (and gotten head from) many guys. So I was pretty surprised when we were talking and she referred to herself as both celibate and a virgin! She is not! This isn't something I really care about (I think people should have sex with whomever they want, whenever they want, without judgment), but she is factually wrong to think that she is a virgin. Should I correct her on it?

—It's Not Important How Wrong You Are

///////////

If you truly don't care about it, let your actions follow your feelings and do nothing.

• • • •

It can be quite tempting to hurt someone one is angry with—often for excellent reasons—under the guise of sudden "concern" that was nowhere to be found before getting angry. But there are equally excellent reasons not to mislabel anger as something else, not to gussy up a resentful motivation in a shiny coat, and to be honest with oneself about one's desires.

////////////

Dear Prudence,

A dozen years ago, I met a man through my work. He was older, married, and had a young child. Nevertheless, I fell hopelessly in love with him. We had a brief but intense affair but lost touch after I moved to a satellite office. Over the years, we reconnected a few times at company meetings, and the affair was always hot and heavy, followed by total radio silence once he was back home with the wife. For nearly a decade, I believed this man was the love of my life and that he would finally realize this and we would live happily ever after. When I finally woke up and smelled the coffee and realized he would never leave his wife, I was hurt and felt like I'd been strung along for all those years.

Not long after, I discovered he'd been using drugs. He was fired some months after I reported him to the company. While I think this was the right thing to do (we work in an environment where impairment of any kind can jeopardize the safety of everyone), I did it for the wrong reasons. I did it because I was hurting and not because I was concerned about safety (I did not tell anyone this, of course).

It's now been several months since he was fired, and my ex-lover has emailed me to say that he wants to reconnect. He says he understands that I did what I had to do and that he's actually happier now in his new job. I'm still in love with this man and probably always will be. I'm wondering if I should tell him what I did and why, or is it better to leave well enough alone and not respond to his email, since the end of our affair brought out the worst in me. I still wish for that happily ever after.

—Right Decision, Wrong Reasons?

I think I can tell you with relative certainty that there is no happily ever after available for the two of you. "After an on-and-off affair, during which she got me fired for using drugs . . ." is never going to make it into a really solid, everlasting love story. This is a mess, and while you seem fairly aware of that at present, if there is any part of your brain that thinks maybe this time it will be different between the two of you, then that's a part of your brain you need to carefully ignore.

Let's go with your theory that you'll probably always be in love with this man. Okay! That's definitely a bummer. I hope that's not the case; I hope that, with some real time and distance (not just waiting for him to call again once he's bored with his wife), you'll be able to see him for what he is and not some romantic ideal. But even if your feelings about him never change, I can at the very least promise that you do not have to sacrifice another decade of your life to such an emotional roller coaster that "reporting my ex to his company for using drugs" and "maybe getting back together" sound like two good ideas. You absolutely should not respond to this email, because there is no conversation you could have that would make things okay between the two of you. There's no explanation, there's no shared confession, there's no long-overdue articulation of feeling that would make your relationship equitable, loving, or healthy.

Do not answer that email, get yourself to therapy, and spend some time figuring out how to make the next dozen years of your romantic life look different from the last. You do not have to keep your life latched on to his.

• • •

There's a world of difference between "I want my relative to stop demanding I buy his self-published books" (an eminently reasonable goal) and "I want my relative to stop thinking he is a good writer" (impossible to achieve—and even if it were possible, hardly worth doing).

////////////

Dear Prudence,
How can I help a college-age relative understand that before he self-publishes another book—he currently has four—he desperately needs to have the manuscripts proofread and edited by someone with high-level grammar skills? The writing is cringeworthy. The theme of the books is notable, but you

cannot get through to the theme because you cannot get past the incorrect punctuation, misused words, etc. The books are available for purchase online, and other relatives have seen them. We are all proud of what he is doing, but not how he is doing it. I tried sending him an email in which I mentioned that such notable writers as Ernest Hemingway and Tom Wolfe thought it wise to be guided by an editor. My words might as well have been struck with a sharp red pencil.

I have a bachelor's in journalism and have worked as a newspaper reporter, which he well knows, along with decades spent in the business world. One thing that a journalism professor said to our class was, "Don't fall in love with your words." I understand that it is hard to edit yourself. Once you have crafted what you just know is the most superb set of words in the English language, how could you or anyone else find a reason to cut them down or alter them in any way? I tried providing links to online proofreading and editing sites, but I think I might have offended him. I also offered to proofread future manuscripts. His only response was to ask when I plan to buy his most recent book. Do you have any suggestions as to how to help him help himself?

—A Cringing Aunt

//////////////

I think you should take your nephew's cue and stop offering him advice. He's made it clear that it's not welcome and that he won't follow any of it. You've offered him examples of famous writers who worked with editors, provided free resources to help him seek out proofreaders, and offered your own services, all to no avail; I don't think there's another way you can frame your suggestion such that he'll take it. Accept that your nephew is likely to continue self-publishing embarrassing books for the immediate future and that it's not your job to dissuade him from so doing, nor to encourage him. Adopt an attitude of peaceful nonengagement, focus your energies on more productive avenues, and feel free not to buy the fifth book.

• • •

The next letter has really stuck with me. I can understand how painful and deeply uncomfortable it must have been for the letter writer to suddenly realize they were working with a former bully, to say nothing of having to field an unexpected come-on, and I'd love to have been able to provide them with an answer that didn't involve having to apologize.

///////////

Dear Prudence,
I was pretty badly bullied in high school for my appearance and being two years younger than everyone else. In college I started lifting weights and "blossomed" into my looks, and life got much better. But the emotional scars remained. Earlier this year I started a new job and discovered the administrative assistant for my group was one of my bullies from high school. I know she recognized me because she made a joke about how

much I'd changed and said we had to "catch up sometime." I was cold but polite for the sake of our professional relationship, but she must have mistaken it for forgiveness, because last week at a work happy hour, she apologized again that "everyone" was so rough on me in high school—then she hit on me.

I was so infuriated that I ended up being very cruel and mocked her until she left in tears. It turns out revenge doesn't feel so good after all, and I've been avoiding her entirely. I'm afraid my boss is going to start asking why I'm wasting time on things the admin should be doing. Still I don't feel like apologizing to her, because what kind of jerk hits on someone they used to treat like dirt? Should I tell my boss what happened? I know he values me highly, so he might be willing to let me work with his administrative assistant, but I'm afraid that might come off as childish.

—Did I Bully My Bully?

////////////

I don't want to rub your face in what might have been, but you could absolutely have brought this issue up with your boss before the incident occurred. Had you told him it would be difficult for you to work with your former high school bully, he might have been able to set you up with his own administrative assistant before things got to the breaking point. Now you have two issues: One is whether you will be able to work with a person who treated you terribly all through high school. The other is how

to apologize to a coworker you reduced to tears in public. The
former has, I'm afraid, absolutely nothing to do with the latter.
You had the right to refuse her come-on, you had the right to
tell her that she made your life very difficult as a teenager and
that you were not interested in developing any sort of after-work
friendship with her, but whatever your residual feelings toward
her, you should have been able to refrain from berating her in
front of your colleagues until she fled the room crying. I don't
doubt it was painful to be picked on as a teenager, but you're
a professional adult now, and this can't be how you handle
personal issues with coworkers.

So the first thing you have to do, I'm afraid, is apologize to
her. You can keep it brief, but you need to apologize for behaving
cruelly and mocking her in public. Don't mention the fact that
she bullied you in high school—good apologies don't include
justifications or explanations (as we've just seen) but focus on
the relevant behavior and offer to make good. Tell her what you
said was inappropriate, that you're sorry, and that you won't
do it again. You don't have to be her friend or beat yourself up,
but you absolutely do need to say you're sorry, then drop the
subject and leave her alone unless you have something work-
related to discuss. If you're both willing and able to move ahead
and treat each other like disinterested colleagues, so much the
better. If you (or she) can't—if the history between you two is just
too tangled and painful—then you should talk to your boss and
ask for his help finding alternate arrangements, even if it feels
embarrassing to ask for help. It's already fairly apparent that you
two are having difficulty interacting with one another, so the time

to worry about what the situation looks like has passed.

• • •

Sometimes there are letters to which the only response is "Oh, dear."

//////////////

Dear Prudence,
I had a professor last semester who I am really, literally in love with. She's married with a kid and I think straight, so it's not something I would ever even attempt to act on. I'm fairly sure she knows I have a crush on her—it's not subtle—and my guess would be that she finds it flattering. She just offered to be my adviser, and I was obviously ecstatic and said yes. The problem is, I have a couple of tattoos related to her. One is a small word in her handwriting, which is a really cute, distinctive handwriting, that I got sort of in the spirit of unrequited love and because it was a positive affirmation she'd written on some of my work, and having her say something like that about something I wrote just meant a crazy amount to me. The other is a line from some of her published writing; I'd sent an artist friend of mine a list of poems and articles and essays and other things that meant a lot to me, including some of this professor's work, and asked her to turn it into a tattoo, which she did. My question is: Do I need to make sure to keep them covered whenever I know I'm going to be seeing her? (They're

on my foot and ankle, so not super difficult to hide.) Will she be creeped out and hate me if she sees them?

—Teacher Tattoos

Oh, dear. I'm torn between a desire to give you a hug and talk you out of every recent decision. I have a lot of sympathy for your feelings, but there's nothing we can do about those now; let's go ahead and tidy up your actions. I'm glad, at least, that you are aware that your married professor does not return your feelings and that it would be unwise to offer romantic overtures she would have to politely reject. If she is a responsible person, she would not have offered to be your adviser if she knew the extent of your infatuation. I want to tell you to find another adviser, but I'm worried that's advice you simply won't take. I think you should find someone else to advise you immediately— yesterday of immediately—but at the very least, yes, cover up your tattoos when you are around her. Do not put her in the supremely awkward position of realizing she's sitting with a student who has had her compliments permanently etched into her skin. That would move your crush from "flattering" to "impossible."

I wish you a speedy recovery from your feelings.

• • •

So much of what went wrong for the next letter writer was

small-scale, perfectly understandable, and easily fixable in the moment, but it somehow compounded into a trip-wire maze of resentment and indignation. "If only someone else had prevented me from making this error" is an alluring oasis when faced with missing a meaningful and relatively rare event to celebrate a close friend, but it's a mirage.

///////////////

Dear Prudence,
About a month ago I received a text message about an upcoming bachelor party for a close friend. Due to my own forgetfulness and being quite busy with grad school and work, I forgot all about it and didn't reply. I completely forgot about it until the day before the event, when the groom told me that something was planned for him the next day, but he didn't know what. I contacted the person planning the event to see if it was too late for me to attend and sadly discovered that it was.

I know that I am to blame for not responding to the event, but I'm feeling a little annoyed at the planner. One text? That was all I got. Doesn't a bachelor party require a little bit of effort on the organizer's part to coordinate with friends (a group email, or at least a second text to remind the person)? In addition, my partner is equally good friends with the groom and didn't get a message at all (only a mention in my first text). Now both of us are missing a very good friend's bachelor party because of one missed text. Does this land squarely on my shoulders? I'm feeling angry, but maybe I am just mad at myself for forgetting.

/////////////

I think you are mostly just mad at yourself for forgetting! It's very rare in life that we are 100 percent wrong while someone else is 100 percent right, but don't let the fact that there are always imperfect scores to be doled out on all sides obscure the pertinent fact, which is that you failed to respond to the initial invitation. It would have been great if the organizer had followed up with a reminder, but the primary breakdown in communication originated with you, and no subsequent rudeness on anyone else's part can change that fact. You missed out on something you wanted to attend because you didn't prioritize it. I can certainly sympathize! That's happened to me. Let the sting of missing out propel you to change the way you respond to future invitations.

• • • •

/////////////

Dear Prudence,

Recently, while visiting my friend "Nancy," I was chatting with her while she put away dishes from the dishwasher. At one point I noticed that she'd left a cupboard door open, so I helpfully closed it. She then turned around with her arms full of plates, for some reason expected the cabinet door to be open, and clumsily dropped some of the dishes. I honestly thought she was done in that cupboard and helped her clean up the mess. I also suggested that next time she put things away one or two pieces at a time so that she could keep the doors neatly shut in between. Nancy never complained to me but must have told our friend "Paul" because he told me that I owed Nancy an apology and should offer to pay for her broken dishware. I admit that open cabinets and drawers are a pet peeve of mine, but I find it ridiculous that I should apologize or pay for attempting to be helpful. Do I owe Nancy anything here?

—Bull in a China Cupboard

I don't know that I have a formal, official ruling here—you were trying to be helpful, but closing a cabinet door while someone else is in the middle of unloading the dishwasher is not practically helpful. You say that "for some reason" Nancy expected the cabinet door to be open when she turned around with an armful of dishes; this was because she'd left the cabinet door open mere moments ago and therefore had a very good reason for expecting it to stay open!

Why don't you speak directly to Nancy about this if you're unsure of what she wants? Maybe she told Paul herself that she's angry with you and wants an apology, or maybe she merely mentioned what happened to Paul and he decided you owed her repayment. The only way to find out what Nancy thinks is to ask her directly—although I don't recommend (for obvious reasons) that you start with, "Nancy, I find it ridiculous that I should have to apologize to you. Do you want me to apologize?"

For what it's worth, apologizing doesn't mean you have to don a hair shirt and take full responsibility for what happened. It was an accident, and just because you're sorry that you (however indirectly) contributed to the dropped dishes, it does not also follow that you think you were being wholly rude or irresponsible. If you don't want to offer to pay for new dishes, then don't make the offer, although it would be a kind gesture between friends.

The one thing I would advise you to reconsider is what you did after Nancy dropped the dishes. You don't describe apologizing in a general sense ("Oh, how awful! I'm so sorry"), just that you offered her unsolicited advice about how to put her own dishes away. If you like closing and reopening cabinets repeatedly while you unload your own dishwasher, that's your affair, but others don't, and there's certainly no one right way to put away dishes. Next time you're visiting a friend who's doing chores, if you want to be useful to her, ask her if there's anything you can do to help— don't decide you know what she should be doing better and make the decision for her.

• • • •

I remember the next letter with a great deal of tenderness, not least because this letter writer wrote to me later with an update on his family's progress. I have no way of knowing whether most people who have written to me end up taking my advice, either wholly or in part, or even whether they've seen that I've answered their question, so I'm delighted to get a second letter merely to satisfy my own curiosity about what happened next, even if they don't take my suggestions. And I'm deeply grateful to have been useful to a parent who fears the world will be unkind to their child if they transition and wonders if discouraging transition might not be the kindest response. Unsurprisingly, I don't believe that it is, but I understand that in this case at least, the letter writer's desire to look out for his daughter's best interests was sincere and loving and that it was only a question of shifting perspective rather than changing his entire attitude toward her.

////////////

Dear Prudence,

My stepkid (she's been my stepkid since she was one, and her bio dad isn't around much) just told us that she is a trans girl. We're doing our best to be good parents. The thing is, as she moves forward and talks to doctors about being a girl at school and with her friends, I just want to put the brakes on. It's not the medical stuff so much, but the social side of things. She's brave enough to do it, but I'm scared to death. She's a kid, people are horrible, and schools don't always deal with bullying in a good way. I just feel trapped because I don't know what I should do. I go from "In the end it's her decision" to "She's ten—there's a reason we have to oversee her decisions!" My wife thinks we can deal with whatever comes, but she was popular and well-liked. I was put in bins and beaten up. So we have different expectations for how bad it could get.

I just want us to make the best decision for my stepdaughter, but I don't know where the reasonable line between wholehearted support and ruled by fear lives. Any ideas?

—Transition Time Line

///////////////

I think a helpful thing to ask yourself while parenting is, "Am I responding to my child's childhood in this moment, or to mine?" I'm so sorry you were beaten up regularly as a child. That stays with you in a very real and painful way, and it's understandable that you want to do anything you can to spare your daughter from the kind of bullying you experienced. The answer to that, I think, is to spend a lot of time working closely with your daughter's medical team, teachers, and school administrators developing a safety plan designed to support her—and to spend a lot of time talking to her, asking what she's worried about, what she's excited for, what she thinks she'll need. She goes to that school every day and likely has a pretty sophisticated understanding of which kids get bullied, and what for, and she's decided that it's worth the risk.

You're absolutely right that as her parent you're there to guide her decisions, but it's also true that she is the ultimate expert in her gender. What she needs from you is love and support. You may feel like it would protect her to say, "Why don't we revisit this in a few years," but that's not taking into account the pain it causes a trans person to go back into the closet. Not transitioning at school is as big a decision as transitioning at school, and it may very well be more painful than getting bullied, which, by the way, may not

end up being as big a problem as you fear! Times have changed
since you were a child.

The more you work as a team, I think, the less panicked you'll
feel about her safety. I hope you have a therapist or a close friend
you can occasionally share your fears and feelings with, because it
can be a difficult road to navigate. I wish you all the best.

//////////

Dear Prudence,
I wrote in a few weeks ago about my concern that transitioning
at school would endanger my stepdaughter. I appreciated your
advice, but I did think you were wrong at the time, so my wife
and I decided that she should wait, explained that to her, and a
few days later realized that it was the wrong thing to do. She was
unhappy and not talking to us about it. So I sat down and told
her I'd made a mistake because I was scared, bargained for a few
more days to get everything set up at the school, and now she's
a girl 24-7. It's been awful, and fine. Which describes basically
everything since she learned to walk, I suppose. My wife took a
few days off work so she could hang out in a nearby coffee shop
during the transition period. I got permission to keep my phone
with me all the time at work. My stepdaughter was annoyed that
the girls' soccer team is rubbish at her school. People have been
mean, but my stepdaughter says they were mean about stuff
anyhow.

So . . . it was the right choice. She's happy. Sometimes I miss the little boy I thought I knew, but mostly when I look at her now, I realize how unhappy she was before. So thanks. You were right.

—Transition Time Line, Part II

////////////

I'm so glad to hear that your daughter is doing well and that you and your wife have been able to take the time to support her as she transitions at school. It's so clear that you love her and want to be there for her, and I think that will continue to serve you well as she grows up. Thanks so much for letting us know how you're all doing, and best of luck improving that soccer team.

• • •

I've read countless letters from people who desperately wish that closeness were transferable. *If I love my partner and like her sister and think her sister's attempts to repair their relationship have been sincere, then surely if I can just communicate my feelings in a sufficiently eloquent way, my partner will come to share them.* That's a tempting prospect, but it's unfortunately rooted in a profound misunderstanding of how feelings operate, not to mention the difference between getting a general sense of someone else's childhood and experiencing said childhood directly.

////////////

Dear Prudence,
I'm very close to my family. I tell my parents and siblings about nearly everything and receive their support. My fiancée is not and does not. We have, for the most part, reached a compromise where we each control the flow of information to our respective families. The problem is this: We both like her sibling-in-law, and while I understand the hostility she feels toward her sibling based on their past, what I have seen is her sibling trying to rectify that past. Her parents are a separate issue, and I agree with her handling of them, but I don't know what to do when I can't see the malicious intent she attributes to her sibling's actions.

—The Ties That Bind

////////////

If you're hoping you can repair your fiancée's relationship with her sibling in order to spend more time with your pleasant in-law, I think that's a dream you should let die on the vine. I don't know how much input your fiancée wants from you when it comes to interpreting her relative's actions; you can certainly ask questions along the lines of "Can you tell me more about this? From what I saw, it seemed fairly innocuous. Does your sibling have a history of __? Is there something else that I'm missing?" and "What kind of relationship do you think is possible with your sibling? Does it feel like your sibling's attempts to make up for the past are genuine and make a real difference, or do you think there's a limit to how much can be repaired?"

Questions you shouldn't ask include *"Why are you so upset about this? It seemed fine to me"* and *"Why can't you just let this go? The past is the past!"* Ultimately, even if you don't understand or share your partner's reaction to her sibling, it's not your relationship to manage, and you should restrict yourself to a supportive, rather than a directive, role.

• • •

Dear Prudence,

Due to depression and the miserable state my life is in, I've completely lost all sexual desire. This has been going on for over a year. My husband is clearly suffering. I've told him that he can sleep with whoever he wants, that we can have an open marriage, that we can get divorced, etc. He refuses and says he loves me and will wait. I know he thinks he is being patient and kind, but it just makes me feel worse for not having sexual feelings. Whenever I bring up the idea of an open marriage, he thinks it's a trap, like I am going to use it as an excuse to leave him. Counseling didn't work. He really doesn't deserve to live like a monk because I am broken. How can I get it across that I'm trying to help him out?

—Open Marriage for Him

I don't think the most pressing issue in your marriage right now is that your husband isn't having sex even though he would like to— although it does, of course, matter. I think the most pressing issue in your marriage is that you need more medical and therapeutic support for your severe depression and feelings of worthlessness. Calling yourself "broken" and thinking your husband deserves better than you because you're suffering isn't the voice of truth. That's the voice of depression telling you that he's good and you're bad and the best thing for him is to draw back from intimacy with you. I don't know what kind of counselor you two saw together, but if the focus of those counseling sessions was your sex life and not your untreated depression, then I don't think it could possibly have helped you. You deserve treatment and help, not in the interest of immediately restoring your sexual desire, but because you are a person worthy of support and shouldn't have to deal with these feelings of worthlessness by yourself.

• • •

I'm less persuaded of my own rightness than I was when I wrote the next answer, so here's my chance to join the "less correct than previously hoped" camp. The letter writer doesn't say much about how long she dated her husband before getting married and moving in together, so it's entirely possible that they did take things slowly, and she simply found over the course of the years that she was far less suited to farm life than she'd thought after even an extensive trial period. While I'm all for taking serious commitments slowly, I also realize that it's not possible to perfectly and permanently prepare for a significant life change, that there is no way to guarantee we'll never experience serious doubt or regret, and that I should have been about 30 percent less high-handed with this letter writer.

///////////////

Dear Prudence,

All my life I've dreamed of living on a farm. I never thought it would really happen, but a few years ago I took a great leap of faith and married a man I met via a dating website for farmers. The trouble is that farm life isn't like I thought it would be. My husband has to work really hard, sometimes twelve to fifteen hours a day, especially during the harvest. And every day he has to get up before dawn to milk and do other chores. Plus, the work is dirty, so he is always filthy. He's really good about not tracking dirt into the house, but it is still annoying. This really isn't how I pictured farm life, and I kind of want out. But my husband is such a great guy that I don't want to leave. I doubt he'd want to start another career that could take us back to the city. I just don't know what to do. Can you see a way out?

—Farm Fatigue

///////////////

I think this is an important warning for other farm-fascinated urbanites thinking about moving out to the country on impulse. Try visiting for a week or two first, or joining a work-study agricultural program, rather than going straight from "apartment-dweller" to "farmer's wife." I'm not sure why you were surprised to find that farm life is both dirty and difficult, but it's hard to muster a great deal of sympathy for your situation, given that you performed so little research before making such a drastic, life-changing decision. You do, at least, have the option now of putting forth a bit more effort toward understanding the new life you've chosen with your husband. Admit to him that you've found it more of a challenge than you anticipated. If all you're doing right now is scowling at the dirty boots out on the porch, try doing more with your time—either try to help out around the farm, or find some other work or passion project to keep yourself occupied. Give this "lifelong dream" a good-faith effort before bailing on it completely. If you have to go, you have to go, but maybe you don't have to. Give this a try. I don't think you've given it your best shot yet.

• • •

//////////////

Dear Prudence,

Nearly twenty years ago, when we were both young adults, I acted toward my partner at the time in ways that I now recognize as abusive. I have grown considerably since then and feel genuine remorse for the behaviors and mindsets I had back then. I have run into my former partner a few times over the years when visiting my old hometown, and our interactions were brief and polite. We are otherwise not in contact. I would like to apologize to them for my past behaviors, but I am worried that it might do more harm than good by making them relive past trauma or feel obligated to respond. I am not looking for forgiveness or ongoing communication with them. Should I send a note of apology, or leave the past where it is and focus on being a good partner and working for a more just world in the present? If an apology is appropriate, would an email be the right format?

—Better Late Than Never?

///////////////

The desire to apologize for past abuse is a good one, but it's definitely not something that you should pursue without expert supervision and counsel. Did your past abuse ever involve something like insisting upon continued contact or boundary-pushing after your partner said no? Did any of it involve monitoring their communication with others, stalking, or demanding forgiveness on your timetable? In such instances, I'd encourage you to turn your energies toward the kind of repair that does not involve renewed contact and to set your goal as not compounding past harm by contacting your former partner.

Have you shared any of your new realizations about your past abuse with a therapist, with your friends, or with any of your subsequent partners? What steps have you taken to ensure that you do not repeat this abusive behavior? It's a good indicator that you're prepared for a nonresponse or for your ex not to forgive you, but I think you should run this plan past multiple people whose judgment you trust and who can offer you ongoing support (at least some of that support should be therapeutic, I think) with a clear-eyed perspective of the past abuse. Only after such preemptive work should you even consider the possibility of a note—and such a note should not, I think, contain an apology but instead ask whether your ex is interested in the possibility of hearing an apology from you, since that offers them the freedom to decide for themselves whether they want to hear from you on the subject. Please move forward very carefully, and double-check your impulses and desires with someone experienced in ending abusive cycles.

Chapter Eight

The Other Shoe Just Dropped, and Coming Up with Bad Ideas

Letters with a sudden fall from grace: Realizing that you had no idea what was going on for months or years. Coming to terms with a sudden revelation. Dealing with secret second lives. "I thought everything was fine . . ." Floundering, searching for purchase, and second-guessing what originally sounded like a great idea.

A ny letter including the phrase "I thought things were fine" is, without fail, immediately followed by the most improbable and distressing revelation imaginable. "I thought things were good" or, worse still, "I thought we were happy" only ups the ante. Shoe dropping of this magnitude, whether it has to do with a romantic betrayal, a revelation at work, or a bust-up between friends, thoroughly destabilizes one's sense of options. "How could we have experienced the same relationship so differently?" follows quickly on the heels of "How could I not have known?" If *this* can be true, then all bets are off and all imaginable responses, including those previously thought unimaginable, are newly on the table.

///////////

Dear Prudence,

For my mother's sixtieth birthday and Mother's Day (same weekend), my parents and younger sister came to visit me and stay at my place. We had decorations, flowers, and a custom-made cake ready when they arrived—a joint effort among me, my sister, and my husband. My husband and I treated the entire group to a very enjoyable (and expensive) dinner one of the nights. My sister paid for pedicures the next day, and my father treated everyone to a late lunch and a musical later that night. My sister and I made Mother's Day breakfast on Sunday at my place before the three of them departed. It was a lovely weekend, and imagine my surprise when I received a long email from my father telling me how disappointed he was that we didn't also get my mother a gift (implying that she was disappointed by the weekend). He told us to not bother doing anything, experience or gift, for his upcoming birthday or Father's Day. I am embarrassed and upset, and I don't know whether to say anything to him and/or my mother (apologize? Be offended that our best efforts weren't enough?).

—Disappointed Mother

////////////////

I wonder if your mother knew that your father sent that email. I don't know if she has a history of asking him to be the bad cop and relate her disappointment to you kids, or if this is a one-off, but I think you should get in touch with your mother directly. Tell her that you were really surprised to hear from your father and that you'd had a wonderful time hosting her and thought it was mutually understood that her gifts this year were primarily experiences rather than tangible objects. You can also ask, "If you'd rather open a gift, please let me know, because I'd be happy to adjust how I plan presents for you," if you think next time around she'd rather ooh and aah over a sweater or a watch and have something to take home with her rather than go out to a few nice meals in a row. It may also help to ask your mother whether she knows anything about your father's email before deciding how to respond to him.

Without totally closing off the possibility that he's nursing a real (or at least real-to-him) sense of hurt, I think your father's way of communicating his desires to you is pretty childish, and I'd call him rather than respond over email, so it's a little harder for him to sign off in a huff. "I was surprised to see that you were so upset after Mother's Day weekend that you don't want us to get you anything for your birthday. I thought we'd all enjoyed ourselves, and we were happy to spend time and money planning a lovely dinner, customizing a cake, ordering flowers, and hosting everyone for the weekend. Can you tell me a little bit more about what you were thinking? Your email really surprised me. Of course, if you don't want anything for Father's Day, we won't force you to celebrate, but I'd like to know more about your expectations and hopes for family celebrations, since ours seem to be very different."

• • •

There's something almost charming about the idea of sending an anonymous letter to a friend you know to be sensitive about the possibility of being talked about. Destabilizing and unhelpful, yes, but almost charming too.

////////////

Dear Prudence,

I just found out that my very close friend's eighteen-year-old son has a fake Snapchat account to sell drugs. My friend is very private and would not only be devastated that her son has been lying and engaging in criminal behavior but also humiliated that people are talking about this. I feel like sending an anonymous letter because a) I'm chicken, b) I want to preserve our friendship, and c) she won't be as humiliated. Is this a good idea?

—Anonymous Anxiety

I have to say, it doesn't sound like a good idea when I say it out loud: "I sent my friend an anonymous letter to let her know her eighteen-year-old sells drugs on Snapchat." It sounds unnecessarily clandestine, avoidant, and messy; plus, if she doesn't like being talked about, she's definitely not going to like wondering which one of her friends or acquaintances or colleagues sent the letter. If you actually think there's a substantial, immediate threat to your friend's safety, tell her straightforwardly. If you don't think there is one, or if you're not certain that it's him (if it's fake, how can you know it's really him?), wait and reflect before making a decision. I'm not quite sure what you mean when you call the Snapchat account "fake"—is he just pretending to sell drugs? Do you mean that it's anonymous or that he uses a different name? Is he still living at home with your friend, and is he publishing their address or otherwise obviously putting her at risk? Do you know her son personally, and if so, have you considered letting him know directly that he's not covering his tracks very well? Generally, you should consider anonymous letters to be measures of absolute last resort; I don't think you're at that stage right now.

● ● ● ●

It's always risky to tell someone you've found an actor you think looks "a lot" like them, even if you believe the comparison is complimentary; I've nursed more than one resentment over "You know, you look a lot like [famous person]" from someone who expected me to be flattered or at least pleased.

People can be awfully proprietary about who they think they look like, and while I don't want to assume that every girlfriend on the planet would be offended or scandalized by hearing her boyfriend thinks she looks like a particular porn actress, I do think it's important to proceed carefully.

////////////////

Dear Prudence,
I have found a porn star who looks a lot like my girlfriend. I have watched her videos often. I want to show my girlfriend her "twin." Do you think that's a bad idea?

—Bawdy Double

////////////////

I suppose my answer depends on the following: Do you and your girlfriend have a history of talking about porn with one another? Do you think she would be flattered or interested? Do you think she would get anything out of this conversation, or do you think you would find it erotically charged and are overwriting your feelings for hers? Are you pretending that she might like something you like so you don't have to take responsibility for expressing your own desires? Have you prepared yourself for how you'll handle it if your girlfriend is not impressed and is in fact turned off or even hurt by this revelation? What will you do if you say, "I'd like to show you a porn actress who I think looks like you?" and your girlfriend says, "No, thanks. I'd rather not"? What will you do if your girlfriend does *not see the resemblance? There are a lot of questions you'll need to answer for yourself before you decide to bring this up with her, and I can't possibly answer them for you. (Good luck figuring all this out!)*

· · ·

A great deal has been written about the "We have a great relationship, but . . ." problem, including the always popular "My boyfriend is wonderful, but . . ." variation. While I don't think it's necessarily a prelude to an obvious deal breaker, the "great" part doesn't have much bearing on whatever follows the "but." The implied argument is something along the lines of "If our relationship is otherwise great, then this particular problem / impasse / set of conflicting desires cannot possibly lead to a breakup," but that's not always the case. Sometimes mostly great relationships end for necessary and important reasons if there's no suitable compromise both parties can agree to. A breakup doesn't retroactively invalidate whatever made that particular relationship lovely or meaningful.

///////////

Dear Prudence,

My boyfriend and I have a great relationship. However, I want to get married, and he does not. He says that he loves me but that he can't promise to love me "until death do us part." I say that I can't make that promise either but that I wish to love him for the rest of our lives, and I wish that he would feel the same way about me. He says that he can't separate "promise" from "wish" and that we will therefore never get married. I think that he's being stupid and selfish. No one can promise lifelong and unconditional love to someone other than his or her child, right?

—Willing to Work It Out

//////////////

Whatever your boyfriend is being, you're not going to persuade him to marry you by coming up with a better argument. Your boyfriend has made it clear that he doesn't want to marry you and that he can't promise he'll stay with you for the rest of his life. If you can live with that, stay and adjust your expectations. If you can't, find someone else who's willing to offer you what you want. What you shouldn't do is try to wear down his resistance by coming up with a list of extremely good reasons why marrying you isn't really that bad and why people don't really mean it when they promise "'til death do us part," so he shouldn't either. This isn't a question of semantics, so don't get caught up in thinking that if you can just persuade him not to mind that particular expression, he's going to want the same things you do.

//////////////

Dear Prudence,
By the time I turned thirty, I already had two marriages and divorces under my belt. I've spent a lot of time thinking about my

part in those relationships' ends, what I overlooked at the time, and what I want (or don't want!) for myself and my child now. I've been with my current boyfriend for two years. We both said early on we could be together, but we would never marry. Now, we've started to talk about marriage, and it freaks me out. It's not that I don't love him, but what if it doesn't work out? I took big financial and personal hits in my divorces. I'm just feeling like I'm in a good place. I know the statistical likelihood of a third marriage working out, and it terrifies me. At the same time, I feel like there is a certain seriousness afforded wedded couples that I miss having. Should I even consider marriage, or should I stick to my original inclination to be happily together but not married?

—Happily Unmarried

I'm curious about the gap in your letter between "we would never marry" and "we've started to talk about marriage." What changed, aside from the passage of time? Going from "never" to "maybe" is a big shift, and while you're both entitled to change your minds, I wish I knew more about what prompted this new conversation. If the only reason you've started talking about it together now is because you've been together for two years and have a vague sense that married couples are afforded "a certain seriousness," I think the best thing to do is revisit your founding principles as a couple and see if you can't reaffirm them. Your reasons to postpone or avoid marriage altogether are reasonable, specific, and grounded in practical experience; they have to do with self-sufficiency, debt, *not wanting to get tied up in court again, and prioritizing the stability of the home you share with your child. Your reasons for considering marriage are largely unclear, but what you have said about them suggests they have more to do with a fear of how others might perceive you than anything that's directly relevant to your relationship. Stick to your original inclination, at least for now.*

If in another year you both find your thoughts turning more and more often to marriage, you can always revisit the subject. But don't rush this! Give yourself time to enjoy being in a good place after years of turmoil. If getting married really is a good idea, it'll still be a good idea a year from now.

• • •

Sometimes I think "Everything was fine" is interrupted not by a surprising revelation the letter writer struggles to contend with, but by a sudden and impish desire on the letter writer's part to upset the applecart—*l'appel du vide* on a smaller, pettier scale.

///////////////

Dear Prudence,

I live in an apartment complex geared toward young adults (college students looking for a quieter environment, grad students, young professionals, and a few young families). Last year, the young woman across the hall lost both her parents in a freak accident, and her little brothers were sent across the country to live with family. She already had one (admittedly very well-behaved and well-trained) dog, but she took in both of her parents' dogs. There is a two-dog limit that I was informed was "strictly enforced," but she apparently appealed for special permission given the circumstances and received it because one of the dogs is "elderly." I feel bad for her circumstances, but it's been a year and she still has three dogs, so apparently the "elderly" one wasn't so old after all. She seems to be a responsible pet owner, but I think it's unfair that she's had three dogs and will for the foreseeable future. I think she used everyone's pity for her family tragedy to get around the rules. Would it be wrong of me to complain to management?

—A Few Paws Too Many

//////////////

Yes, it would. Management is already aware of her situation, and you have no new information to offer it—you don't say that her dogs are behaving badly or that she's started hoarding animals. Your complaint would be nothing more than "I don't like the arrangement that you, management, have already approved," which is just too damn bad. She hasn't "gotten around" anything; she asked for an official exemption and received it. Dogs don't always die on schedule; surely you understand that this woman could hardly have promised her landlord that her elderly dog was guaranteed to die in the next year. If you truly believe that your neighbor has somehow "gamed the system" to get an extra dog by losing her parents in a freak accident, you may have just set a new record for the unkindest, least reasonable Dear Prudence letter of all time. Mind your own business, attempt to cultivate joy in your own heart, and leave your neighbor alone.

. . . .

There's often an immense pleasure to be had in entertaining an idea one *knows* to be bad, even self-destructive, and I am an enthusiastic supporter of pleasure. But I must come out against poison-pen letters in addition to being against anonymous letters to friends about their sons' hypothetical Snapchat accounts. If you wouldn't be willing to tell someone off in person because you know it would make your life worse, don't write the letter.

//////////////

Dear Prudence,
My work environment is horrible. Executives are demeaning and degrading; colleagues are territorial and passive-aggressive rather than empathetic and collaborative. My bosses have totally abandoned me and refused to promote me despite recently admitting I'm overqualified and regularly deliver high-quality results. Well, I'm moving to another city soon, and even though I don't have another job lined up yet, I don't want any references from these people. Part of me wants to leave everyone with a sharply worded handwritten note on my way out, so they know exactly how I feel about their terrible behavior. The other part of me wishes I could be content

enough to quietly slip out and let this place implode on its own. What's the best route to take?

—Bridge Burning Beckons

////////////

Leaving a poisonous letter in your wake is almost never the best route, unless you are an actual Borgia and willing to fully commit to the lifestyle. You might not want references from these people, but you may very well end up needing them if any future employers decide to call your most recent manager (a fairly common practice), and I can't imagine getting an offer letter after someone hears, "He seemed great, until he left a note on his desk letting us know we should all go to hell." You would be tanking your future career in order to insult former coworkers without even having the pleasure of watching them read your words. On some level, too, you must know that none of them are self-aware enough to take your words to heart—they'd dismiss you as "crazy" and embittered before they got to the end. You're moving away and moving on, and you don't ever have to see these people again. Let that be enough.

• • •

I have lots of sympathy for anyone who spends a great deal of time and energy training to become the architect of their own misfortune, possibly because I have done so myself on more than one occasion. Sometimes the most carefully thought-out and minutely planned ideas are the best worst ideas of all.

////////////

Dear Prudence,

I'm in college and have spent the past year trying to set up my roommate with one of my classmates (they are perfect for each other). It now seems as if that will finally pay off, as they have a date coming up—I'm so psyched for them! There is one problem though: I've been sleeping with said classmate. Both of us have been going through a rough patch and have been using each other as comfort, but there are no feelings involved whatsoever— we are just very good friends. (I have an amazing long-term boyfriend, who knows and understands all of this.) Now that my roommate and classmate are getting together, the sex element of my friendship with my classmate is over, but there's already been awkwardness with my roommate—I think she wants me to stop hanging out with my classmate (who's also my best friend here). Is there a way I can reassure my roommate that I'm not interested without having to lose my best friend?

—Love Triangle

////////////

This sounds like an unusually fraught situation. You've orchestrated your ex-lover's next relationship with the woman you live with, who's already uncomfortable with how close you are with said ex-lover. You think your roommate wants you to spend less time with your classmate, but you don't know for sure. You've ended your sexual relationship, but until the subject actually comes up, I don't think it's your responsibility to demote your friendship with your classmate.

However, I do think it is your responsibility to reduce your future meddling by a good 85 percent. It may work out between them and it may not; you have already put the ball in motion and now must let it roll. Mentally categorize their possible romantic relationship as "none of my business" and keep from worrying too much about reassuring—or losing—either one.

• • •

Revelations like the next one are doubly devastating, not just on their face but because they draw into sharp relief just how serious a loved one's emotional deterioration has become. It's incredibly painful to try to support someone deeply in need of help while also attempting to recover from a horrifying, unfounded accusation that cannot help but taint one's other family relations.

////////////////

Dear Prudence,

I live at home with my five siblings (I'm the oldest) and mom and dad. For about a year now, my mom has been going through depression and mental health issues. One night at the dinner table, my mom said that I may be having an affair with my dad and that she cannot trust us being together alone in one room. It's not true. Not only did my dad and I not see this coming, but neither did any of my other family members. We talked for hours explaining that this accusation made all of us very uncomfortable. I expressed how much I respect and love her and my dad way too much to ever do anything like that. I cried. My siblings cried. My dad cried. Nothing we said seemed to help. I decided to stay out of my parents' way, especially my dad's, to make her feel comfortable and to trust me.

Recently, I took a trip with my mom and my sisters to my country. It was great, and I had no issues with my mom. I even got married on that trip. My husband lives in that country and could not travel back with me, so I had to come back home alone with my mom and sisters. I thought things would be different after that trip and marriage. But as soon as we returned home, my mom started acting suspicious and said she still felt my dad and I were having an affair. I was devastated. I decided to stop speaking to my mom. My dad agreed with me and supports me on this decision. He has apologized for her behavior toward me and has expressed that he also struggles with this accusation. I cannot move away due to financial issues. I love my mother and want a relationship with her for myself and my future children, but I cannot take her accusing me of such behavior. I have not told anyone, even my husband, about this matter. I'm ashamed to bring it up. What can I do?

—Mom Thinks I'm Sleeping with Dad

//////////

This is profoundly sad and disturbing, *and I can't imagine how difficult it must be to stay in the house with her right now. I don't know if your mother is currently being treated by a doctor or mental health professional, but if she is, you should encourage your father to discuss her latest symptoms with them, because* *they're a sign of a disturbing break from reality. Do you have any other family members living nearby or friends who might be willing to host you in a guest room or on a couch for a few days? Getting even a temporary break from staying in your parents' house would be good for you, and if you don't feel prepared yet to share the sensitive nature of your mother's paranoid delusions, you can just say that you're going through a difficult time with your family and need a little space. In the long run, saving up as much as you can so you can eventually move out is going to be necessary, and that might include speaking to your husband directly about this so the two of you can prioritize getting you out of there.*

. . . .

Sometimes a shocking revelation has unexpected advantages—if things weren't previously "fine," there can be a sort of relief in learning something that might in other circumstances prove dismaying.

////////////

Dear Prudence,

Last year, at forty-seven, I accidentally discovered that my mother had been lying to me about my biological father for my whole life. She married the man who raised me when I was six months old and swore the entire family to secrecy. I found my biological father, and we are both devastated to have missed out on a lifetime of love and family connection. His family has welcomed me with open arms. He apparently proposed to my mother, but because she was much younger than him and not ready to grow up (in her words, the power dynamic in the relationship was in his favor), she declined. She told him she'd had multiple partners and there was no way to know whose I was. She confided to me that she didn't want anyone else having a voice in how I was raised, and she told my aunt that she married my adoptive dad because he was a partying hippie and she wanted to keep living that life.

My mother is also mentally ill and has been barely functional most of my life. She abused and neglected me and my younger brother our entire childhoods and still plays the victim every chance she gets. Everything is all about her. I've handled things like chores and bills for my parents since I can remember. I love my dad, but he's only ever made excuses for her. This time, I'm simply not prepared to forgive and forget. She had plenty of time to tell me the truth and never did. I don't want to fracture my family, and I'm being urged to forgive her, but I don't see how I can. To complicate things, my dad (who raised me) is dealing with a progressive disability, and my parents are aging. They will need increasing care as time goes on. I'm struggling. I won't have the means to get regular counseling for a few more months. What do I owe my mother and father after this? Is this something I can reasonably consider a relationship deal breaker?

—Where Do I Go from Here?

Let's start with what you owe yourself first: you get to be angry, take time and space away from your parents, prepare to start counseling in a few months, push back against the idea that you should quickly forgive your mom, and spend meaningful time with your new family members. I want to leave open the possibility that your mother was on the more difficult end of an uneven power dynamic with your biological father at the time and felt pressure from various fronts. I don't want you to think of your mother as someone whom you have to make excuses for or clean up after or as a bad actor and a manipulator whom you stop talking to. She may very well be a complicated mixture—suffering and self-centered, frightened and manipulative, in genuine need and also looking to drain you of energy.

The important thing is that you have been abused and pressured into taking care of your parents for your entire life, and now that you're finally contemplating taking a break, you feel responsible for planning and managing their retirement. I think this will be profoundly helpful to discuss in therapy, but that's still a few months off. In the meantime, consider allowing yourself to prioritize the family relationships where you feel cared for over the ones where you are forced into a caretaking role.

//////////////

Dear Prudence,
My boyfriend (twenty-eight) and I (twenty-six) have been living together for seventeen months now and made a cross-country

move six months ago. I thought everything was great and was looking forward to getting engaged soon, because he is the love of my life. As it turns out, he thought I would change my mind about not wanting kids—and I thought he was just fine with not having kids. We've been through several (pandemic) months of very tough conversations and a lot of crying on my part. I burst into tears watching an episode of *House Hunters* yesterday in which a couple got engaged.

I think we all know the pluses and minuses of having a child, so I won't go into them, but my top concerns include the fact that I don't really like children, I want to have as much alone time together as possible, and if something happened to my partner or we got divorced, I would be stuck raising a child instead of being free to do whatever I want. The thing I attach to on days where it sounds better is the thought of sharing my religion, which means a great deal to me, with my child. But she might not adopt it herself, and my partner is of a different religion and isn't willing to raise her with only mine. If I wouldn't have a child if we weren't together and it's not my preference, is it something I should just never consider, full stop? Or is this scenario something to think about over the next five years?

—Child-Free in Albuquerque

//////////////

I think you have considered having children more than once, especially in the last few months. It's one thing to grant yourself a period of open-minded exploration when your feelings are unclear, but you don't seem to have unclear feelings at all—only incompatible ones. You don't want children, and you don't want to lose your partner, who does want them. But "I really hope we don't have to break up over this" is not the same thing as "Sometimes I really do want children." The strongest, warmest, most positive feeling you've been able to generate on the thought of having children is "My religion is really important to me, and I'd enjoy sharing it with someone else." You don't like children, you don't like spending time with children, you want to be free to set your own schedule, you want to prioritize time with your partner over time with dependents, and in the event of divorce or bereavement, you'd feel shackled and resentful at the prospect of having to look after a child on your own. I don't think there's much here to reconsider or that's likely to change in five years' time. I think you know fairly clearly that you don't want children. I don't want you to have a child against your own instincts in the hopes it will keep "the love of your life" close, only to find yourself feeling stuck, frustrated, isolated, beholden, and without options. That would not be a good life for you, and it would not be a healthy environment for your child.

If your partner were willing to take "Well, I don't really want one, and it's not my preference, but if it means losing you otherwise, I'm willing to have a child" as an enthusiastic entry into child-rearing, then frankly I'd be concerned about his values and general fitness as a parent. I don't know why he believed you were likely to change your mind, nor do I know what he said or did to give the impression that he didn't care about having children. That's probably worth discussion, even if it means more crying in the short term. But kicking

this can another five years down the road won't spare you tears or
heartache. It's a hard decision, and there's no avoiding it. But you
two have to make it together and arrive at it honestly.

• • •

Then there are moments where one very much wants to believe that a particular situation is fine because it doesn't seem
like a very big deal! I do, however, have plenty of sympathy
for the next letter writer inasmuch as I think it's draconian
and unfeeling to forbid tenants to have pets.

////////////

Dear Prudence,

My husband and I have lived in a condominium complex for
more than twenty years. We are quiet and respectful, pay our
condominium fees on time, and keep up our mortgage and
property. We also have a homeowners insurance policy and
otherwise try our best to follow all rules and regulations. Our
daughter was brought up here and now lives in another part of
the state, close enough to visit once every one to two months.
She and her spouse adopted an adorable terrier puppy, who is
sweet, friendly, and seems to love people. They always pick up
after the dog, keep her leashed, recently had her spayed, etc.

About a month ago, they came for a visit and stayed two
nights with the puppy. Within a week, we received a notice from
management to remind all residents that dogs are not allowed

to visit the property, EVER. During their visit, my daughter and son-in-law took their dog out to the back of our unit at 2 a.m. to make sure she didn't have an accident during the night. One of the neighbors observed them, and my daughter told me how weird it was to see this person doing their laundry in the middle of the night (supposedly, this is against the rules and residents are supposed to observe quiet time between the hours of 10 p.m. and 7 a.m. There are signs specifically asking us not to do laundry during these hours). She also noticed the woman was not friendly and pointedly watched them with the dog. I find myself feeling furious, knowing that they carefully pick up after the dog with bags they have ready at all times.

There is a neighbor with special permission to have their "emotional support" animal (a dog that frequently and annoyingly barks). Do I take this further with management? Insist to have special permission? I find myself getting annoyed about it and really angry at this nosy neighbor as well as the feeling that we are being singled out. Our dog visitor never barked or bothered anyone. We kept her very close and leashed; she did not run up to anyone or otherwise cause any problems during the visit.

—Puppy Problems

/////////////

You have a neighbor who slightly annoys you! If I believed that anything like peace or happiness lay on the other side of meticulously documenting her own infractions, like using a dryer after formal laundry hours are over, I'd tell you, but I really, really don't believe anything of the kind lies in that direction. Your daughter's dog sounds great! But you also knew the complex rules don't allow visits from dogs, so I don't think you should work yourself up listing all the ways in which this dog is extra special. It's kind of annoying that your neighbor didn't speak to you directly, but all that's happened is that you've received a bland reminder from your management company. This neighbor doesn't have the power to hurt you, so don't expend too much energy on resenting her.

If you want to email your management company and ask for future dispensation on overnight visits from a particular dog, I think that's fine, and there's a decent chance they'll hear you out. But if they say no, they say no, and your daughter will either have to find a dog sitter on future visits or book a room at a pet-friendly hotel.

• • • •

One doesn't necessarily *expect* one's husband to cheat, but there's at least an accepted social script for how to handle it. However, realizing that your couples' counselor has been aware of your husband's cheating while facilitating an "organic" conversation about nonmonogamy feels like an over-the-top plot twist.

////////////

Dear Prudence,

My husband, "Barry," and I have been married for twenty-three years. We have four children. I thought we were happy until, about a year ago, Barry began picking fights with me. I finally convinced him to join me in marriage counseling. We saw "Dr. Mary" individually and as a couple. Slowly, Barry admitted that he'd like to open our marriage. Dr. Mary was supportive of this and encouraged me to open my heart to the possibility. As Barry and I began communicating more healthily, I warmed to the idea. Then I discovered evidence that Barry had started cheating on me around the same time he started picking fights. When I confronted him, he told me everything—that he tried to find faults in our marriage to justify cheating and, even more shocking, that Dr. Mary knew about his infidelity. She told him to keep the affairs a secret, explaining that it could destroy our marriage if I found out.

I'm shaken to my core. For the sake of our children and the preceding twenty-two good years, I want to make things work with Barry. But I'm furious with Dr. Mary. When I confessed that I thought Barry could be cheating, she discouraged me from mistrusting him. I was vulnerable to her and paid her to help my marriage, and she recommended nonmonogamy, knowing we'd start off on a bad foot. Sex-positive therapists are difficult to find, but her behavior seems highly unprofessional to me. Should I bother relaying that to her—and, possibly, to the board that licenses her? Or am I misdirecting my anger?

—Undermining Therapist

I think you could certainly direct some more of your anger at Barry! That doesn't mean you have to leave him, but if you've already decided you have to make it work with Barry because of the children and your previously happy marriage, I think you will be tempted to make Dr. Mary a scapegoat.

What she did was unkind and baffling—it's one thing not to reveal a confidence that Barry shared with her to you in your joint sessions, but it's quite another to encourage him to lie about his infidelity while also supporting the prospect of an open marriage. It's certainly worth checking with her governing board to see if any of this violates her professional code of ethics, and you have every right to be upset that she encouraged your husband to lie to and manipulate you.

But your husband is the one who lied to and manipulated you. Your husband is the one who started having affairs, then started picking fights with you in order to distract himself from his guilt over his affairs, then lied to you in therapy, then tried to convince you that what you two really needed was an open marriage. You were vulnerable to him, and he recommended nonmonogamy despite knowing you'd start off on the wrong foot. So don't let your anger flame out on Dr. Mary so that your husband can go back to being the good guy. There are serious problems in your marriage, and your husband has seriously abused your faith in him. Those twenty-two years may have been good together, but his behavior over the past year wasn't simply a one-time lapse of character. It was ongoing, concerted, and profoundly unloving. I wish you all the best in finding a therapist you can trust.

Chapter Nine

It's Fine If You Want to Transition, It's Just That...

Letters with a shared theme of attempting to displace and disinherit discomfort: "Transition's not the problem—it's just the way you decided to transition that bothers me." "I think it's great you're bisexual. I just don't know why you want to tell people about it."

Perhaps unsurprisingly, the balance of transition-related letters I received during my tenure as Prudence shifted significantly in light of my own transition; I heard more and more often from people contemplating transition for themselves, where I had previously heard more frequently from cis people with questions about their trans partners, children, and friends. It can be difficult to release a proprietary sense of expertise about somebody else's gender, and yet such a release is vital if one hopes to preserve a loving, compassionate relationship. Someone else's transition is not an argument in need of evaluation for persuasiveness.

////////////

Dear Prudence,

My off-and-on boyfriend told me he's going to transition. He said he let his hair grow a bit long, and then just looked in the mirror and saw a woman. I don't want to be insensitive to whatever he's going through, but I don't think this is a real trans case. The trans people I know say they have felt trapped in the wrong body since at least adolescence. Should I express my concerns to him?

—Ready to Put My Oar In

////////////

You should not tell your "on-and-off" partner that she is not really trans, no. Lots of trans people are acutely aware of a sense of dysphoria from an early age, but that's not the case for everyone, and the "trapped in the wrong body" narrative is far from the only way to describe such an experience.

Sometimes when a person is beginning to come out, they can't immediately and perfectly find the words to distill an inchoate longing, desire, or identity, and whatever your erstwhile ex's process has looked like, I can promise you her transition is not a mere whimsy of the moment that came after she looked at herself in the mirror and saw long hair. What she is trying to tell you is not "I grew my hair out and thought on a whim that it might be fun to

*transition in a world that is not kind to trans women," but rather
"I saw something in myself, something I may not have understood
well before or felt comfortable articulating; it was something
meaningful and rooted in identity, presentation, and appearance.
I saw myself in the mirror, and something was different, and that
something was also consistent, and I want you to know about it."*

*If nothing else, bear this in mind: any trans person who has
reached the point of telling their family and friends has absolutely
asked themselves the question "But am I really trans?" a million
times over. This question has absolutely occurred to her, and she's
decided the answer is yes.*

●●●

It's deeply moving to hear from parents who are prepared to
affirm and support their trans child, and I'm keenly aware
of the magnitude of such a project, seeking to balance one's
responsibility of care toward a young person who might experience moments of great doubt, momentary certainty, anxiety, and ambivalence. It's a tall order indeed, and my own
experience transitioning as an adult in my thirties doesn't
always provide relative expertise.

////////////

Dear Prudence,
My thirteen-year-old came out to my husband and me as
nonbinary/transmasculine two years ago—they use *they/them*

and *he/him* pronouns. They have been incredibly open and communicative; we have a terrific and affirming therapist as well as supportive friends and family. My kid knows we're not invested in any particular "outcome" when it comes to identity or transition and that all we care about is supporting their best life. Next month our kid will turn fourteen and will be able to start HRT [hormone replacement therapy] if they want to. But they can't decide—they go back and forth on the question, they cry at night before bed, freaking out about the gravity of the decision, and they worry about whether they'll miss a window. I don't know what to do. I just want my kid to feel safe and supported. We've listened to a few episodes of your podcast together and appreciated your insight. Do you have any advice for my child as they make a decision, or for me in supporting my kid in turn?

—Want to Help Make Decisions About HRT

While our circumstances may be quite different in some respects, I can certainly relate to going back and forth on the question of starting HRT, of panicking about the possibility of missed opportunities, and of letting "I dare not" wait upon "I dare." You know, I think, that I can't promise you one decision or the other will be the right one for your kid—but I do think information gathering can be a really useful, practical response to panic and uncertainty. Encourage your kid to speak to people who started HRT at different ages to get a sense of the depth and breadth of possible experiences. Are there any support groups for trans/

nonbinary/questioning youth in your city that your kid could visit? What do you and your kid know about the physical effects of HRT? What potential changes does your kid find the most interesting, appealing, and desirable? What potential changes do they feel uncertain or ambivalent about? What potential changes do they find distressing? Bring these questions up with your kid's doctor, therapist, and any medical professionals working in trans health care willing to take your call, and keep a written record of what you learn. Remind yourselves that there are no stupid or inconsequential questions when it comes to HRT. Encourage your kid to keep written notes on their biggest fears, especially ones that lead them to cry. What are some of the worst-case scenarios currently rattling around in their head, and how can you reality-test them?

It may help, too, to remind your kid that this is not the single moment of decision-making that will govern the rest of their life. Yes, there may be some changes that HRT can provide most effectively or even exclusively during adolescence, but HRT will still be available at sixteen or eighteen or twenty-two or thirty if they decide to give it more time. The most important thing to stress, I think, is that no single option will perfectly eliminate ambiguity, uncertainty, or the possibility of regret. These three things are part of the business of living with a body. That doesn't mean we can't make informed decisions, act in our own best interests, or separate internalized transphobia from meaningful ambivalence, but it might feel a little bit freeing to treat the possibility of regret not as a shocking sign that you've definitely made the worst possible decision but as emotional information.

It also helps to have a plan in place for acknowledging and incorporating regret into your life. "If you started HRT and experienced [whatever outcome your kid's most worried about], what would your options be?" That's a practical question with real, concrete answers—anything from "I'd decrease my dose" to "I'd talk to my doctor about [finasteride/electrolysis/etc.]" to "I'd go off HRT for a while" to "I'd ask for advice from other people who've experienced the same thing." A useful guiding principle before making any decision might be "Do I have sufficient support in place to do this, and if not, how might I get it?"

•••

Some aspects of transitioning can be incredibly complex. Luckily, this isn't one of them: there's nothing inappropriate about discussing one's own transition with young people. Transitioning is not an "adults-only" topic of conversation, and adults who want to use children as cover for their own feelings of discomfort or transphobia are acting wrongly.

//////////////

Dear Prudence,

My sister-in-law is mad at me for coming out to my thirteen-year-old niece. I have always known that I was trans, and at fifty-four I am finally starting the process to make this happen. One of the first people I told was my niece, who changes her orientation on a weekly basis and thinks it is cool to have an aunt who will now be an uncle. I did tell my brother about it and he did not have a problem with it, but now his wife has found out and is very concerned about me having this inappropriate conversation with my niece. It was actually my brother and my niece who advised not saying anything to my sister-in-law. Now she wants to discuss this with me. What is the best way to approach this?

—Came Out Wrong

////////////

You won't be surprised to learn that I don't think it's inappropriate to tell a thirteen-year-old that you're going to be transitioning, especially since you're, you know, planning on transitioning and she was probably going to figure out something was up somewhere between changing your name and having everyone else start calling you Uncle. Under other circumstances I might give some space to the possibility that your niece's mother might have a nontransphobic reason to want to be more involved in that conversation, or at least to have a heads-up about when it took place so she could do some follow-up parenting, but if both your niece and your brother "warned" you to keep who you spoke to about your transition a secret from your sister-in-law, I think we can go ahead and safely assume that what she considers "inappropriate" about that conversation is the fact that you're transitioning. You may want to proceed diplomatically if you're worried she'll attempt to keep you from seeing your niece (I don't know if she's likely to take things that far, or if you think you'd lose your brother's support should she become openly hostile; you know the specifics of these relationships better than I do, so follow your own judgment there), but you don't have to apologize for being straightforward about your transition or concede that it's an adults-only topic of conversation.

You weren't asking your niece to scrub in on your top surgery; you were letting her know you were trans. Being trans isn't inappropriate; hold your ground on that one, and enlist your brother's support if you can. Good luck!

•••

Attempting to maintain a proprietary sense of control over a partner's identity is not merely a bad idea, it's also an unwinnable battle—it's wrong on its face, yes, but it's also impossible to achieve and quite often counterproductive. It's especially egregious when one misinterprets "bisexual" as "looking to cheat on me" or "dismissing my own identity."

////////////////

Dear Prudence,
I am a woman in a relationship with another woman. We have been together for four years, married for one. Recently, I have noticed that oftentimes when people (and especially men) refer to her as a lesbian or us as a lesbian couple, she insists on correcting them: "Actually, I'm bisexual." We end up having conversations with friends like, "Jenny, as a lesbian, what do you think of Hillary Clinton?" "Actually, I'm bisexual." She says that

she doesn't want her bisexual identity erased and that there is nothing wrong with her wanting people to have a correct understanding of her sexuality. I think it's weird that she mostly does this with men. It seems to me like she is putting it out there so she can in some sense remain an object of desire to these men. Plus, she married a woman—she should get used to people assuming she is in a lesbian relationship. Which of us is right in this situation?

—Wife Insists on Telling Men She's Bisexual

Oh, I'm afraid I'm not going to be able to give you the answer you want. I'm sorry! If your wife briefly corrects someone during a conversation with "Actually, I'm bisexual," it hardly sounds like attempting to remain an object of heterosexual desire to me. If she went around saying, "Actually, I'm still very interested in men, particularly you, you massive dose of sexual charisma," you might have a case, but she doesn't. She tells people, including men, that she's bisexual because she's bisexual. She's not orchestrating a stealth future-cheating campaign. Imagine if your wife had red hair, and people occasionally and mistakenly referred to her as a brunette. You wouldn't panic if she told them, "Actually, my hair's red." You wouldn't wonder what it might mean. It's a piece of morally neutral information.

Your wife says, "Actually, I'm bisexual," and you hear, "I'm only half in love with my wife and hoping to keep my options open while I look for a heterosexual exit." But all that she's saying is that she's bisexual. That's it. You're adding a lot of assumptions, fears, and insecurities to the mix. She's in a relationship with a lesbian, but that doesn't mean she's going to identify the same way. She's bisexual, and that's important to her. Nothing you've told me suggests she neglects you or flirts with men in order to stoke your jealousy. I think you need to figure out why you feel so threatened by the fact that you married a bisexual woman. Were you hoping she'd change her mind or get over it? Why is it so important to you that she let other people assume she's a lesbian? She's with you. She married you. She's out. She's your wife. Nothing about your identity or your relationship is threatened by her sexuality in any way; it's time for you to let go of this.

•••

Second verse, same as the first.

//////////////

Dear Prudence,

I'm a bisexual man in a happy, monogamous relationship. My wife is fine with my sexuality but does not want me to talk about it with other people. She especially does not want me talking about it around her friends, many of whom are gay men, for fear that they would start hitting on me. (I think maybe she also worries that they would make fun of me—although we all get along great.) She also does not want me to contact an ex-lover, who was also my best friend for a long time (although admittedly this was years ago). I'm not particularly bothered by these "conditions," but I would like to speak to this guy at least once again in my life, and it might be nice to have people with whom I could openly discuss my sexuality.

—She's Honestly Fine with It

///////////////

I disagree that your wife is "fine" with your sexuality. If she wants you to keep your sexuality a secret and thinks any gay man who learned of it would be unable to keep from either mocking or trying to seduce you, I think she is in fact deeply uncomfortable with and resentful of your sexuality, which is a shame. It's one thing for her not to want you to get in touch with an ex, which is understandable though high-handed; it's quite another for her to forbid you from even talking about the fact that you're bisexual. If she thinks the only thing keeping your friends from trying to destroy your marriage is a mistaken belief in your heterosexuality, then she has insufficient faith in both your marriage and the character of your friends. Tell your wife that you're not going to hide who you are from those close to you simply to keep her comfortable. Her version of protection and support looks an awful lot like a closet to me.

•••

For those who might be inclined to treat bisexuality as tantamount to nonmonogamy, here's a useful reminder that opening up one's relationship to additional partners does not necessarily and immediately resolve any fraught feelings about bisexuality. Once again, the question of "How does my partner's bisexuality reflect on me?" arises, and while I'm not interested in dismissing anyone's feelings about a partner's bisexuality right out of the gate, I think it's important to avoid treating someone else's sexual identity as an automatic revision of one's own identity. The next letter writer might be experiencing an understandable degree of anxiety about possibly encountering homophobic reactions secondhand, especially if she's only previously been in straight relationships, but I was glad to see she felt prepared to move ahead and support her partner's coming out regardless.

////////////////

Dear Prudence,
I've been with my current partner for almost seven years, and we started an open relationship about two years ago. We are in it for the long term. My partner has struggled to come to terms with being attracted to men, and he's finally ready to embrace it and come out as bisexual. I am completely behind him on this, and I don't want him to be anything but his true self. Since our relationship is open, he will have the chance to explore that in a more secure way too.

I have to admit, though, that it took some time for me to wrap my head around it, and I can tell he senses my uneasiness. Overall, I feel extremely confident in the strength of our relationship, but at the same time I'm still processing this change and feel unsure of how best to support him. Moreover, he wants to start coming out to our friend group and select family, something I'm also supportive of—but we both have the feeling that it will inevitably bring discussions of our open status as well. We are selective with whom we tell because we know it's not something everyone will understand or approve of. But coming out is something he really wants to do, and recently he even said he was waiting for my permission to start. I feel overwhelmed, but I don't want to drop the ball on this. I know he needs my support now more than ever. How do I do this?

—Sort of Supportive

////////////////

You can start by saying to your boyfriend, "I don't want you to wait for my permission to come out, although you certainly have it." There's a limit to the utility of "processing time," and it sounds like you two have already spent months, if not years, thinking through this solely as a duo. If your boyfriend is ready to come out and you feel "extremely confident" in your relationship, I think the time is ripe (or at least as ripe as it's going to get).

As for your worries that his coming out will necessitate conversations about your open relationship that you're not sure you're ready to process, please go easy on yourself. I do hope that your friends and relatives will not overstep themselves and ask intrusive questions about the nature of your relationship after your boyfriend comes out, but if they do, their idle curiosity does not merit a personal response, merely polite correction.

For example, if your boyfriend says, "I've been wanting to tell you this for a little while. I'm bisexual, and it's taken some time to get to terms with it, but I'm ready to come out. [Letter Writer]'s been great, and I'm really happy to have her support," the polite response is something along the lines of "Congratulations! How wonderful!" or "Thank you for telling me" or "I'm here for you." If anyone's response gets out of hand and includes something like "Bisexual? That means two or something, right? Since your girlfriend is only one person, does that mean you're going to start sleeping with other people? Are you now or have you at any time been in an open relationship?" you do not owe them a polite response. One needs a better reason than "I'm curious, and you've just come out" to ask such a personal question. If you want to remain politic, either of you can say something like "Nothing else is changing—we just wanted you to know because it's been meaningful on a personal scale for [Boyfriend] to come out." Good luck, and congratulations!

•••

There are relatively few upsides to encountering vicious, explicit homophobia from one's relatives, but at least it frees one from worrying about how to respond politely. A silver lining for every raincloud.

Dear Prudence,

A few months ago, one of my aunts sent me an email telling me
how wrong my "lifestyle" is and how much I'm hurting my parents
(I'm gay and marrying my love) and attached a list of Bible verses
about whore-mongering and such to help make her point. When
I sent a calm reply explaining that I am happier than I've ever
been and at peace with my sexuality, she replied with an email
that said, among other things, that I make her glad she never had
children.

I haven't had to see her since, and I don't know how to react
when my parents mention her and her husband in conversation. I
think that if they know anything about it, it must be minimal. But
my question is this: She's just sent me a Facebook message saying
that she misses me and loves me. I feel like my replying would
be an invitation for more abuse (and since I've worked hard to
get out of their conservative fundamentalist worldview myself,
it's painful to deal with people who try to tell me my sexuality is
sinful), but at the same time, I hate feeling like I'm abandoning my
family and treating them like they could never change. How do I
reply, if at all?

—Poison-Pen Aunt

*People certainly can change, but usually not within a few months
of telling their niece that her being gay is such a blight on their
own happiness it makes them relieved to be childless. Had she sent*

you an apology, that would be one thing, but I think you're right to intuit this is a gambit designed to get you to let her back into your life for another round of How Your Lifestyle Disgusts Me. Don't think of this as a situation where you have "abandoned" your aunt. Being unwilling to accept abuse is not abandonment.

If you decide to reply to her message—it would be perfectly reasonable not to—tell her that you're sorry to hear that she misses you, but you're rather surprised to hear it so soon after her last note and that you won't be able to maintain a relationship with someone who periodically accuses you of being an affliction and a disappointment to your family. My guess is that when you refuse to apologize for her cruelty, she will switch tactics again and go right back to calling you names. You are not treating someone unfairly if you refuse to take their abuse; what you are doing is demanding that, at the minimum, the barrier to entry for being a part of your life is not sending you abusive screeds about your sexuality and intimating that it would have been better for your parents had you never been born.

////////////

Dear Prudence,

A decade ago, I began dating an incredible woman, "Hannah," a single mother to her newborn "Max." Max knew from the beginning that I wasn't his biological father, but he's always called me Dad, and I legally adopted him when he was four. Hannah and I were discussing marriage when she was killed by a drunk driver.

It was the worst year of my life. I only got through it because I knew Max needed me. I tried to include Hannah's parents in his life and even offered to move closer so they could see him more, but they said they didn't want me "foisting a kid on them." For Max's sake, I try to be friendly. Two years ago, I started dating a wonderful man, "Luke." (I'm bisexual.) Our relationship is great, and Max loves him. Luke moved in with us shortly before lockdown, and it's been a godsend having someone to look after Max when I'm at work. (I'm an essential worker.) Hannah's parents were appalled to find out I was dating a man after I told them last year and suddenly wanted to become "involved" once Luke moved in.

When they found out that Luke looks after Max while I'm at work, they called CPS [Child Protective Services] and reported that I had abandoned Max with a strange man and "potential predator." Luke and Max actually received a visit while I was at work, which established that Max was safe but [that] also terrified and distressed both of them. I have now received several calls from social workers who have been told that Max lives with "two strange men," neither of whom are related to him, and that his grandparents are "frantic" about his safety. Hannah's parents say they're going to sue me for full custody because I had "nothing to do with their grandchild." I'm at a loss. They've always been low-key homophobic, but this is so extreme and out of the blue that I'm concerned for their stability. Aside from consulting a lawyer (which I'm doing), what should I do? How do I explain to Max, who loves his grandparents, what is happening? I don't see how I can ever see these people again after their behavior. I have been exhausted since lockdown began, with increased pressure at the hospital, Luke struggling to work from home, and Max's education, and this has honestly broken me. I feel overwhelmed just thinking about it.

—Not a Stranger

///////////////

I'm so sorry Max's grandparents are putting you through this nightmare scenario. I don't wonder that you feel exhausted and overwhelmed. I'm thrilled to hear that you're talking to a lawyer, which is the most important thing you can do right now. Not because your not-quite-in-laws have a solid legal case for disrupting a lifelong relationship between you and your son on the basis of your having a boyfriend, but because they've made it clear they're willing to stoop to any levels to harass and intimidate you, and you deserve robust legal defense and counsel. You might also contact the National Center for Lesbian Rights, which advocates for all LGBT people, publishes guidebooks for LGBT parents, and offers a legal hotline for further counsel.

I hope this goes without saying, but do not allow Max's grandparents to have any further contact with him. There's a small but real chance they might try to kidnap him, not to mention the distress and pain it might cause your child to hear, "Your dad and his boyfriend are dangerous and trying to hurt you." These people are trying to take your child away—a child they had previously ignored—because you're bisexual and in love with a man. They do not have Max's best interests at heart, their homophobia is all-consuming, and you never have to see them or speak to them again. If your lawyer recommends you keep a log of their harassment, do so, but otherwise I think it's time to start blocking their numbers and email addresses.

Obviously, you don't want to overwhelm Max with painful details, but he's already aware that something's going on, and kids have a pretty good radar for trouble. He's already experiencing the violence and cruelty of homophobia, and he's not too young to hear you talk about it. I know you've tried to speak kindly about your in-laws in the past for Max's sake, but they're putting him in danger, and it's not retaliatory or unfair to be honest with him about the danger these people pose. If you and Luke have any friends in the area who can help, either by dropping off dinner, coordinating with other LGBT advocacy groups, taking notes during your calls with your lawyer, or just offering you a shoulder to cry on, please lean on them. You need (and deserve) all the help in the world while you protect your family.

•••

I heard from many people, some cis, some trans, some wildly uncertain, who feared that any period of questioning the possibility of transition (either their own or someone else's) was akin to hitting a countdown timer, and that if they had not come out and started transitioning by the time the clock had run out, their period of exploration would retroactively become fraudulent, somehow dangerous to other trans people, or otherwise inauthentic. I don't believe that's true! Nor do

I believe that any individual acts of modification, presentation, or identification remain the exclusive property of certain types of trans or nonbinary people; if someone wants to try wearing a binder, tinkering with their hormone levels, or changing their wardrobe, hairstyle, name, or pronouns, they should do so for as long as they like and feel profoundly free to change again in the future if they particularly wish it. The goal ought not to be "following through" with earlier choices, as if one is putting down a security deposit on an apartment and is now legally on the hook for a lease, but to pursue an expanding sense of freedom, autonomy, and possibility in one's own life.

//////////////

Dear Prudence,

My twelve-year-old came out as bisexual about a year ago. Since then, she and her friends have adopted the use of gender-neutral nicknames with one another. She uses female pronouns and asks that I use her new name in public. I took her to her first Pride march recently, and she was very happy. This has opened up a conversation about using binders. She's very developed for her age. I am not opposed to this, but I am thinking about the root of this desire—if it comes from the beginning of a transition versus an expression of being a girl uncomfortable growing into a woman's body. Therapy is definitely on the table, but I want your advice on how to approach this to be able to support her on her journey. Does the root of her request change how we move forward? How do I bring up therapy without making assumptions about her gender or the reason behind her binder request? How do I help her be comfortable in her body whether she transitions or not?

—Binding Prospects

////////////

You sound like a thoughtful and supportive parent who's spent a lot of time carefully considering your responsibilities toward your daughter. When it comes to therapy, don't overthink it—just tell your kid that if she's ever interested in seeing a therapist to help her process her goals, desires, or feelings, you'd be happy to set that up. I wouldn't peg the therapy to the binding, because that might make the process seem a bit transactional: "See a therapist X number of times, and I'll let you order a binder" doesn't exactly foster a sense of curiosity and open-mindedness.

I think you can be a bit easier on yourself when it comes to trying to divine the origins of this request. It's not necessarily worth trying to ground an interest in low-stakes body modification as being trans-related or not. That can imply, "If you end up being trans, it's fine to want to alter your silhouette with a binder, but if you're not trans, you just have to learn to love yourself in a bra." Learning to love one's body is a worthwhile project, and loving one's body and choosing to modify the appearance of one's bustline are not incompatible (with the caveat that it's worth checking with her pediatrician and researching techniques for binding safely). If she starts binding and ultimately transitions,

*great! But if she tries it out and comes to think of it as a matter
of personal autonomy, that she was granted age-appropriate
freedom to play with her gender presentation, and develops a
concrete sense that you can love your body and choose to present
in gender-nonconforming ways, that's a good outcome too.*

•••

The next letter was a bit challenging for me because I'm not
inclined to be especially sympathetic toward someone considering the possibility of joining a community they feel a
certain degree of a priori contempt toward. I do hope this
letter writer eventually reconsiders some of the knee-jerk
assumptions described here, particularly the idea that trans
women shouldn't play sports (which is rather extreme and
puts the letter writer at odds with such organizations as the
NCAA, the Association of Boxing Commissions, the International Tennis Federation, and the Union Cycliste Inter-
nationale, none of which can be described as progressive
trans-rights advocacy groups) and the idea that "parents" as
a class have a proprietary interest in shielding children from
queerness, when parental homophobia is at the root of some
of the most serious health crises in the LGBT community,
including teen homelessness and domestic violence.

But the pursuit of transition is a fundamental compo-
nent of bodily autonomy and a basic, unalienable right. It
is not something one can either earn or forfeit on the basis
of personal or political commitments, good or bad behav-

ior, or even a sense of solidarity with other trans people. If nothing else, this question serves as a useful reminder that identity categories themselves are not automatically grounds for group solidarity and that what people often call "the LGBT community" is not a single coherent community in any meaningful sense. Merely choosing to transition does not immediately put one in community with anyone else; *identity* is not a synonym for *solidarity.*

//////////////

Dear Prudence,

As a recreational cross-dresser, I'm increasingly feeling like I want to transition, which would make me trans and a lesbian. However, I have serious doubts about some "LGBT rights." I am firmly against allowing trans women to compete in women's sports. I am against forcing bakers to participate in celebrations that they don't agree with. I am even sympathetic to concerns about an "LGBT agenda" being pushed on children and parents. On the other hand, I have used the ladies' restroom while en femme and am grateful for LGBT protections that may make my life easier going forward. I used to think that a middle ground was often good, but now I'm not sure whether such middle grounds are really viable. Would it be wrong to transition while holding lukewarm views on LGBT rights?

—Transitioning While Not Fully Supporting LGBT Rights

//////////////

For my part, I think it's good to have robustly progressive views on LGBT rights, but they're not a necessary precondition for transitioning. Caitlyn Jenner is one of the most famous trans women in the world, and she's rather well known for her lukewarm-at-best views on the subject. If you're concerned that you may find yourself on the outs with other trans people by espousing these views and therefore may not have the strong community support you need during your transition, then I'd encourage you to spend a little time preparing for how to deal with conflict graciously and respectfully. Perhaps you might spend time learning more about how rights that might not seem desirable or beneficial to you might be so for other members of the community.

You are free not to participate in any sports professionally or recreationally, to only patronize the bakers you like, to ignore all children and parents, and generally to sit out the push for any rights you don't support. It may help for you to think about the causes you do support and find ways to further them, rather than worrying about causes you don't. If you were to move from having certain private qualms to actively campaigning, say, against an "LGBT agenda being pushed on children" (I'm not quite sure what that would look like—forced calendar updates?), you may very well find your life quite lonely, alienating both transphobes and trans people alike. But none of that would have any bearing on whether you ought to transition. That's your call to make.

•••

Like some of the earlier letters in this chapter, this one falls into the category of "LGBT people are all well and good, and I suppose they have the right to exist in a general sense, but any immediate proximity to someone I know makes me feel deeply uncomfortable, as if I'm being asked to concede something about myself." Such discomfort doesn't necessarily mark one as an irredeemably bad person—ambient homophobia is everywhere, and it's hardly remarkable to notice its effects in oneself—but it's worth careful investigation and eventual release.

////////////////

Dear Prudence,
My heterosexual twenty-eight-year-old daughter told me that she recently started a relationship with a trans man. I've always been supportive of LGBT issues, but I feel a little wary. I didn't know if "trans man" meant a man that used to be a woman, a man transitioning to a woman, or something else. Whenever I asked my daughter any questions, she acted like they were rude and out of bounds. When I met her partner, they (their preferred pronoun) were distinctly male with long hair. But their behavior really confused me. They looked and acted extremely, flamboyantly, and shallowly like a gay man. It seemed like attention-getting behavior to me.

I feel like my daughter is being used as a testing ground. Her partner doesn't have a job, a stable lifestyle, or seem grounded in any way. I don't know what my expectations should be. Do I keep my mouth shut? Do I ask gently probing questions? I'm really more concerned about the quality of their relationship than the nature, but I don't understand the social parameters around these issues.

—Not Around My Daughter

//////////////

The important question here is "What do I do when my twenty-eight-year-old daughter dates someone I'm not wild about?" And the answer, I'm afraid, is "Not much." Your daughter knows she's dating an unemployed person with a somewhat "unstable" lifestyle, and for now at least, that's not a problem for her. Absent signs of abuse, there's not a lot for you to do other than be polite and friendly when spending time with your daughter's partner and privately heave a sigh of relief afterward that at least you don't have to date them. This is a general rule for anyone your adult child may date: Be polite, be friendly, be open-minded within reason, and remember that your ability to influence who your kid dates wanes with every year past about thirteen. Let them make their own mistakes, enjoy things you find baffling, and generally wend their own way through life.

When it comes to matters of gender, I think there are two issues here. One is your genuine lack of familiarity with terms, identities, and what's within the limits of polite discussion. That's fine—everyone starts somewhere—and if your daughter isn't available to help you learn the basics, I'd encourage you to visit PFLAG's glossary page for a primer.

The other issue is your deep-seated discomfort with someone whose interpretation of "maleness" is playful and flamboyant. I'm not sure what you think acting "shallowly" like a gay man is, but it clearly unsettled you, and the idea of someone behaving that way while also dating your daughter made you anxious, defensive, and unhappy. That's really interesting! I think the person you should be asking "gently probing questions" of in this case is you: "Why do I interpret flamboyant behavior as inherently attention seeking? Why do I assume stereotypically heterosexual behavior is not attention seeking? Is attention seeking always a bad thing? Why do I assume my daughter is being 'used as a testing ground'—testing ground for what? In what ways am I attempting to draw a distinction between my heterosexual daughter and her partner, whose gender expression is hard for me to locate and contextualize? What am I really afraid of here, what do I want to control that I can't, and how will I maintain inner peace and calm if my daughter continues to date someone who makes me feel so off guard?"

• • •

Whenever one is faced with the unhelpfully broad question "Am I being a bad or a good ally?" it's usually a good idea to ask smaller, more specific questions, like "Did anyone ask me to do this on their behalf?" and "Can I think of a particular person I have just helped?" If the answer to both questions is no, one needn't immediately don a hair shirt and go on a pilgrimage of repentance, but it's often a sign that one can probably stand to relax a little. Just being cool and doing a little less are often valuable acts of allyship when uncertainty reigns.

//////////////

Dear Prudence,

Recently I joined a dating app to spice up my solo quarantine and try to find straight men who were interested in Victorian-style epistolary romance. I matched with a professor at a nearby college whose second message told me he was "transamorous." Did I do the wrong thing by reporting his account to the app? I'm not trans (not that it was any of his business). The term really rankled, and I can only imagine how it might affect someone else. I was left in a swirl of questions about how I present and how people see me versus who I am. I regret not directly challenging him in the moment. "Transamory" is fetishistic bullshit, right? Should I have said something? I reported him, but I did not reach out to his employer, who I was easily able to find with a Google search. Ugh! I'm just trying to find love and wear utility ponchos.

—Was I a Bad Ally?

//////////////

Reporting someone's profile simply because he's interested in dating trans women, regardless of how clumsily he might put it, is not an act of solidarity with trans people. Some cis people (and trans people!) do fetishize and objectify trans women, but simply expressing an interest in dating trans women is not itself "bullshit," and I don't think it merits a report for violations of terms of service. It certainly doesn't merit contacting his employer. This man didn't ask you invasive questions about your body, speak to you in a dehumanizing fashion, or threaten your safety. That doesn't mean you're obligated to like him. But you had no idea how he treats the trans women he approaches or dates, whether he's a respectful partner, or anything else. Nor did reporting him improve the lives of any actual trans women. I think the reason you're second-guessing yourself now is because you're aware on some level that you were offended that this man thought you might be trans, and you sought to punish him for it. But that won't remove your discomfort, and it doesn't help trans people either. Only introspection can do that.

I don't want to be too hard on you. I also want you to be able to find love and fun and companionship, and I believe you when you say you want to support trans people. But there's no universal consensus among trans people about whether cis men who describe themselves as "transamorous" are meaningfully different from garden-variety chasers. The fact that chasers sometimes go on to transition themselves is also complicated, as is the fact that different trans people have varied reactions to the concept of chasers. I'd encourage you to seek out a variety of perspectives from trans women who have written on the topic, such as Kai Cheng Thom, Diana Tourjée, and Janet Mock. And if you're interested in being an ally, consider making a donation to trans-led organizations such as GLITS, St. James Infirmary, or Compton's Transgender Cultural District today.

Chapter Ten

My Kids Are Growing Up. Can Someone Please Stop This?

Letters with a common theme of unrecognized powerlessness:
Problems you can't solve on your kids' behalf anymore.
Problems your kid has with you in particular. Problems
that stem from being well-meaning. Problems that show
up only after you try to let go. Problems you can't take
responsibility for, and problems you probably should.

I always hope that anyone writing to me about a problem
with their children, regardless of age, is also canvassing
their fellow parents, since I have no children of my own and
have a necessarily limited perspective on parenting as a result. I still vividly recall the time a close friend off-handedly
referenced toilet training one of her kids, and I unthinkingly

replied, "Is that still going on? I thought that happened when they were a year old or thereabouts"—a conversation she has never once let me forget. I have experience *being* parented, of course, and am happy to share general principles that might be useful to anyone, but my expertise is pretty tightly circumscribed. I'm able to speak with more confidence about issues one might face as a child grows into an adult, particularly on occasions where the well-meaning desire to intervene become impossible and counterproductive, about anticipating the nearing end of one's direct authority, without fearing it also spells the end of closeness, tenderness, or intimacy.

///////////

Dear Prudence,

I'm twenty-seven, and my mom and I grew up very close. It was often just me and her. I've supported myself since graduating college, and she now lives about twenty-five miles away. In the past few years, she has started escalating simple questions into situations she can control. For example, once I asked if she had any jumper cables she could lend me to jump my partner's car battery. She told me she was calling a tow truck to take his car to a mechanic. She assumed the car would be unsalvageable, so she was also booking a rental.

Another time, I asked her for the title of a book she'd mentioned a while ago, and she said she was ordering a copy of it to my house. Whenever she does this, I try to calmly tell her to stop, since that's not what I asked her for and (in some cases, like the car) not her place. She usually doesn't listen. Then I get flustered and end up repeating myself with less eloquence and more distress. Then she ends up crying, saying that she knows more than me, that I'm being unreasonable, and it's "mean" to reject her help. When things cool down, I apologize, try to explain why I rejected her plans or "favors," and ask her to please take things I ask for or about at face value. Then she just says that I'm wrong and insists on further apology and empathy for her. I don't know how to stop this beyond never asking her for anything, even the title of a book, ever again. How do I break this pattern?

—Above, Beyond, and Overboard

//////////////

I think no longer asking your mother for things is an excellent idea, and I second the motion heartily! If you need jumper cables, text a friend or call roadside assistance yourself. If you can't think of the name of a book she mentioned, do your best to google whatever elements of the title you can remember, or call a local bookstore and ask for help tracking something down. That's a much simpler approach than trying to have the same conversation for the two hundredth time and hoping for different results.

I don't want to overstep myself or venture too far from the scope of your question, but it's a little unusual that you frame the idea of not asking your mother for help regularly as something extreme and better avoided if possible, instead of a perfectly natural part of growing up. I also notice that you say that "my mom and I grew up very close," as if the two of you were peers, instead of a parent *and a child. If the "closeness" between the two of you has always been dependent on a certain deference to her feelings and giving in to her demands, it might be worth considering what other kinds of distance you might enjoy from her.*

• • •

It's pleasantly surreal to be invited to comment on someone else's advice! In the following case, at least, it's possible that the letter writer's advice might be perfectly reasonable, but there is very little advice (outside of general rules of respect and kindness) that is universally applicable in all dating situations. Besides which, it's entirely possible to think *My mother normally has great judgment* and *I think she's wrong on this one* at the same time without fear of contradiction.

////////////

Dear Prudence,

I am a college student who decided to try online dating this summer. I matched with a guy who I guess I can say is my "type," with a sense of style I find attractive. However, I later discovered that he harbors anti-abortion sentiments and questionable ideas about race. Both of us are people of color, and he is likely just uninformed. Still, I'm very pro-choice and strongly against his beliefs about race, so I unmatched with him, since I did not think I would get along with him long term.

I shared what happened with my mother, who I am very

close with, and she disagreed with my decision. She said that she had boyfriends and even close friends that previously held ignorant views whom she "educated." I told her I personally do not feel that I am in a place where I would be patient enough to educate a guy I am dating, especially one who would be upset if I got pregnant accidentally and wanted to seek an abortion. My mother said I was being too harsh, that he might be a good person outside of his views, and that I probably won't ever need to seek an abortion anyway. I want to trust my mother's advice, since she normally has great judgment, but I feel as if this guy's views may have made us clash. For future reference, was I being too restrictive?

—Mom's Dating Advice

I don't think it's a question of whether you were "too restrictive" or not; I think it's a question of who would have to actually go out with this guy, you or your mother? And the answer is you, so it hardly matters whether your mother agreed with your decision. If she's been willing to spend a lot of time "educating" her dates in the hopes that they will come round to her worldview, then that's something she's free to do. If you prefer to date someone who already shares your core values on some pretty big-picture issues, then you made a reasonable choice.

There's also no guarantee that you can educate someone into seeing things your way while dating—the odds are just as good that you could make your case persuasively and not change your date's opinions a whit. Moreover, your mother's dismissal of whether a guy's views on your right to choose has any bearing on your romantic relationship with him seems flippant to me. Most people don't think they're going to need an abortion until they do, and saying, "I probably won't ever need an abortion, so I don't care if my potential partner is anti-choice," seems awfully blinkered and shortsighted. You don't have to trust your mother's advice 100 percent of the time, and just because you think she often demonstrates good judgment doesn't mean she's infallible or that you have to be guided by her when you date.

• • •

It's delightful and freeing to realize it simply doesn't matter what your aunt wants you to do with your inheritance! It matters as much as what, let's say, the prime minister of Ruritania wants you to do at your next optometrist's appointment.

////////////

Dear Prudence,
My father died last month and left everything to me. Thing is, I have two sisters and a brother whom he cut out of his life for one reason or another. Likely bad reasons; he wasn't a loving father but a very petty man. Not really sure how I stayed on his good side. So I told my siblings: Don't sweat it. Regardless of the will, I'm splitting the inheritance four ways between us. Here's

the problem. My aunt heard, and she's outraged that I would undermine her brother's will. She says Father had his reasons for disinheriting them, and I should respect them. She implies she knows something I don't but won't say. Me, I'm guessing she's as petty as my father. But she has my wife convinced there's something to what she's saying. And it's not a small amount of money I'm dividing up, so "fair's fair" doesn't have the strength it should as an argument. So I guess I'm looking for affirmation. Fair's still fair, right?

—Sharing the Wealth

///////////////

I'd encourage you to double-check with an estate lawyer in case they have some specialized knowledge that contradicts this, but hell yes, fair's still fair. If your father wanted your aunt to handle his money after he died, he would have left it to her. He didn't. He left it to you, and you get to use it as you see fit. If you wanted to buy a life-size statue of your father made out of soap shavings and launch it into the Pacific on a raft made of two-dollar bills, you'd have the right to do it. Your aunt can be as outraged about your generosity as she wants to be. I'd bet half your inheritance that your aunt's vague insinuations are totally baseless and have more to do with pettiness and jealousy than they do with some unforgivable secret sins your siblings have committed. It's your money and you want to help your siblings with it. Good for you.

"Everything would be so much better if you would just let me fix it" is an extremely tempting vision—I've fallen prey to it often myself, especially in the course of my years as an advice columnist. But it's rather like saying, "Everything would be so much better if reality as it currently exists were completely different," which is to say, it's both true and slightly nonsensical. I can't know what it's like to watch your child suddenly flounder in college after seeming to do well in high school, and I have no doubt the next letter writer simply wants to help her daughter get back on what she sees as the right track, not micromanage her every decision. But it's not a question of whether Sarah might someday thank her mother if she tried to get her back into college, or even a question of whether her mother would actually have any grounds to lodge a proxy appeal on a student's dismissal (I suspect she wouldn't, but I could be wrong)—it's a question of whether this letter writer can foist her vision for Sarah's future onto Sarah, and the answer to that question is a straightforward no.

////////////

Dear Prudence,

My daughter "Sarah" is twenty-one. She did extremely well in high school and had her pick of colleges. She chose to attend a great college about two hours from home. Sarah, her father, and I were all happy with the choice. College didn't go well, though.

Sarah had issues with her roommate and had to move out of the dorms because her RA sided with her roommate. She struggled in classes and was under academic probation when she was accused of plagiarism. Sarah says the plagiarism was inadvertent, and I believe her. It was, however, the final straw for her, and when the college moved to academically dismiss her, she didn't fight their decision. Our plan was that Sarah take a semester off and regroup, then begin applying to other colleges. She agreed to this course of action, but now that the time has come and gone for her to start applying, she refuses to do anything. She says that her record will follow her wherever she goes, and she has no chance to get in anywhere.

I want to go to her old college and attempt to get her reinstated. I have read over its policies online, and I believe it might take Sarah back. My husband does not want me to do this and says Sarah needs to make her own decisions. For the record, Sarah does have a job as a waitress and her own apartment that she pays for. But I know she would like to get back into college. I think she would thank me in the end for appealing her dismissal once I get her back into school. Do you think that it is wrong to go against my husband and do this for Sarah?

—Just Let Me Fix This

////////////

It would be a mistake. Your daughter is twenty-one years old and ought to be learning how to handle adversity on her own; your job as her parent is to offer support, criticism, and/or advice when appropriate, not to make interventions on her behalf. I can imagine it must be distressing to watch your child respond to a crisis with a defeatist attitude, but fighting a battle she has already forfeited will not do her any good. Regardless of whether Sarah would someday thank you for your actions, the most important thing to ask yourself is this: Would my attempt to get Sarah's old college to reinstate her help her cultivate resilience? Honesty? The ability to deal with the consequences of her actions and to acknowledge when she has done something wrong? Would it increase her self-sufficiency or improve her ability to tackle her own problems head-on? Or would it just make me feel more comfortable? I'm inclined to believe your desire to wipe away the problems of Sarah's past has more to do with your inability to acknowledge that your child might fail—or, at the least, flail—than it does with anything else. Your daughter is currently working and able to provide for herself; she is in no immediate danger. Let her forge her own path.

////////////

Dear Prudence,

I'm a twenty-five-year-old woman getting married in the summer. My mother is very old-fashioned and proper and does not believe in sex before marriage. She also believes that my husband and I are virgins and will remain that way until our wedding night. Both of us have been sexually active since high school! My older sister told me that my mom is planning on giving me a sex talk and explaining how everything works and "how to please a man" before my wedding. I would like nothing less than to listen to my mother explain sex to me, but I'm worried she'll be angry if I tell her I'm not a virgin. What should I do?

—Not a Virgin, Mom

There are more possible responses to "Darling, I'm going to explain sex to you now" than either "Sounds great! I've definitely never had sex" or "It's too late! I've been deflowered!" Tell your mother, if she brings the subject up, that you're well-informed about the mechanics of sex and don't require a "birds and bees" conversation. While I don't think you should be living in fear of your mother finding out you've had sex before marriage, it's also none of her business how much or what kind of sex you've had. It's perfectly appropriate to tell her that you're up to speed on what goes where, and that you don't want or need any wedding-night instruction from your mother, without confessing your sexual history.

• • •

People often love to offload their judgment and annoyance toward a relative on the relative's spouse, especially when that spouse is a woman who dares not to want children (*groan*). But why on earth this letter writer should assume her nephew shares her "heartbreak" about the possibility of not having children is beyond me, to say nothing of the idea that the entire family should climb into their marital bed and start offering suggestions about reproduction.

////////////

Dear Prudence,

Our whole family is very worried about my nephew. He is a
terrific thirty-year-old who has wanted a home and family since
he was at least ten. He finally found the love of his life. The two
of them have a lot of fun and adore each other. But she was clear
from the beginning that marriage was not her goal, and neither
were children. Much to the amazement of the intended bride (I
think) and delight of my nephew, she accepted an engagement
ring. She also compromised on the location of a house they
bought together (*groan*). When family, friends, and fiancée try to
discuss wedding dates and plans with her, she leaves the scene.
Now my nephew and her BFF are making the wedding plans.
Also, whenever she is around children, she is kind to them but
obviously has no intrinsic interest in them. They don't fascinate
her or appeal to her. Apparently, they have talked about children,
but she will only go as far as to adopt—no pregnancy for her. This
whole thing looks like heartbreak in the making for our beloved
nephew. Do you see any way the family can assist without
alienating my nephew or making the situation worse? So far, we
are all on the sidelines.

—Reluctant Bride

////////////

I think "on the sidelines" is a very appropriate place for you to be in relation to your nephew's marriage. Whether he and his bride-to-be have had sufficiently frank discussions about their goals and what they're willing to compromise on or not, you're not helping anyone by monitoring your future niece-in-law's response every time a child drifts into view. What would you say? "Lesterton, we've noticed that Skamaranth seems insufficiently fascinated by passing toddlers. Have you considered breaking off the engagement?" I'd leave the scene, too, if I could feel my extended family-to-be scanning my face for signs of baby and/or wedding fever every time someone brought up invitation cardstock and place settings. (And why the groan at compromising to purchase a house together? That sounds like a perfectly reasonable decision for a couple about to be married.)

If you and your nephew are genuinely close, and you are truly concerned that he has not listened to his fiancée's lack of interest in having children, you might consider bringing it up with him—once. Tell him you're concerned because you know he's always wanted a wife and children, but you're not sure that his intended wants the same thing, and then genuinely listen to his response. What looks like "inevitable heartbreak" to you may feel like commitment, compromise, and love to him.

• • •

It's not always mere projection that can cause tension between in-laws and a new spouse, of course, but it's important to continue to resist the temptation to problematize a child's partner for any conflict or change to the parent-child relationship (aside from extreme cases of abuse, forced isolation, financial control, etc.). Sometimes an adult child who might have previously hesitated to argue with a parent on their own behalf is newly emboldened to object after getting married and establishing a great degree of distance—that doesn't mean the spouse is pouring poison into their ear and turning them against "the family" through sheer cussedness.

////////////

Dear Prudence,

Since my daughter married "Chris," she has turned into a different person. It started on her wedding day, when she got drunk and screamed at me for "always putting her down" after I made a (not insulting!) comment about her nontraditional dress. That was four years ago, and things have gotten worse since then. She and Chris have spent every Christmas with his parents rather than me and my husband, she ignores calls and texts, and she has gone from attending every pre-pandemic family function with thoughtful gifts on birthdays to missing all but funerals and sending gift cards as Christmas presents. She has spoken to us twice since February, and on one of those occasions ended up screaming abuse at us until my husband hung up.

I found out the worst news recently and cannot process it. My daughter is pregnant, and not only had she not told us, but she didn't plan to. I only found out, mortifyingly, because a friend saw something on social media and asked me about it (I'm not on social media). My husband and I tried getting through to our daughter, but she has changed her personal number and only Chris answers the house phone. When confronted, he told us that she no longer wanted any contact with us, and that "they" did not want us in their child's life. My husband accused Chris of controlling our daughter, at which point Chris hung up. I have since called and pleaded with him to let me talk to my daughter, but to no avail. He has always been a cold person, but I never thought he would do something like this. I know that my daughter has some responsibility for her choices here, but I agree with my husband that Chris seems to be a powerful influence in isolating her from us in this extreme way. We are at a loss as to what to do from here. I cannot bear the thought of never meeting my own grandchild, and part of me can't believe that our daughter would be so cruel as to follow through with this plan to keep us from them permanently. Is there anything I can say that might get through to Chris or that I could put in a letter begging my daughter to reconcile? My husband and I miss the sweet, warm girl that we raised and feel as though we've lost her to a cold, angry stranger.

—Heartbroken

////////////

I want to leave open the possibility that someday you and your daughter might be able to reconcile, or at the very least have an honest conversation about your relationship that doesn't devolve into a screaming match. But I don't think you're going to get there

by assuming her husband is running interference between the two
of you without your daughter's knowledge and input or by trying
to contrast her adult self to the "sweet, warm girl" you knew years
ago. (Would you like it if someone said they liked you better when
you were a little child?) It sounds like your daughter has asked her
husband to serve as a buffer, likely because of how badly the last
few direct interactions between the two of you have gone.

In your letter, there's a thread of unwillingness to consider your
daughter an adult actor capable of making rational decisions.
You say that she has "some responsibility for her choices," when in
fact she has total responsibility for them, and you seem unable to
connect the dots between anger she directed at you the last few
times you spoke and the fact that you two no longer speak. It's not
extreme to stop speaking to someone when your relationship has
deteriorated to the extent you describe. It may be painful, and you
might not like it, but one follows the other quite logically. None
of this is to say, by the way, that your daughter's reasons for not
wanting to speak to you must automatically be good ones or that
all of her resentments must be justified.

But you seem more defensive than curious about those
resentments, and it seems to me that you've spent all your
energy attempting to make Chris the bad guy rather than
reflecting on your relationship with your daughter and trying to
see things from her point of view. You say you didn't think your
comments about her wedding dress were insulting, but it's fairly
clear that she did, and more than that, that she experienced
it as part of a pattern of demeaning comments. Did you stop
to consider whether there might have been some truth to her

experience, even if you might have wished she'd brought it up in a calmer fashion? Did you ask her to tell you more about how your comments have made her feel over the years? What made her start screaming during that last phone call? You say you're at a loss, and it's clear that you feel bewildered, but it doesn't sound to me like you're working without any information. It sounds more like when your daughter gets angry and tries to get some space from you, you try to circumvent that boundary, blame someone else for it, dismiss her frustrations, and then act shocked when she doesn't respond well.

I don't think you've yet cultivated the kind of distance and emotional curiosity that might produce a useful letter asking for reconciliation. Besides which, it's pretty clear that your daughter is not interested in that at this point. I think you should try to change your tactics and actually listen to what she's saying. She doesn't want to talk to you, which includes writing her letters, begging her husband to change her mind, claiming she's being "controlled" by said husband, or trying to find out her new number. Spend some time leaving her alone. If you feel sad or angry or misunderstood, then seek the advice of a therapist, and tend to your own feelings with care. Try to open your mind to the possibility that you have played a part in the deterioration of your relationship with your daughter, that she was not simply brainwashed overnight by an evil husband. If you think you will not be able to bear the pain of not meeting your grandchild, then seek out whatever emotional support from your own friends that you need in order to bear it, because I'm afraid you're going to have to. Whenever you're in doubt or experience turmoil over this loss, err on the side of not *repeating old behavior and trying to force unwelcome contact with someone who's made it very clear they don't want any.*

. . .

Sometimes there's nothing to say but "I share some of your bewilderment here, and I wish I could offer more insight into what might be driving your child's recent decisions, but I'm afraid I can't," and focus on the limited remaining available options while hoping something may change in the future. It's cold comfort, I imagine.

///////////

Dear Prudence,

Our nineteen-year-old daughter decided to ghost us. She goes to college eight hours away from our home. We set her up in a dorm, paid her tuition, sent her money, and talked to her almost every day. After she complained about her roommates, we agreed she could move to a more independent-style dorm the next year. She then told us she was staying at school for a summer internship (turning down a good internship in our hometown to do so). When we traveled with her siblings to surprise her for her birthday, we were shocked to find out that she did not live at the address she gave us. After a number of calls, she finally told us she had moved out and started living with a guy she met at a coffee shop near campus. We took her to dinner and said we wanted her to stay safe and focus on finishing college. We tried not to show our anger and disappointment, but she refused to tell us anything about the guy—not even his last name.

She said she would continue school and would work to pay her share of the rent. We tried to talk to her about her options and not rushing into adult responsibilities. She agreed to come home after her internship and spend two weeks with us. That was a year ago. Since then, she's taken all the money we ever gave her out of her bank account. We had to cancel her credit card after she maxed it out. She doesn't speak to any of us, even her old and ailing grandparents. We all call and text her almost weekly, but the only time she ever responded was a message about her health insurance (we are still paying for her health insurance and cell phone).

For me, her silence is painful, being her mother. I cannot imagine what I, her father, or any of us did for her to callously disconnect from her family. When people ask me how she is doing, all I can say is she's well, and then I want to sit somewhere and cry. We saw on Facebook that her boyfriend is twenty-six, not in school, and works at a hardware store. He also has posts of him smoking pot. She now has two jobs and is still enrolled in college. I am sad because that is not the college experience that I was hoping for her. At this point it's hard to pretend like I don't care because I do, and I miss her beyond words. I am making excuses to her brothers and sisters and grandparents when they want to know why she doesn't want to be a part of our family anymore.

—Ghosted by Our Grown Daughter

I'm so sorry for the pain and bewilderment you're experiencing right now. The good news, as you say yourself, is that your daughter is safe and well. No, she's not having the college experience you envisioned for her, but she's working hard, (mostly) supporting herself financially, and still attending classes. And while you might not have chosen this particular boyfriend for her, she's healthy and functioning and has made the choice to continue living with him.

I hope you will stop pressuring yourself to come up with cover stories when family members ask you about your daughter. If her siblings are very young, I wouldn't encourage you to be overly blunt, but you don't have to make up excuses. You can simply and truthfully say, "Sometimes people pull away or need space, and they don't always tell us why. I don't know why [Sister] is distant right now, and it does hurt, but I hope someday we can talk about it, and I'll be here for her when that day comes." If friends ask you about her and you feel like going off to cry, please give yourself permission to do so. You have every reason to be sad about this, and you shouldn't always try to mask your grief—find appropriate outlets for it, and let it out. Please consider seeing a therapist. Not so you can find someone else to explain why your daughter has pulled away, or agree that you've never done anything that might merit her sudden silence, but so you can honor your own grief and figure out what you need to do in order to build a life that's relatively serene and useful whether or not your daughter answers your calls. You should also scale back on how often you try to contact her. Since she almost never responds, it's a counterproductive habit that doesn't actually get you what you want and probably just increases your agitation and stress.

I have no idea if your daughter is going through a rebellious and insensitive phase that she'll later regret or if there are more serious reasons behind this estrangement. It may be that, as you and your therapist go deeper into the history of your relationship with your daughter, you are able to identify parts of the story you want to take responsibility for or can acknowledge you did something harmful. That doesn't mean it's your job to assign immediate blame to yourself. But since you're not going to be able to force answers out of your daughter, the most productive source of insight is going to be your own memory and your own psyche.

• • •

I feel rather cold advising a mother to dwell less on her fond memories of her daughter as a child, and I certainly don't want to encourage anyone to forget the past or draw a veil over happier days. But previous forms of relation that might have worked or felt good between a parent and a young child won't necessarily translate into a healthy, happy relationship between two adults, and seeking renewed closeness with a grown child by reminding them of what a sweet toddler they were often only pushes them further away. Parental memories of childhood can be sweet, of course, but they're not necessarily building blocks for connecting in the present.

///////////

Dear Prudence,

My younger daughter was quite extraordinary as a child—observant, empathetic, sweet, and kind. Her dad and I tried to raise her as a caring, loving person, and it worked. For a while. During her teen years, she was greatly influenced by close friends who didn't have good behavior modeled for them at home: swearing, no manners, obnoxious behavior. We are quite liberal, and she normally embraces our values but seemed to turn away on other things. She lost the sunny disposition she once had.

Her senior year she started dating a girl we knew very little about but who seemed to make her very happy and, as she said, "made her feel beautiful" (I'm biased, I know, but my daughter is gorgeous). The most I could find out was that her girlfriend had a rough homelife, but their teachers praised my daughter for being a good influence on her. Her girlfriend came to school more and did her homework, as urged by my daughter. That made me proud. Then, tragedy. On an evening when she promised to come watch my daughter's game, she didn't show. Turns out, she got into a car with a bunch of other friends who were on a mission to steal drugs and money from a home. Armed robbery and murder followed. Within a couple days, all of them were arrested. My daughter was devastated but stood by her. I tried to talk to my daughter about them having no future now, as her girlfriend pleaded out and is going to prison. But due to COVID, her sentencing has been delayed, and she's still at home. In addition to this, I see signs of jealousy, manipulation, and control. How do I help my daughter see this is not a healthy relationship? I've never felt so helpless.

—Worried Sick

/////////////

Feeling helpless is very difficult. But the path to something like (relative) serenity begins by acknowledging the people and situations you have no power over. You cannot force your daughter to stop loving her girlfriend, to break up with her, to consider their relationship unhealthy, or to abjure the company of people her own age who may swear, behave obnoxiously, or otherwise act out. The harder you try to exert your will in those areas, the more thwarted you'll feel and the faster your daughter will pull away. You'll have limited, circumspect opportunities to share your concerns or ask thoughtful questions, and if you navigate those opportunities with a light hand, you'll likely get a lot further with your daughter than if you try to push. Offer your daughter support where you can; don't offer her advice unless she asks you for it; and seek out friends and/or a therapist when you need to vent or cry about your baby girl.

I will also offer caution about dwelling on fond memories of your daughter's childhood, which can sometimes be a barrier to establishing an honest, emotionally balanced relationship in the present. It seems like you may be longing for a time when you were readily able to keep your daughter safe and close, but for her that would mean longing for a time before she was able to make her own decisions, fall in love, or cultivate her own values. Trying to appeal to your daughter by reminding her what a great kid she used to be will likely make her feel as if you're questioning where she went wrong or are unwilling to see her as an adult, so I'd save those trips down memory lane for another time. All your feelings here are perfectly understandable, but you can't process them with your daughter, who is striking out on her own as an adult.

• • •

In my junior year, I played Grandma Kurnitz in a no-budget high-school production of *Lost in Yonkers*, complete with a bad wig and a worse attempt at a German accent; the climactic confrontation between Grandma Kurnitz and her daughter Bella occurs toward the middle of the final act, where I delivered the line, "Go—open your restaurant, live your life, have your babies. If it's a mistake, let it be your mistake," words as true today as they were then.

///////////////

Dear Prudence,

My daughter and her boyfriend are both openly bisexual. We adore him, and their relationship seems to be full of genuine affection. They are each other's best friends, and I literally saw him step in front of a moving car to pull her to safety. All good, right? Well, he comes from a strict religious tradition. I grew up in this tradition too, so I'm familiar with it, and I know just how insidious the worldview is and how hard it is to throw off. It's extremely homophobic: the only acceptable life is to be straight, marry, and have children, preferably while young.

Recently, I learned that they've never had sex. My daughter's perfectly willing, but he is not. They have been together for three years. We live in a part of the country where a lot of people pay lip service to premarital virginity. You can probably guess my worry. I think my daughter represents a road to a conventional life that he's always envisioned. I know he wants children. I am petrified that in the future (maybe after marriage and kids) he will realize that he's not bisexual, he's gay, and that he has locked himself into a life that isn't right. I've seen this train wreck before, and it is devastating for everyone. And here I am, her parent, so everything I might say is loaded like an atomic bomb.

—Train Wreck Incoming

I understand your concerns, but I think this is something your daughter and her boyfriend are going to have to figure out for themselves. You were able to extricate yourself from the same worldview and become (it sounds like) a happy, well-adjusted adult; have some faith in this young man's ability to do the same. You may not have made the same choices around intimacy that he has, but it's not your place as his girlfriend's mother to give him advice concerning his sex life. They're not yet married—they're not yet even engaged—so you're getting pretty far ahead of yourself in assuming it's only a matter of time before they've had several children and he's leaving her for a man. Trust your daughter and her boyfriend to make their own decisions, even their own mistakes, and take the evidence you've seen that they love one another at face value. If you find that these anxieties become overwhelming, I recommend seeing a therapist who can help you deal with them without trying to control and manage your daughter's sex life.

////////////

Dear Prudence,

I'm a senior at a local university, commuting from home, and my younger sister is leaving soon for a distant school. It's just me, my sister, and our mother in the house, and I'm worried that I'll be smothered now that Baby Sis is going away. Mom's a single parent and does everything she can to keep us close so that she's not lonely (this includes asking us to sleep in her bed for weeks at a time, and it's been this way for years). Now that my sister is leaving and it's just me, I already feel bad about leaving Mom to do homework on campus or stay after class or anything else that keeps me out of the house. At the same time, I don't want to be stuck at home with Mom for my entire senior year. Is there any middle ground so that I can get out of the house and be a little more independent while making sure Mom's not too lonely?

—Lonely Mom, Stuck Daughter

////////////

I would argue that it is not your job to make sure your mother isn't lonely. Studying on campus, going out with friends, and generally being out of the house are entirely normal behaviors for a college senior, and you're not neglecting your mother or in any way causing her loneliness by trying to build a life of your own. There's no need for you to look for a middle ground here; your mother has to figure out how to be happy without clinging to her grown children. Children are supposed to leave their parents. Leaving isn't abandonment, and you should not feel bad for a minute about leaving your mother to lead a normal life. Your mother's loneliness is way beyond your ability to fix, and she should seek professional help. Even if she refuses, consider seeing a therapist on your own and getting support in building a life that doesn't involve sleeping in your mother's bed just because she can't stand the thought of sleeping alone.

////////////

Dear Prudence,

My husband and I have been married for three years. I am about to turn thirty, and we are discussing the possibility of having children, although we are both leaning [toward] no. I have never felt a maternal need for kids, though I would love to have a dog. I have friends with children, and while I love playing the part of auntie, I am exhausted after spending a day with them. When I think about kids, I mostly think about the negatives: they are expensive, we won't be able to travel, and I have a family history of mental illness and some other diseases I would hate to pass down. There is one thing that keeps me from saying no, and that is that I am afraid of being alone when I am old and can't fend for myself. I see my grandmother and have no idea what she

would do if it weren't for my mother and her siblings. I recently
visited my old nanny in a state-run nursing home, and it left me
with nightmares. Should we have a child to make sure someone
is there to care for us? Should we look into the Hemlock
Society? I should add that I am generally not a strong person
and have told my husband many times I pray that I die before he
does.

—Don't Want to Die Alone

/////////////

*I have a lot of sympathy for anyone willing to admit they're terrified
of dying alone. But you should not have children. Wanting a child
for the sole purpose of creating a future nurse is no reason to start
a family. Any child of yours would pretty quickly pick up on the fact
that you find them exhausting, expensive, and a burden—things
that are true of all children but in your case would not be balanced
by parental love. My guess is that child would not then leap at the
chance to provide you with round-the-clock care in your declining
years.*

*You must know on some level that having children does not
guarantee anyone a peaceful death. Many people outlive their
children. Many people with living, healthy children are still put
into nursing homes for a variety of reasons. Having a child now is
not insurance that you will be given the kind of death you want.
Address your fear about end-of-life care directly by planning
ahead. Establish a living will, start a retirement/medical fund
that will help pay for private nursing, but don't bring a child*

into the world just to alleviate your desire to avoid institutional
care. Consider seeing a therapist to confront your (very normal!)
concerns about your own mortality and what the end of your life
may look like; you owe it to yourself to face these fears head on,
rather than try to build a baby escape hatch and run away from
them.

• • •

I'll never know where people continue to get the idea that
good parents can be forged by badgering people who don't
want children into giving in. If I ever find the source, I'll
brick it up.

/////////////

Dear Prudence,
We are concerned our only son isn't having children. Every time
we bring it up with him, he seems to have a new excuse. Recently,
when we tried to discuss this with our daughter-in-law directly,
she said her high-powered career would be severely impacted
if she didn't plan childbearing carefully because she doesn't get
paid parental leave at her workplace. We tried to encourage her
by saying that she doesn't even need to work since our son is
very successful and we have considerable means. This seems to
have offended her greatly. How do we convince them that we
only want them to be happy?

—Son Won't Have Children

//////////////

A great way to convince your children that you want them to be happy is to stop directly contributing to their unhappiness by repeatedly badgering them about their life choices and assuming you know what will make them happy better than they do.

Apologize to your son for pressing the issue, take his excuses at face value (what you consider "excuses" may be, to him, excellent reasons to delay or avoid having children altogether), apologize to your daughter-in-law for presuming she should quit her job and have children simply because you would find it convenient, and then drop the subject entirely. You have forfeited the right to ask innocently about whether or not they're planning on having children because you have repeatedly failed to do so politely, respectfully, and appropriately.

Chapter Eleven

Alone Together

Letters with a pandemic theme: working from home, not working from home, dealing with a partner who's working from home, cabin fever, not having anywhere safe to go, health and medical issues, self-distancing protocols, mask wearing, risk management, collective cooperation, trying to leave a dangerous living situation when almost everywhere is dangerous, alternatives to calling the police.

I have little to say about the pandemic that feels useful, new, or interesting; it's as exhausting to discuss as it has been to contend with. Sometimes it's simply amplified familiar, pre-existing problems, and sometimes it's introduced new ones.

///////////

Dear Prudence,

A while ago, I started chatting online with guys because I'd been single for a while and the pandemic has of course limited other

forms of contact. When I say chatting, I mean genuinely trying
to find connections—I'm in my late thirties and way past the dick
pic stage. I had seemingly gotten really close to this guy when he
suddenly ghosted me. I was stung but had been forewarned that this
sort of thing happens, so I quietly nursed my ego and moved on.

Lo and behold, a few weeks later and who do I see appear
under a different account? So in a moment of unbelievable
stupidity, I messaged him under a fake account and got him talking.
I wanted to know what I had done wrong by asking about "previous
relationships" and intended to let it go after that. We've gotten
really close. He still has no idea of my real identity. He's told me the
last girl he was with (definitely me—same age, same state) came
across as a little too needy for him so he ghosted her and was
ashamed of it. He's even promised to go to family therapy after we
spent all night talking about his anger issues with his daughter. Last
night he told me he loved me, and I was making him a better man.
And to be honest, I'm getting strong feelings for him too. I cannot
see a way out of this. I did something so wrong, and I continue to
propagate this wrongdoing every day. But I risk humiliating and
upsetting this man who, in short, doesn't deserve it. I know that
you're going to be brutal, and I deserve that, but how do I get out
of this without destroying him?

—Catfish Gone Wrong

*I don't want to be brutal, but I do think the reality of your situation
is a brutal one—you know that this is not a healthy or workable*

foundation for a real or lasting relationship, and that fact makes you very sad. You know that this man found your needs excessive and that he chose to respond to that realization by ghosting you. The fact that you've gotten close under an assumed new name doesn't change that emotional reality, nor has it really addressed the underlying hurt. You've reestablished a new kind of emotional intimacy, but promising someone you've only messaged online that you're going to go to family therapy isn't the same thing as a truly honest reconciliation.

Frankly, I think you should ghost him now, not as retribution for his past ghosting, but because there's simply no way forward from here and because I think the best sort of help you can receive will come from a therapist and from sharing what you've done with some trusted friends and asking for their support as you figure out how to behave differently in future relationships. If the idea of ghosting him seems unbearable, another option is to tell him the truth and prepare yourself for a likely breakup. If that seems unbearable too, your other option is to keep the fiction going until he figures it out. That option to me seems the worst of the three, and I'd encourage you not to pursue it.

•••

It has been interesting to revisit the archives and see when people started referring to "the middle" of the pandemic, when they started referring to the "early days" in retrospect, and when what used to be "the middle" was eventually relegated back to the early days in turn.

////////////

Dear Prudence,

I moved in with my boyfriend in the middle of the pandemic. I didn't realize until now, but he drinks almost every day. He rarely gets drunk during the week, but he almost always does during the weekend. We've been dating almost three years, and I've never seen him sloppy drunk or doing anything regrettable. As far as I can tell, he just gets a bit more extroverted when he's drunk.

I'm worried about this behavior. My father was an alcoholic, but he had a very different personality. He was a fun-loving guy but got angry pretty easily, more so when he was drunk. My current boyfriend doesn't do that. I know your advice would be to talk to him about it; I've just heard so many stories of alcoholics who will constantly shape up when their significant other talks to them but slowly slip into their old habits. I'm wondering if I should just leave without talking to him. I don't want to continue in this relationship for months or even years only for him to develop full-blown alcoholism. What would you advise?

—Drinks Too Much

////////////

I'd advise you to base all your decisions on the following principle: you are absolutely allowed to leave your boyfriend because of how his drinking makes you feel. That doesn't mean you have to consign him to "definite future alcoholic" status, place his drinking on par with your father's, or make a universal claim that anyone else would see his drinking as similarly problematic. If you decide that, based on your own history with an alcoholic parent, it's not possible for you to safely and happily live with someone who drinks every day and gets drunk most weekends (even if their drunkenness results primarily in exuberance and does not result in anger), then ending your relationship is a perfectly reasonable option. And it's not a reasonable option because you know for certain what his drinking will look like in the future—you don't know that—but because you know his drinking habits right now set off primal fears rooted in your own childhood about volatility and loss of control and inhibition. It's not a question of "either your partner is 100 percent bound to become an alcoholic like your father," in which case you have to leave him for your own safety, or "your partner's drinking is fine and therefore you have to stay in this relationship and learn to accept it." It's a question of what makes you feel safe and able to connect, and it's perfectly reasonable to say that even if he's sweet and friendly when he gets drunk, you don't want to be in a relationship with someone who gets drunk most weekends.

I would encourage you to have some sort of conversation with your boyfriend before initiating a breakup, if only because I think it would provide you with meaningful peace of mind, but you don't have to have that conversation in your home or all by yourself or with the goal of getting him to agree with your perspective. If you want to enlist a friend or two to check in with you before and after the breakup, please do; it might help to feel like you have someone in your corner and a safe place you can stay the night afterward. You can make it clear that the issue is one of compatibility; it doesn't sound like you want him to drastically amend his relationship to drinking and stick around to see if it works for you. It sounds like you want to end things and look for future partners who drink very little or not at all. That's eminently reasonable. It might help to attend a few Al-Anon meetings (or SMART Recovery or any of the other support group alternatives to Al-Anon that appeal to you), if you haven't already. Even if you're only able to attend meetings online, you can start to think about your limits around alcohol in terms of your own needs, rather than simply "Is it fair for me to be upset by [X]?" Of course, you certainly don't have to attend meetings in order to take the next step here.

///////////

Dear Prudence,
I am writing because my spouse's workplace has become increasingly abusive toward its workers since the pandemic started. She is working from home, and her department has gotten more understaffed and overworked to the point where she regularly works extra unpaid hours just to catch up. Her supervisors are at best willfully ignorant of this fact, as she sends emails and submits work after 5 p.m., while always being clocked out at 5 p.m.

What is my role here? My spouse is openly hostile to the suggestion that she say something or just stop working and do what work she can by 5 and pick it up the next day. I have considered attempting to anonymously report her employer to the Department of Labor, but I'm not sure what effect that would have, and I am sure she would be angry if she found out I did, as she very clearly does not want to make waves.

—Work-Life Imbalance

////////////

I think you're right not to make an anonymous report, not only because you know it would anger your spouse but because it's possible that she could still be targeted for retaliation if her employers suspected the report came from her. As awful as this situation sounds, I don't think your spouse is in the kind of danger that might merit an intervention that overrides her wishes, and that should be your guiding principle when it comes to something like making a report to the Department of Labor.

Instead, I think you can ask your wife for guidance: What does she need from you in terms of support or distance right now? Conversely, are there some limits you need to set for yourself, either in terms of how much you're prepared to hear her complaints about work or in terms of encouraging her to look for work elsewhere? Does she have reason to fear she'll be fired if she just stops working at 5? If so, I don't think your advice to "just stop working" at 5 will be very effective, even though I wish it were. You don't have to pretend that this is a healthy situation, or even one that's sustainable in the long run, but I think you should confine your position here to asking questions, trusting your wife's sense of her job security, and encouraging her to come up with backup strategies.

////////////

Dear Prudence,

My wife and I are polyamorous, and apart from some mishaps
early on, we are happy with the arrangement. She started dating
a new girlfriend a few months ago. I have met the girlfriend a
couple of times and like her, but my wife wants us to socialize
all together more often, something that I'm not really interested
in doing. I certainly support my wife spending time with her but
don't see a need to have a close relationship with her girlfriend.
Because of COVID, we have to restrict who we can see in person,
so I understand why my wife wants to include her girlfriend in
social events. Even so, I would still rather have a pleasant but
acquaintance-like relationship with my wife's girlfriend. What
should I do?

—Why Must We Be Friends?

////////////

*Reiterate your boundary ("My goal is to have a friendly but
limited relationship with your partners; I'm not interested in a
close friendship for [X] reasons"), and ask your wife to talk a little
more about why this is important to her. Maybe it's just that her
dream of a polyamorous relationship is one where everyone's very
close to one another, and you two will have to deal with the fact
that your two ideals aren't in perfect alignment. Or maybe it has
something to do with your earlier mishaps, and she thinks this is
the best way to avoid future problems. Maybe it's a question of
convenience, because seeing someone outside of your household*

during a pandemic is fairly complicated, in which case you might have a right to express resentment over being instrumentalized. Maybe she just thinks you two would really like each other, and you'll have to clarify that your desire to keep some space between you two isn't due to hostility but the need for room to work through (present or potential) complicated emotions in safety and privacy.

If you both want different things, that's not a sign of disaster, but an opportunity to really hash out (in writing, if possible) what you can both reasonably offer each other, how you might strive to meet needs the other isn't prepared to fulfill, and what "good enough" looks like. It's possible for people in an open relationship to get seized with a utopian vision of the future where everything feels good all the time, and it can be really useful to ground yourselves in practical expectations. Just because your wife loves you and is really into her new girlfriend, it doesn't necessarily follow that you're going to become the Three Musketeers. That's not an impediment to your wife's happiness or an indicator that her desires are bad or shameful or Pollyannaish. It's just a check-in.

////////////

Dear Prudence,

Four years ago, I had an affair with my cousin's husband. The fallout was exactly what you'd imagine: god-awful. I felt terrible about it at the time and apologized immediately. My cousin severed ties with me and most of my immediate family. Recently our grandmother died from COVID, and we were all together

for the funeral. My cousin was perfectly polite, and I was
reminded of my immense guilt that I hurt her and broke up her
marriage. I would like to send a note apologizing for my part in
the dissolution of her marriage but am not sure it's a good idea.
I also realize sometimes it's better to let sleeping dogs lie and
don't want to bring up a painful memory for her unnecessarily.
I would ask my parents, but I don't want to open an old can of
worms with them. We've moved on, but I know they feel pain at
losing their niece at my hands. Any advice you can give would be
appreciated.

—Family Fallout

///////////////

*The key here is that your impulse to send this apology note did
not arise from a realization that you had failed to apologize
comprehensively four years ago, nor from an indication from your
cousin that she was interested in reestablishing a relationship or
in having a conversation that went beyond basic politeness. You
were simply reminded of your guilt. That's understandable, given
the circumstances, but I don't think it's a very good reason to try
to contact her. She was fairly clear about not wanting to speak to
you (or anyone in your family) four years ago, and since she hasn't
followed up after the funeral with either you or your parents, it's
reasonable to assume she still feels now the way she did then, and
the only reason she spoke to you at the funeral was because she
didn't want to violate social conventions. Were you to try to speak
to her again, I fear you would only cause her additional pain and*

make her feel responsible for managing your guilt. The kindest thing you can do for your cousin, the clearest way you can honor your commitment to not add to the pain you've already caused her, is to respect her wish not to speak to you.

If the idea of not saying anything to anyone feels unbearable, or if you worry you're going to endlessly punish yourself, I'd encourage you to speak with your close friends or a therapist about your feelings. You might even consider the possibility of revisiting the subject with your parents. You say you don't want to open an old can of worms with them, but since they are in a relationship with you and your cousin isn't, there's much more room there for potential honesty, making amends, and healing. You can proceed cautiously and begin by asking them if they're even interested in speaking on the subject again. Speaking with these other people instead of your cousin may not fully address your guilt, but it will go a long way toward treating her with respect and compassion. You deserve relief from your guilt—you do not deserve to spend the rest of your life in shame and self-loathing—but you cannot seek that relief from the person you harmed, since she's already made her wishes very clear on that front.

•••

I don't want to put too much pressure on any single letter writer, but for everyone's sake, I sure hope that the rare upside described in the following letter remained a positive and that everything worked out.

///////////////

Dear Prudence,

In one of the rare upsides to the pandemic, I have reconnected
with a friend. We've been video chatting every two to three
weeks for the past few months, and it's been great. The first time
we talked, it somehow came up that I had recently realized I was
bi. They mentioned that they had recently begun dating women
and nonbinary people. (For context, I'm a cis woman, and this
friend is nonbinary; historically, we have both only dated cis men.)
I'm developing feelings for this person and feel like they have
recently been subtly signaling romantic interest in me. But I'm
not sure if I'm reading this right. We live on opposite sides of the
country and are not the sort to travel during the pandemic. Also,
I have a pretty low sex drive and am worried about disappointing
them in that regard whenever we might actually be able to see
each other in person. Another worry is that I don't have a lot of
sexual/relationship experience for someone in their thirties.

On the one hand, this is the first time I've developed romantic
feelings for someone in a long time, so I sort of want to say
something. On the other hand, I'm worried about ruining our
friendship if I'm reading this wrong. And even if it turns out we
are on the same page, I'm not sure how we would make this work
in a pandemic without a clear end in sight. How do you think I
should approach this?

—Pandemic Pining

///////////////

Approach this with the assumption that signaling possible romantic interest is not an automatically friendship-ruining proposition! You may decide you're not ready to say anything until after the vaccine has been made widely available (or some other pandemic-related milestone), which would be perfectly reasonable. But plenty of friendships have survived a brief conversation about romantic possibility, and what you're contemplating telling them is relatively low-risk. It's not as if you've been desperately in love with them for years and don't think you can continue your friendship if they don't return your feelings. You've recently reconnected, you're in the habit of discussing unexpected changes in your dating lives, and you have reason to think they're at least a little interested in you. You don't yet know what expressing such interest might look like, which stands to reason, because you haven't discussed it with them yet, and your present circumstances are a little unusual. Again, that's a good thing, not a reason to keep your mouth shut.

I often hear from people who want to ask out a friend but feel like they shouldn't unless they have a perfect sense of how such a relationship would proceed. That is too high a barrier to expressing interest! You can cross those bridges when you reach them, but don't assume that a relatively low libido or a relatively small number of exes precludes you from ever trying to date someone you like. Give yourself permission to express romantic interest at some point in the future. You don't have to do it today if you don't feel ready. But neither do you need to exhaustively map out an entire romantic future, ensuring a road ahead that's free of any bumps or complications, in order to say: "I think we've been flirting a bit lately, and I've really liked it. What do you think?"

• • •

It's one thing to take pandemic-related stressors into account when giving friends, families, or colleagues a break, but pandemic-related stress doesn't cause racist tirades. The question of how to handle full-time work and full-time childcare in light of a pandemic is a serious one, but it's entirely separate from questions about the nature of the blowup (left carefully vague here), and it would be a serious mistake indeed to believe addressing the latter would do anything to address the former.

////////////////

Dear Prudence,

My wife was in a very stressful situation about a month ago when she was at a park in our hometown. After trying to balance a full-time job while caring for our three children for four months, she honestly just kind of lost it. She snapped. My wife is now the subject of a "Karen" video that made the rounds last month in our town (luckily, it didn't spread beyond that). She was, and still is, horrified by her behavior. She is seeking counseling for both the "snap" and the underlying thoughts and attitudes that came out in the video.

In the meantime, how do we get back to our normal life? Many folks around town are understandably freezing us out, and some of my kids' friends' parents are refusing playdates. This is only adding to the loneliness and isolation our family had already been feeling because of the pandemic. I hate to see my kids suffering because of my wife's unconscionable actions. Short of moving to

a new town, what can we do to rebuild the relationships that used
to keep us grounded in this awful time?

—Frozen-Out Family

*Presumably your "normal" life was the one where your wife was
trying to balance a full-time job while caring for your three children,
a situation that so overwhelmed her that she "snapped," so I don't
think you should be too eager to return to it. (One obvious change
there might be for you to take on the greater portion of childcare for
the foreseeable future.) More than that, your "normal" life was also
one where your wife apparently harbored certain vague thoughts
and attitudes that horrify her—that's nothing to want to hurry back
to. (Do they horrify you?) What have you two communicated to your
kids about this, beyond simply "Something happened, it's horrifying,
but we can't go into detail"?*

*I would love to know more about the specific "underlying
thoughts and attitudes" that came out in the video, because that
would help me offer meaningful, context-driven advice. What in
particular is she sorry for? What does she now think she could
have done differently at the time? How much damage did she
cause others? Was she merely rude, or did she threaten someone
else's health and safety? What has she done to try to make
amends beyond seeing a therapist?*

*Presumably whatever she did in that park was not related to
her stressful full-time job; presumably you referenced "Karen"
without going into even the barest of details because she said or did*

something racist, but you didn't want to say what it was. Why was
your wife's response to stress to do or say something racist? Is this
something she's discussed with her therapist? Has she apologized
to any of your friends or neighbors, and if not, why? What do they
want from her, and from you, before they can answer the question
of whether they're ready to rebuild? You cannot demand that your
friends rebuild relationships, and you cannot use your kids' loneliness
to pressure others into forgiving their parents. But you can ask the
people you know and love, sincerely and nondefensively, what you
can do to start to rebuild trust together. Sometimes that might mean
giving others time and space or the freedom to say, "I can't accept this
apology," but you have to be willing to respect that. Otherwise it's not
an apology at all, but a demand to forget whatever happened.

//////////////

Dear Prudence,
My mom divorced my father when I was young and raised me
alone for a few years before remarrying and starting a new family.
I've always received different (worse) treatment than my half-
siblings from my mom. Friends and boyfriends have remarked
for years on how she treats me—she ignores me or attributes
my words to my husband, insults my appearance, and questions
my life choices whenever I see her. I've kept my distance but
maintain a veneer of politeness.

When the pandemic hit, she started texting me every day to
"check in"—but in practice she uses it as a chance to vent. Open

questions like "How are you doing?" have given way to questions with room for only blandly cheerful responses, like "What are you grateful for today?" If I reply to her with something positive, she second-guesses me. If I reply with something negative or complicated, she ignores it and talks about what's on her mind. I've taken to answering with short, ambivalent replies to give her very little room to maneuver.

The thing is, I'm having a terrible time in quarantine and really do need someone to talk to! My husband has been tweaking his depression medication and has been having frequent panic attacks, and a lot of my coping mechanisms feel very far away right now. When I check my phone in the morning and see her text, it feels like my day is off on a bad foot before it's even started. I'd like to ask her to stop pretending to care how I'm doing while making me help her process her quarantine feelings, but I'm worried it will blow up and exhaust me even more. What do I do?

—Too Many Texts

////////////

If I thought there was any chance your mother could be guided or pushed into being the sort of person you could talk to when you're going through a hard time, I'd do my best to advise you on how to do so, but she seems to be remarkably consistent and implacable in how she treats you. I think the best you can hope for in your relationship is to minimize how much time and energy you spend on her. That may sound bleak, but I think it's a good foundation for hopefulness. You can find kind people to vent to, develop new coping strategies, reground your relationship with your husband, restructure your relationship to your phone, and gain valuable insights into your patterns with your mother, all without looking to her for support or guidance. If that means setting her texts to "Do Not Disturb" and ignoring 80 percent of them, do that; if that means spending thirty seconds each morning telling her something bland, repetitive, and formulaic so as to give her no conversational purchase to keep going, do that. If that means saying, "I don't have the energy for these conversations. I'll let you know when I'm free to talk," and ignoring whatever her response may be so you can go do something genuinely relaxing and meaningful, then do that. (My vote's for No. 3.)

In the long run, I hope you can find ways to disconnect the idea that if your mother blows up at you, you therefore have to exhaust yourself trying to placate her. I realize it's not a change that can be made overnight, and no matter how relentlessly and reliably she tears you down, part of you might always wish that your mother will finally say something kind, loving, and nurturing to you. But I think whatever you do next, you should behave as if you knew without a doubt that your mother's response is going to be unreasonable, unloving, demanding, and critical. Painful as that assumption may be, I think it will free you up to pursue what's best for you, rather than try to tiptoe around her in the hopes you can avoid something that sounds fairly unavoidable.

//////////////

Dear Prudence,

How do I get past my anger at friends who created a "social bubble" during the pandemic that didn't include me? And then they're always inviting me to attend parties ... that I can't attend because I'm not in their social bubble. Then they send me pictures of what I've missed or call me crying because of how much they miss me! I've never asked my friends to change their lifestyles. They have kids who have friends who visit them; they've got other friends they visit too. They've celebrated every birthday and holiday with other people since the pandemic started. They have traveling houseguests, and they crisscross the state monthly to visit each other. One kid's thirteenth birthday party back in the summer had at least twenty people in the pool, eating at the same tables, without a mask in sight. And yet they all complain about how they can't wait to get back to normal "when it's over."

As far as I can see, their lives haven't altered much. Sure, their youngest children started remote schooling. But they still played with neighboring children after class ended, had sleepovers on weekends, and had lots of people in their "bubble." I can't do any of those things. I don't want to risk my health or the health of my parents. But I'm angry that my friends didn't work harder to see me safely if it was that important for them. How can I move past my anger when I realize it was also my choice to keep my own bubble small? I don't want to yell at my friends once we can actually socialize in person again. But honestly, even my siblings haven't been maskless around me and our parents or each other's households. We've firmly committed to it.

//////////////

I hope you can balance two slightly competing truths as you consider renegotiating your friendships postvaccination. The first is that you're perfectly entitled to your frustrations about the past year, and you don't have to immediately sweep them out during an emotional spring cleaning. The second is that it may very well be possible that your friends didn't change their daily habits in the same ways that you did, but that doesn't necessarily mean the pandemic hasn't altered their lives "very much," either. Whenever possible, consider your friends' choices with as much tolerance and generosity as you can, especially when you consider how disruptive and overwhelming having young children suddenly attending school from home every day must have been. That doesn't mean you have to cosign every risk they took or affirm that every birthday party and overnight houseguest was planned according to the most rigorous and thoughtful safety protocol. Nor does it mean you have to pretend to feel good about things! You can be honest about your own isolation and resentments, particularly as they relate to your friends' decisions to call you crying about their inability to include you in their social lives. But your goal should be to work through those frustrations without litigating each child's birthday party or last summer's weekend houseguests down to the letter. Continue to stick to your own commitments, talk to your friends honestly about your experiences now (instead of waiting to yell at them in person in a few weeks or months), and give yourself a break. You've been through a lot.

////////////

Dear Prudence,

My daughter is now almost four and will be four and a half by the time our second child will be born later this year. She is excited for the new baby boy and often kisses my belly and says hello. Due to the pandemic, I've had to transition to working remotely, so I've spent a great deal of time with my daughter at home. She has gotten very attached and used to me being there all the time. Oftentimes she will get jealous and will not allow me to talk to others or even go to the store alone. She wants me all to herself. Is this a sign of her feeling that someone new will come into "her" territory and she is becoming possessive of me and envious of this unborn baby, or is this a phase that too shall pass?

—Worried Mother of Two

////////////

I'll start with the important caveat that I have no children, so I can't speak to just how common or uncommon this might be. I canvassed a friend of mine with two kids and got this incredibly world-weary response: "It's a phase. It's always a phase. Everything annoying your kid does turns into some new annoying thing in a month." It will almost certainly pass at some point—it's very unlikely that your daughter will still insist on accompanying you during every errand when she's fifteen and thinks you're an idiot—but I don't think you have to simply write this off as an inevitable, fixed stage of development such that intervention is impossible. If anything, I'd take your daughter's increased dependence not as an indicator of her feelings about the new baby but as an indicator of just how challenging living through a pandemic is for little kids. The size and scale of her social world has shrunk amazingly over the last year! You can affirm her need for reassurance and remind her that you're there for her, but you don't need to give in to her every demand either. If you need to talk to someone else and she's distressed about it, be patient but encourage her to practice being by herself for a few minutes.

"I think a lot of parents forget to tell their kids about their own needs and feelings, but she's old enough to start thinking about the fact that you sometimes need a little time to yourself too," my world-weary friend adds. "'I know you're sad I'm talking to someone else. I really want to hear what they have to say, and I'll talk to you when we're done.' It's a good way to help prepare her to think about her little brother's needs when he comes along too." Your four-year-old will still sometimes get jealous or demanding, won't be able to fully incorporate your interiority the way a fellow adult might, and won't always be able to immediately call upon her reserves of patience and self-reliance when you want to do something without her. But you can start to schedule small periods of time throughout the day where you two aren't joined at the hip, and encourage her to think of a little "alone time" as something both parents and kids need and enjoy. Good luck! It's a lot to deal with, and I hope your daughter's next developmental stage is something like "helps with the dishes without being asked" or "quietly reads in her room."

Chapter Twelve

A Worker Among Workers

Letters with a fluorescent tinge: problems that are uniquely work-related, problems only a boss could cause, problems only a union can solve, problems HR was supposed to handle, problems your predecessor was supposed to fix, problems your coworkers were supposed to address, loud snacking, public nail-clipping, unbearable working conditions both physical and relational.

I'm sympathetic to anyone, like the following letter writer, who has trouble with names (I sometimes do myself) while also having to speak to dozens of new patients and colleagues a day, but I agree that calling your coworkers "dear" is overly familiar, even though it's clear the letter writer isn't trying to make anyone uncomfortable on purpose.

////////////

Dear Prudence,

I am a young woman and physician-in-training. I am terrible with
names and work with a rotating team of nurses, social workers,
nursing assistants, and other physicians. I work at several hospitals
on several teams. I tend to refer to people as "my dear" or "my
love." This includes everyone: my patients, other doctors I work with,
social workers, etc. The other day at work, I was speaking with a staff
member. I said, "Thank you so much, my dear, for your help earlier."

Later that day she told me she doesn't like nicknames and asked
me to call her by her name. I apologized and thanked her for telling
me. In the future, I will call her by her name (which I won't forget)!
Is this a practice I should stop for everyone? I mean it kindly, and
my intention is to be warm. I am cognizant of my role as the doctor
with nurses and social workers (even if I am in my first year of
training) and don't want to come across as patronizing or make
anyone uncomfortable. This interaction has made me second-
guess myself. Am I no worse than a creepy male boss?! Is there a
kind term of endearment that would be more neutral?

—Need Neutral Nicknames

////////////

*I have no interest in ranking you on a scale of creepy male bosses,
but yes, you should stop calling other people who work at these
hospitals "my love." And you definitely shouldn't be calling your
patients "my love," either—that goes beyond warm and friendly
and into "pet names for a significant other" territory. Just say*

"Thank you so much" when you don't know someone's name, or ask them for a reminder of their name. You don't have to apologize to everyone you've ever used a term of endearment with—just knock it off. You can maintain a sense of warmth by using eye contact, smiling, and saying thank you, but leave the "my dears" and "my loves" for your friends and loved ones.

////////////

Dear Prudence,

I recently got a position at a company that apparently still has a 1960s-style *Mad Men* relationship with alcohol. I belong to a nondrinking church. I had always thought it wrong to bring religion to work. Therefore, at the first office "Friday Bash," I simply declined to drink, thinking that it would be no big deal, especially in this health-conscious day and age. I was then set upon by people trying to force drinks upon me. I was eventually rescued by a coworker, who came over and said she couldn't drink either on account of a medication interaction. What she doesn't know is that they call her "the nutcase on medication" behind her back. And that's just the excuse she came up with to get them off her case! At the following "Friday Bash" I again declined to drink and, when pressed, I finally said, pleasantly and nonjudgmentally, "My church doesn't allow it." I then got called in and told not to bring "religion" to work. I just don't want to drink, and I want to be left in peace. I know, legally, I have that right. What should I do? Is it too soon to job-jump, as my minister has suggested?

—Not a Lush

////////////

I suppose I can understand why hearing "My church doesn't allow me to drink" might have startled some of your coworkers, but I absolutely cannot understand why it is so difficult for some people to hear "No thanks, I don't drink" as "No thanks, I don't drink." There's no reason to demand a justification when someone says "No thanks" about food or drink, especially at work. "No thanks" stands on its own. If you feel comfortable following up with your boss, tell them that while you're not interested in pushing your religion on anyone, you felt repeatedly pressured by your new colleagues to furnish an excuse for not drinking, and you'd prefer that, in the future, you not have drinks forced into your hand by your coworkers. (An eminently reasonable request from an employee!) It sounds like this is the kind of office that knows how to make work confusing and unpleasant for anyone who doesn't fit in with the frat-house vibe; I don't think it's too soon for you to start looking for a job somewhere else.

• • •

Perhaps my favorite type of letter begins with the phrase "I have a coworker I cannot stand." I am instantly drawn in, immediately invested, and awash with the memory of every coworker I have ever grown to dislike in an artificial, forced proximity! It's as sincere and simple a shameful pleasure as any I can think of, and while my goal remains spreading sweetness and light wherever possible and discouraging nursing petty, distracting grudges, I feel a rush of sympathy for anyone in such a position.

////////////

Dear Prudence,

I have a coworker I cannot stand. We'll call her "Alice." Alice is constantly in everyone's business and gossips all day long. We are a small department in a large company. Alice constantly bashes the two fathers of her children and talks about what an amazing stepmother she is to her boyfriend's kids. She constantly complains about her sons' stepmothers and custody battles.

Now to backtrack: About three years ago a good friend asked if I would babysit for her neighbor, who'd had a baby with her friend. The father was unfortunately in jail, and the mother (her neighbor) was MIA. I babysat the sweetest, most beautiful baby girl who ended up being adopted by the father's brother and wife. I recently found out that Alice is the mother of that baby. I had briefly mentioned the girl I once babysat and how the girl's mother had just left her with family and never came back, and I used the girl's first name. I've never seen someone's face go so pale. Alice looked terrified and asked if I knew anything about the mother. I told her no, and she looked relieved and walked out of my office. This confirmed to me that she was the mother. She comes to my office daily to complain and gossip about coworkers in other departments, as well as the issues with her children's fathers. I get so angry hearing about this when I know she abandoned her daughter. Can I shut her up by letting her know what I know? Or do I go with the morally safe option of putting up with her?

—Shut Up or Shut Her Up?

//////////////

The best advice I can give you in the middle of this (very dramatic) soap opera is this: talk to Alice much less. I know it's not always possible to opt out of gossip in a small office, but I think it's worth giving it your best college try. You might not like Alice—from the sound of things, I don't much like her either—but I don't see how it would improve your work life if you let her know you think she's a bad mother, especially because the only "confirmation" you have at present that she is indeed the mother in question is the fact that her face went unusually pale. If this were a Victorian novel, that would be all the evidence you need, but as it is, I don't think you have quite the open-and-shut case you think you have.

Maybe Alice is the mother of the girl in question. Maybe she isn't. Either way, there's nothing to be gained by letting Alice know that you know. It won't improve the little girl's life, since she's already been adopted by someone else, and since Alice abandoned her daughter several years ago, finding out that her coworker disapproves is hardly likely to persuade her to change her ways. If you don't like hearing her gossip, you don't have to throw her long-lost daughter in her face in order to get her to stop. Try: "Alice, I'm afraid I'm very busy, and if you don't have anything work-related to discuss, I'll have to get back to my project." Repeat as necessary, and punctuate your point with headphones as often as possible.

• • •

The next letter keeps me up at night, I'll admit. Three times? *Three times*, in as many months? There must not be a fourth time, even if that means developing a complicated *Memento*-style series of Post-it note reminders all over the bathroom mirror and a series of randomly timed smart-phone alerts throughout the workday saying, "Don't ask anyone if they're pregnant today, especially not Sandra." It may have been too late to avoid an HR nightmare, and frankly I'm not so sure I'd want to help the letter writer avoid one.

////////////

Dear Prudence,
Three months ago, "Sandra" started working at the same company as me. I'm not going to come off well in this story, and it's too late to hope for Sandra to like me. Basically, I have asked her three times if she is pregnant / when the baby is due. I'm forgetful by nature and often ask family, friends, and coworkers the same question—although never a question this offensive. Sandra is overweight and sometimes wears dresses that I mistakenly think are trying to emphasize the bump. Sandra has been gracious but increasingly less happy answering me, and I feel like an ass each time. I apologize profusely but by now she thinks I'm making fun of her. How do

I convince her otherwise / prevent this from becoming a HR nightmare for me?

—Foot Forever in Mouth

///////////

You say you're "forgetful," but if you're genuinely so forgetful that you're incapable of remembering that a coworker isn't pregnant on three separate occasions in as many months, I worry about your memory and cognition skills and encourage you to speak to a doctor. The most important thing for you to do right now is leave Sandra alone. Unless it's work-related, don't ask her any questions at all. Write it down if you have to—"Don't ask women if they're pregnant." Write it discreetly on your arm under your sleeve every morning if that's what it takes. I promise, if a woman is pregnant and you need to know about it, she will tell you. Your thinking her dress "emphasizes a bump" does not qualify you as needing to know, and you're in danger of creating a hostile work environment. You've already apologized, so don't go overboard trying to pressure Sandra into thinking you're a good person. Just leave her alone.

• • •

While I never want to encourage excessive passivity at work, I think it's generally wise to adopt Marcus Aurelius's attitude: "Begin the morning by saying to thyself, I shall meet with the busy-body, the ungrateful, arrogant, deceitful, envious, unsocial." One needn't agree with his idea that the root cause of such encounters is always ignorance of the good, or get on board with the subsequent claim that "the nature of him who does wrong . . . participates in the same intelligence and the same portion of the divinity" as oneself, such that "I can neither be injured by any of them, for no one can fix on me what is ugly, nor can I be angry with my kinsman, nor hate him." It's really only a very little Marcus Aurelius we need to borrow, leaving the rest to the side for the present. Without assuming the worst automatically, it can make the day a great deal easier if one expects to encounter difficulty, nosiness, annoyance, irritation, and so on, so that they do not come as a shocking injury to what was meant to be an otherwise-unblemished day, but a mere matter of course. Wherever there is an opportunity to say, "Well, sometimes these things happen—it's annoying, but I'll move on," one ought to take it.

////////////

Dear Prudence,
I work for a large behavioral health organization in admissions. I coordinate scheduling with the staff at one of the clinics, including one person who later became front-office manager. She has a rude way of responding to group emails with questions that might be directed at me, but she never addresses me directly the way others do when they ask for my assistance [and never] even uses my name. It's very weird for me, and I have taken to ignoring her in response, although it's confusing to understand if she is

even doing this on purpose. I do not know her well, but what I do know of her is not great. She announced loudly and aggressively in a meeting that "they" (meaning their clinic and front-office staff) do not need "INTAKE" (a reference to me, I believe). Is there a more effective way for me to address her rudeness? I have tried addressing her by her name, but she does not seem to notice or change this way of doing things (like responding in kind as a typical person might do). The majority of my other interactions with clinicians and other staff are more polite, so she is also bucking the norm and seems to ignore these examples of better behavior. I have not been direct with her, due to not even being sure what she is trying to do, and also because I expect a bad reaction and do not want to waste my energy on her.

—Email Etiquette

//////////////

If you're not sure she's referring to you in an email, then give yourself the gift of not worrying about it and let it go. If she sometimes replies to group emails with a general, open-ended question, and you decide not to answer it, I don't think you then have to worry about getting "direct with her," because there's nothing to get direct about. Let someone else answer it, or let her figure it out on her own. If she's asking questions that only you could possibly answer, I can see how that would be annoying. In that case—but only in that case!—let her know politely that you can handle questions along those lines in the future and encourage her to contact you directly. But if these are questions that someone *else might reasonably be expected to respond to and she's addressing the group, my advice is once again to let it go. If you're having an ongoing conversation with her and she's being rude, or if she's come to you with a specific request and she's pointedly avoiding using your name, then by all means speak up. But you don't have to explode in order to let her know you'd like her to ask you directly if she needs something from you. You can (and should!) do so professionally and politely.*

I'm not surprised you expect a "bad reaction" should you confront her over this. Maybe she is insensitive or bad at communicating, but I think you're hanging on to this grudge too tightly. You don't have to like her or go out of your way to befriend her. And it doesn't sound like you have to interact with her very often, and if she's going out of her way to give you a wide berth, why not return the favor? It'll make your work life a lot easier.

• • •

On the other hand, if you simply have to tell a colleague that they smell bad, I think there's nothing for it but to say it directly and get it over with.

////////////

Dear Prudence,

I hired a short-term freelance worker (who is a few years older than me) for a job, and boy does he get ripe toward the end of the day—so bad that I feel like I can still smell him hours after we've said goodbye. The job only requires him to interact with other freelancers and minimal client contact for a few days. My friend says I need to enlist a man to pull him aside and let him know he needs new deodorant, man-to-man. Is it even more awkward if I ask another freelancer to have this talk, or can I do it myself in a way that doesn't make this dude feel terrible?

—Outsourcing Body Talk

////////////

Please don't ask one of your other freelancers to tell this man he smells. That is so far outside the scope of the terms of their temporary employment with you, I'm a little troubled you would even consider it. Do not abuse your status as manager in order to avoid discomfort, and do not ask your freelancers to confront fellow freelancers on your behalf. They're not your colleagues; they're your employees. You'll have to decide if his contract is short-term enough that it's worth suffering in silence, or if you're going to have to have a frank, uncomfortable conversation about personal hygiene at the office.

• • • •

Of course, Marcus Aurelius doesn't really cut it when the "busy-body, ungrateful, arrogant, deceitful, envious, unsocial" you encounter every day at work is also your husband and your employee. In such cases you have my permission to give Marcus Aurelius a miss entirely.

//////////////

Dear Prudence,

My husband and I started our own company in a creative field about three years ago. He was having trouble holding down a traditional job, and I wasn't enjoying mine, so we decided to make the most of his creative talents and my administrative skills. Now I understand why he had trouble in his previous jobs. He blows off deadlines, resents clients (and cannot be trusted to speak to them directly), and complains bitterly and endlessly about the natural constraints of our job. I'm functionally the manager of our company, and it falls to me to make sure everything actually happens the way it's supposed to. He regularly gets upset with me when I enforce the planning and deliverables that are outlined in our contracts, and when I schedule "too much" work for us despite our workload being pretty normal. He's very sweet outside of work, and I love him when we're just hanging out together. We actually perform our day-to-day work tasks seamlessly as a team; it's the management that we fundamentally disagree on. I'm at my wits' end and am seriously considering saying that I want out. I know I could find another job, but I'm not sure he can, honestly.

But quitting our business becomes a question of what happens to our marriage. Do I really want to stay married to someone who I don't think can be an equal partner to me in work, finances, buying a home, or having children? I truly don't know how he would be able to provide for himself on his own. I absolutely love the work we do; it's my dream job. I can't do it without him, and he can't go on without me. I feel so stuck, and I don't know what to do. We argue about this every few months like clockwork, and nothing really changes even though he always admits he could do better. My ideal situation would be to stay married and to keep working in this field, but with him just accepting that we really do need to work forty to fifty hours a week and that it won't always be super fun and immediately rewarding.

—Husband Makes Lousy Employee

//////////////

Your ideal situation does not presently exist. It also seems unlikely that it's going to start existing anytime soon, because your husband has never been able to bring himself to accept that his work requires a weekly forty-to-fifty-hour commitment, that he has to speak politely to clients, or even the general nature of the industry he works in. So it is with a great deal of affection and compassion for you that I say: Let the dream of your "ideal situation" die on the table right now. Nor do I think that you can keep your present situation going indefinitely. It's only been three years, and you're already at your wits' end; what will it be like if five years from now you're still your husband's boss, and he still resents you for reminding him of the terms of the contracts he's already signed? At a certain point it just doesn't matter how "seamlessly" your day-to-day work goes. The rest of your job sounds absolutely unbearable, and you're quite right to worry about how your husband might handle the responsibilities of parenthood on the basis of what you've seen from him at work.

Stop acting as if being your husband's full-time mentor/boss/ babysitter/assistant is a viable lifelong strategy, because it isn't;

you'll eventually get exhausted and frustrated and quit. I don't think a "dream job" has ever involved having to plead with, cajole, or coax your only employee (who happens to be your spouse) into doing their job; getting into regular fights about the contracts you've signed together; or talking to every single client on your own because your only coworker is incapable of having a civil conversation with any of them. What might you have the time and energy for if your husband accepted that you "really do need to work forty to fifty hours a week" and that work isn't always "super fun and immediately rewarding"? What would you prioritize or what kind of career moves would you consider if you relinquished the delusion that you are just this close to convincing him? What if you did not make his employability your responsibility? What if you put the same attention and care toward your own career that you've been putting toward trying to keep his career from foundering?

I realize you two have been in business together for years and that you currently depend on this income; I'm not suggesting you tell him you quit tomorrow and then immediately abandon your existing projects. But having the same fight every few months doesn't change anything, so quit waiting on your husband to change. You say that you want out and that you think you could easily find another job; I think it's just that simple, and you should do exactly that. Figure out a manageable timeline for wrapping up your old projects, and start applying for jobs elsewhere.

• • •

This next letter was unusual by virtue of the source of the inappropriate pregnancy-related behavior: I don't think I've ever gotten another one from someone whose pregnant colleague was violating their personal space on a regular basis. The reverse was far more common, and I usually had to advise pregnant people dealing with invasive questions or unwanted physical contact at work. The underlying principles are the same, of course, but it was a slightly horrifying reminder that life is still full of surprises, even when you think you've heard it all.

////////////

Dear Prudence,

I work in an office with several pregnant people. My partner and I are child-free, but we are happy for others who want to have kids. I made the mistake of confiding to a (nonpregnant) coworker that babies weird me out and that I find the general concept of pregnancy a little terrifying. I know plenty of folks birth babies every day, but the physical aspects of it sound just awful. This coworker told one of the pregnant women what I said, and now she won't stop finding excuses to press her very pregnant belly against me. I have asked her to stop, but everyone gets a good laugh about how much I am bothered by this.

How do I get her to stop? I find it unsettling and am starting to think about switching jobs just so I can get away from these boundary-violating people!

—Baby Bumping

////////////

I'm so sorry you're dealing with something so bizarre and intrusive while you're trying to get work done. If it feels indicative of a larger office culture that you're not interested in being a part of, you can certainly look for work elsewhere. But in the meantime, you don't have to put up with this woman routinely pressing herself against you. "I've told you to stop pressing yourself against me in the past, and you haven't stopped, instead treating my discomfort like a joke. It isn't. There is no professional reason for you to touch me like that at work, especially after I've told you I don't like it. Are you able to stop yourself from doing it again? If you can't, I will talk to our supervisor and HR, and we'll come up with a strategy together."

●●●

Sometimes the longest letters need the shortest answers. This happened to be one of them.

/////////////

Dear Prudence,

I am a married mother of two. Three years ago, I had an affair with my boss, a married father of four and a longtime family friend who is more than twenty years my senior. He even got an apartment close to his business so we had a place to go. The affair lasted almost a year, longer than any other affair he's had, and the emotional affair continued much longer. He ended the physical affair by telling me he was a codependent sex addict and that he thought I had some of those behaviors as well, and then left on a

European vacation with his family. I was devastated. Since then, I have worked very hard with my therapist trying to get to the root of the reason I cheated and how to prevent this in the future.

About a year after the physical affair ended (though the emotional affair continued), I learned he slept with a mutual friend. Because he had promised to tell me if he engaged in these behaviors but had not, I immediately shifted our relationship to work-only and ceased all emotional communications. This was a very difficult time for me as I missed him dearly and felt very alone. After six months, we slept together again on a business trip (those are rare). While we did not continue the physical part, the emotional affair picked back up, and I realized how much I missed him and wanted to be with him. Knowing he would decline (keeping his marriage intact for his children has always been his goal), I confessed my feelings for him and asked if he would leave his wife for me. As expected, he turned me down. I began processing the rejection with my therapist, which brings us to today.

I finally feel some peace at work and in life in general as I'm trying to be accepting of my feelings for him and have worked very hard on treating my past traumas. I love my job, and I am really good at it; in fact, I recently got a large raise. But I'm at a loss on what to do going forward. My relationship with my husband is improving (he does not know about the affair), and I am happy with my job, though it is extremely stressful at times. However, I still have periods when I miss my boss/lover and yearn for him, and he still has moments when he makes sexual innuendos or overshares beyond the boundaries we have established about his personal life. I have to interact with many

of the women he has slept with in the past, though none of them
know about each other or about me. I have to interact with
my boss every day on some level, and we work incredibly well
together. He has been supportive through my quest for mental
health and wants me to continue working with him. Sometimes it
seems utterly impossible to do that, and sometimes it seems like
I have a perfect work situation that I would be stupid to give up.

—At a Loss with Boss

/////////////

*I cannot agree you have a "perfect work situation" that you would
be "stupid" to give up. I think you're in a nightmarish work situation
with the world's worst boss who has a habit of seducing and taking
advantage of his subordinates, and you should leave immediately
for the sake of your marriage and your own emotional well-being.
That doesn't mean you should quit tomorrow with no plan in place.
Start discreetly applying for other positions, and ask your therapist
for support as you do so.*

*By the way, a man who sleeps with his employee, dumps her
by declaring, "I'm a dysfunctional sex addict, and I think you are
too—I'm off to Europe with my family," sleeps with their mutual
friends, overshares with his former affair partner, and uses her as
a surrogate partner at work is not "supportive through [her] quest
for mental health." He's actively sabotaging that quest. Get out of
there as quickly as you can, and don't look back.*

• •• •

It's unfortunately common for a letter writer to learn someone they sort of know does cam work (or makes porn or has some other sex-work-adjacent job) and immediately go from never giving much thought to the conditions such workers might experience to suddenly being overwhelmed with a desire to express "concern" and "warn" them that someone else might make life very difficult for them if they were to find out the nature of their work. It's prurience dressed up as solicitude, and it does no one any good.

////////////////

Dear Prudence,

I am a thirty-eight-year-old single gay man. I often watch guys masturbate on a popular cam site. I don't perform on camera myself, but I like interacting with the guys who do, and I have a number of favorites. A few months ago, I found the stream of an eighteen-year-old guy whose routine I liked a lot. "Cam" quickly became one of my favorites, and I always tipped generously whenever I saw his show. He didn't show his face, but his bio mentioned that he's a high school senior who lives in the same metropolitan area as me and likes daddies. (He doesn't know where I live.) I never suggested meeting up because the fantasy is enough for me.

This is where it gets weird. Cam's voice sounded familiar, but I couldn't place it. He talked about wanting to show his face on camera, and one night he did. I was shocked when I realized he was the son of my coworkers. I've known him since he was about fourteen via various "family night" activities sponsored by my employer. Cam has always been out and proud, and now that he's of legal age, he's clearly decided he wants to be very out. He's an adult, at least according to the law, and has every right to do what he wants on camera to anyone who wants to watch.

However, I worry that Cam could be setting himself up for trouble down the road, as I know that people record webcammers and post the videos all over the internet. I'm also fairly sure that Cam's parents don't know what he's doing late at night in his bedroom. What's more, he uses his real name on his stream, so it would be easy to track him down. Should I tell Cam's mom and dad? Should I somehow tell Cam that I know who he is and that he should be more careful online? I want to make it clear that I'm not looking for permission to ask him out, have sex with him, be his sugar daddy, etc. I have not watched Cam's stream since the night he went fully exposed. I probably won't watch his show again, as it squicked me out a little watching a young man I know putting it all out there. What would you do?

—Webcam Recognition

I don't think you're looking for permission to ask Cam out either—but it does seem like you're planning to intimidate him. How would this conversation even go? "Hey, Cam, I guess legally you're allowed to do this, but people—I won't say who, just people—record webcammers and post their videos all over the internet. What would your parents think if they knew you were doing this in your

*bedroom? I know where that is, by the way, because I've known
you since you were fourteen. You should probably be more careful.
Anyhow, I'll see you around—remember, I work with your parents!"
There's not a version of that speech that isn't intrusive, creepy, and
borderline threatening. You didn't care about whether the parents
of the eighteen-year-old webcammer you were getting off to knew
what he was doing (or, for what it's worth, what you were doing "in
your bedroom," which is such a vile, shaming phrase) before you
realized he was an acquaintance. Nothing's changed just because
you realized you knew Cam outside of his videos. He's already
perfectly aware that people can see him when he's camming—that's
how it works! You wouldn't be giving him any new information he
could use to make money or prioritize his own safety. You'd just be
letting him know you don't respect his boundaries or the implied
shared discretion between the streamer and the stream watcher.
Find someone else to watch whose parents you don't know,
continue to tip generously, and move on.*

////////////

Dear Prudence,
I'm a transgender man with a part-time job at my university. When
I started my job, I was only recently out and had just started
testosterone. I emailed my boss and came out to him in simple,
straightforward terms; he seemed receptive and said he'd inform
my coworkers of my gender. However, for the first four months
at my job, none of my coworkers gendered me correctly and
sometimes awkwardly called me "they." I assumed it was because

they were conservative and pushed through it. It's been over eight months now, and I now consistently pass. I recently learned from one of my coworkers that my boss gathered everyone together after I was hired and told everyone that I was nonbinary and used *they/them* pronouns, which isn't true—I'd been very clear that I'm a trans man who uses male pronouns. I was furious. I felt so isolated and uncomfortable at my job for so long, and it took me months to get my coworkers to understand I was a man. Should I complain to my boss? Or to his supervisor? I'm one of three LGBT workers, and we've all experienced this kind of treatment.

—I'm Not Nonbinary

///////////

If your school has a Title IX office, check in with it before speaking to your boss so the staff is aware of the situation and can offer you and your fellow LGBT coworkers support in case you need to file a report. Then check in with your boss. Be prepared to loop in his supervisor, regardless of how receptive he seems. It's a good thing you emailed him when you started the job because you can refer to something you have in writing. Tell him: "I've recently learned that you told my coworkers I'm nonbinary and use gender-neutral pronouns. If you recall, when I emailed you about this eight months ago, I told you I'm a trans man who uses male pronouns. I'm not sure how or why this apparently changed. Can you explain this to me? I want to make sure it doesn't happen again." If you have this conversation in person, be sure to send an email afterward summarizing what you said ("Just to summarize our conversation

today, we clarified X and agreed that you'd do Y going forward")
so that you have a written record you can show to either your
boss's boss or your Title IX office in case this doesn't lead to a
simple, straightforward resolution. And anything other than "I'm
sorry, I'll correct this with your coworkers, and it won't happen
again" is not a simple, straightforward resolution.

• • •

When faced with a choice between looking out for the interests of a fellow worker, particularly a fellow worker whose health-care coverage rests precariously on the timing of their last day, against the interests of the company itself (or even the shared group workload that will have to be reconfigured afterward), look out for your fellow worker.

////////////

Dear Prudence,
I am starting a new job next week; my last day at my present job is Friday. I gave two weeks' notice and hope to get everything wrapped up so I don't leave anything hanging. My coworker (we do similar jobs, and it's assumed she will cover my position until someone new is hired) is also leaving Friday, and she has sworn me to secrecy. She is afraid our boss will escort her out immediately, and if she works through July 1, she will have health insurance for another month. I can sympathize with her on that point. But I also feel terrible for our coworkers left behind, who will honestly not

have anyone to do this work. I feel like I should warn them, but then, her news is not mine to share. For the record, management here is terrible, and I don't mind them getting the shaft. What do you think? How do I face these people again after next week? I'd like to remain friends with them, and feel bad for the situation they'll be in!

—Giving (Her) Notice

//////////////

Yes, your coworkers' immediate situation after both your departures may be unpleasant, but plenty of offices have lost workers unexpectedly, and they'll have the institutional support of your company behind them. It's the company's responsibility, not your coworker's, to make sure the entire workplace doesn't rely on a single employee remaining in their position forever. You don't have to confess that you knew about her plans in advance; if they gripe to you about it, tell them you're sorry about all the extra work that's recently fallen their way and hope you can take them out for a drink sometime soon to commiserate. If your soon-to-be ex-coworker is counting out her health-care eligibility in weeks, I think you should err on the side of keeping her secret and encourage her to find low-cost coverage after her employment health plan runs out.